YOUTH IN INDIA

This book explores the attitudes, anxieties and aspirations of India's burgeoning young population in a globalised world. Drawing upon time-series survey data of the Indian youth aged between 15 and 34 years across 19 Indian states, it provides key insights into a range of themes along with an overview of the changing trends and patterns of their behaviour. The volume examines the job preferences of the Indian youth, their career priorities and opinions on reservations in employment and education sectors. It measures their degree of political participation and studies their attitude regarding political issues. It looks at aspects relating to their social and cultural contexts, preferences and practices, including lifestyle choices, consumption habits and social customs such as marriage, as they negotiate between tradition and modernity. Further, it discusses the anxieties and insecurities that the youth face, their mental health and their experiences of social discrimination. The essays here offer an understanding of a critical demographic and shed light on the challenges and opportunities that the Indian youth confront today.

Lucid, accessible and empirically grounded, this volume will be useful to scholars and researchers of sociology, political sociology, political studies, youth psychology and anthropology as well as policymakers, journalists and the interested general reader.

Sanjay Kumar is Professor and Director at the Centre for the Study of Developing Societies (CSDS), Delhi, India. He is one of the founding members and currently the Co-Director of Lokniti, a research programme of CSDS. His area of specialisation is electoral politics, though by using the survey method he has been engaged in research on a wide range of themes: Indian youth, the state of democracy in South Asia, Indian farmers, slums of Delhi and electoral violence. He has published several books, edited volumes, contributed chapters and published articles in various journals. His most recent book is *Post-Mandal Politics in Bihar:*

Changing Electoral Patterns (2018). His other publications include the books *Electoral Politics in India: The Resurgence of the Bharatiya Janata Party* (with Suhas Palshikar and Sanjay Lodha, 2017); *Changing Electoral Politics in Delhi: From Caste to Class* (2013); *Measuring Voting Behaviour in India* (with Praveen Rai, 2013); *Indian Youth in a Transforming World: Attitudes and Perceptions* (with Peter R. deSouza and Sandeep Shastri, 2009); *Indian Youth and Electoral Politics: An Emerging Engagement* (2014) and *Rise of Plebeians? The Changing Face of Indian Legislative Assemblies* (with Christophe Jaffrelot, 2009). He also writes regularly for national and regional newspapers, in both English and Hindi. His articles are published in *The Hindu, The Indian Express, The Asian Age, Deccan Chronicles*, *Dainik Bhaskar, Rajasthan Patrika* and *Mint*. He appears frequently on Indian television as a psephologist and political commentator, and has been an international election observer in many countries.

YOUTH IN INDIA

Aspirations, Attitudes, Anxieties

Edited by Sanjay Kumar

Routledge
Taylor & Francis Group

LONDON AND NEW YORK

First published 2019
by Routledge
2 Park Square, Milton Park, Abingdon, Oxon OX14 4RN

and by Routledge
52 Vanderbilt Avenue, New York, NY 10017

Routledge is an imprint of the Taylor & Francis Group, an informa business

British Library Cataloguing-in-Publication Data
A catalogue record for this book is available from the British Library

Library of Congress Cataloging-in-Publication Data
Names: Kumar, Sanjay, 1967- editor.
Title: Youth in India : aspirations, attitudes, anxieties / edited by Sanjay
    Kumar.
Description: Abingdon, Oxon ; New York, NY : Routledge, 2019. |
    Includes bibliographical references and index.
Identifiers: LCCN 2018058194| ISBN 9780815380191 (hardback :
    alk. paper) | ISBN 9780367142001 (pbk. : alk. paper) |
    ISBN 9780367142049 (e-book)
Subjects: LCSH: Youth—India—Social conditions.
Classification: LCC HQ799.I5 Y626 2019 | DDC 305.2350954—dc23
LC record available at https://lccn.loc.gov/2018058194

ISBN: 978-0-8153-8019-1 (hbk)
ISBN: 978-0-367-14200-1 (pbk)
ISBN: 978-0-367-14204-9 (ebk)

Typeset in Bembo
by Swales & Willis Ltd, Exeter, Devon, UK

CONTENTS

FIGURES

TABLES

CONTRIBUTORS

Asmita Aasaavari is a graduate student at the Department of Sociology, University of Connecticut, USA. She is interested in political sociology, development, welfare and labour politics. Previously, she was involved in research on electoral politics, educational inequality, gender and labour. She has Bachelor's and Master's degrees in Sociology from the University of Delhi.

Vibha Attri is Researcher at Lokniti, Centre for the Study of Developing Societies, New Delhi, India. Trained in survey research, her areas of interest include electoral politics, local self-governance, voting behaviour, gender and political participation. She also serves as the Editorial Assistant for *Studies in Indian Politics*. She holds an M.Phil. in Political Science from Panjab University, Chandigarh.

Souradeep Banerjee has worked at the Lokniti, Centre for the Study of Developing Societies, New Delhi, India. His research interests are elections, political parties, migration and electoral reforms, and he has a Master's degree in Development Studies from the Tata Institute of Social Sciences, Mumbai.

Shashwat Dhar is currently pursuing his PhD in Political Science at Vanderbilt University, USA. His primary field of interest is comparative politics, with a special focus on migration, political behaviour and campaign finance. He was previously with Lokniti, Centre for the Study of the Developing Societies.

Arushi Gupta is an independent researcher working and writing extensively on foreign policy and domestic politics in India. She has been previously associated with Lokniti, Centre for the Study of the Developing Societies and the Observer Research Foundation. She holds Bachelor of Arts and Master of Arts degrees in Political Science from Delhi University.

Pranav Gupta is a doctoral student in Political Science at the University of California, Berkeley, USA. His research interests include party politics, voting behaviour and politics of public service delivery.

Sanjay Kumar is Professor and Director at the Centre for the Study of Developing Societies (CSDS), Delhi, India. He is one of the founding members and currently the Co-Director of Lokniti, a research programme of CSDS. His area of specialisation is electoral politics, though by using the survey method he has been engaged in research on a wide range of themes: Indian youth, the state of democracy in South Asia, Indian farmers, slums of Delhi and electoral violence. He has published several books, edited volumes, contributed chapters and published articles in various journals. His most recent book is *Post-Mandal Politics in Bihar: Changing Electoral Patterns* (2018). His other publications include the books *Electoral Politics in India: The Resurgence of the Bharatiya Janata Party* (with Suhas Palshikar and Sanjay Lodha, 2017); *Changing Electoral Politics in Delhi: From Caste to Class* (2013); *Measuring Voting Behaviour in India* (with Praveen Rai, 2013); *Indian Youth in a Transforming World: Attitudes and Perceptions* (with Peter R. deSouza and Sandeep Shastri, 2009); *Indian Youth and Electoral Politics: An Emerging Engagement* (2014) and *Rise of Plebeians? The Changing Face of Indian Legislative Assemblies* (with Christophe Jaffrelot, 2009). He also writes regularly for national and regional newspapers, both in English and Hindi languages. His articles are published in *The Hindu, The Indian Express, The Asian Age, Deccan Chronicles, Dainik Bhaskar, Rajasthan Patrika* and *Mint*. He appears frequently on Indian television as a psephologist and political commentator, and has been an international election observer in many countries.

Jyoti Mishra works at Lokniti, Centre for the Study of Developing Societies, New Delhi, India. She has completed her PhD from the Centre for Political Studies, Jawaharlal Nehru University, Delhi. Her areas of interest are electoral behaviour, democracy, political institutions and governance.

Shreyas Sardesai is Research Associate at Lokniti, Centre for the Study of Developing Societies, where he primarily handles key election-related survey projects. Before joining Lokniti in 2010, he worked in TV news for about seven years. He is a graduate in History from St Stephen's College, Delhi University. He completed his postgraduate studies in Political Science at Jawaharlal Nehru University, Delhi.

PREFACE AND ACKNOWLEDGEMENTS

The fact that India has a budding youth population is well acknowledged. But there also exists a serious lacuna when it comes to empirical research on this subject. This book aims to fill this gap through carefully collected evidence about Indian youth – their attitudes, anxieties and aspirations. The scope of the study is far-reaching: through surveys conducted across 19 states on respondents ranging between 19 to 34 years of age, we can confidently claim to have reached most corners of a diverse country such as India.

A similar study on attitude and perception of India's youth was conducted ten years ago. Ten years is a long time, long enough at least for many economic, political, socio-cultural and technological changes to have taken place in a country. If one were to sum up the changes very briefly, economically, the Indian economy has further liberalised at a rapid pace and has come to acquire the tag of the world's fastest growing economy. Politically, the last decade, especially its latter half, has been rather tumultuous, with India witnessing a major anti-corruption movement that spawned the rise of a brand new political party, and a landmark national election in 2014 that fundamentally changed the nature of the regime ruling the country. Socio-culturally, there have been frequent conflicts between the forces of conservatism and liberalism on various issues such as women's rights, minority rights, LGBTQI rights/decriminalising homosexuality, censorship and freedom of expression, and more recently on the issue of growing intolerance in society. On the lifestyle front, there has been a proliferation of the mall, multiplex and café/restaurant culture across Indian cities and towns, which has radically changed the way urban Indians spend their money and their leisure time. Lastly, tremendous advancements in the world of communications and networking technology in the last ten years have also drastically transformed the way we live, communicate and consume information. In the light of these significant developments in India over the last one decade, this book tries to measure the continuities and changes in the attitudes and practices of youth that may have taken place.

It looks into the job profile, job preferences and career priorities of Indian youth and also their attitudes and opinions on the issue of reservation in employment and education sectors. Beyond this, the book also seeks to explore youth's social and cultural attitudes, preferences and practices with respect to marriage and a variety of aspects relating to their lifestyle and habits. This volume also highlights the various anxieties and insecurities of the youth and further attempts to understand and analyse their experiences of discrimination. It also measures the level of political participation of Indian youth.

This volume is a result of a collective effort of various scholars and researchers without whom this book would not have been completed. The first part of this acknowledgement goes to all the authors who have contributed to this book. They have not merely been the chapter writers, but most of them travelled along with me in this research journey, trying to understand issues connected to the young people of India. I would also like to extend my gratitude to members of the Lokniti Network who were a part of this study and without whom this study would not have been completed. My sincere thanks to Suhas Palshikar, Sandeep Shastri, Hilal Ahmed and Sanjeer Alam for their constant support and guidance. I would also like to thank the CSDS Data Unit, specifically Himanshu Bhattacharya, who was extremely helpful in cleaning the data and providing the authors with data so that they could use it for writing. With this, I also thank the Lokniti team at CSDS, particularly Ananya Singh, Ankita Barthwal, Amrit Pandey, Gayatri Raj and Dhananjay Singh, who helped in different stages of writing the book. I would also like to thank the anonymous reviewers to whom the first draft of the manuscript was sent by the publishers for their valuable suggestions.

Surveys can never be possible without the active cooperation of the respondents. Over the last one decade, we interviewed large numbers of young people living in different parts of India. I must begin by extending my thanks to all the young minds who agreed to spare their precious time by sharing their views on various issues. Thanks are also due to the team of investigators who worked hard in the field for data collection. I would also like to extend my gratitude to all the state coordinators who led the research teams in the various states and successfully completed the survey. The team consisted of A.K. Verma, Anupama Saxena, Bhanukumar Parmar, Biswajit Mohanty, Dhruba Pratim Sharma, E. Venkatesu, Harishwar Dayal, Jagrup Singh Sekhon, K.M. Sajad Ibrahim, Kushal Pal, Nitin Birmal, P. Ramajayam, Prabhat Mohanty, Rakesh Ranjan, Sanjay Lodha, Suprio Basu, Veena Devi and Yatindra Singh.

Research of this nature which begins with data collection and ends with a durable academic product in the form of a book demands lot of time. Since we are mostly short of time, the normal casualty is the family, which often gets the least attention. I must thank my family members for not only being patient but for extending the moral support needed for completing this academic exercise. I would like to first thank my wife Rashmi, who always supported and encouraged me during the entire process of completing this book. My daughters Vishakha Nandini and Manavi Nandini also need a special mention in this book. Both of them have always been a source of inspiration for me. Curious questions from the younger daughter Manavi Nandini about how one writes a book have been very interesting all through these years of my writing. Appreciation from various other family members has also been a source of inspiration for me, and I must acknowledge their invisible contribution to this book.

I would like to offer my sincere gratitude to the Konrad Adenauer Foundation for the grants they made available for this project. I would also place on record our gratitude to Routledge for bringing out this volume in record time and especially to Shoma Choudhury, Commissioning Manager, Routledge India, for her continuous support and cooperation which ensured the timely completion of this book. There may be others who provided different kinds of support to me while writing this book; I may not have mentioned their names, but my sincere thanks to all of them as well.

ABBREVIATIONS

AAP	Aam Aadmi Party
AIADMK	All India Anna Dravida Munnetra Kazhagam
AITC	All India Trinamool Congress
BJD	Biju Janata Dal
BJP	Bharatiya Janata Party
BSP	Bahujan Samaj Party
CPI	Communist Party of India
CPM	Communist Party of India (Marxist)
CSDS	Centre for the Study of Developing Societies
DMK	Dravida Munnetra Kazhagam
ECI	Election Commission of India
EU	European Union
GDP	gross domestic product
IHD	Institute for Human Development
INLD	Indian National Lok Dal
IT	information technology
JDS	Janata Dal (Secular)
JDU	Janata Dal United
JNU	Jawaharlal Nehru University
KAS	Konrad-Adenauer-Stiftung
LGBTQI	lesbian, gay, bisexual, transgender, transsexual, queer, questioning, intersex
LJP	Lok Janshakti Party
MBA	Master of Business Administration
MNC	multinational company
NCP	Nationalist Congress Party
NCRB	National Crime Records Bureau

NDA	National Democratic Alliance
NSSO	National Sample Survey Office
OBC	Other Backward Caste
RJD	Rashtriya Janata Dal
RPI-A	Republican Party of India (Athawale)
SAD	Shiromani Akali Dal
SP	Samajwadi Party
TDP	Telugu Desam Party
TRS	Telangana Rashtra Samithi
UK	United Kingdom
UP	Uttar Pradesh
UPA	United Progressive Alliance
USA	United States of America
VCK	Viduthalai Chiruthaigal Katchi

1

INTRODUCTION

Sanjay Kumar

India stands on the cusp of a major demographic revolution. With about two-thirds of its population aged below 35 years, it is amongst the world's youngest countries today. This youth bulge in India has meant that its emerging economy has a demographic dividend that is not possessed by many other countries, including some of the developed world. However, this is naturally not going to last forever. India's median age is expected to rise from 25 to 30 by 2025, and to 39 by 2050. This means that both the youth bulge and the promise of a rich demographic dividend will gradually subside.

There has been a growing corpus of rich empirical work on India's youth. Nakassis (2016) in his study on youth presents the literature on liberalising India and examines the everyday talk about status, value and aesthetics, which revolves around the reformation of youth culture. It subjects intimate social hierarchies in college and how it destabilises older hierarchies. This helps us understand the recurring anxieties, attitudinal change and perspective towards life. The intimate social hierarchies of cultural practices which travel across time and space are crucial in understanding the 'horizon of avoidance and desire' (Nakassis, 2016) in everyday life of a youth. Similar empirical work has been done by scholars such as Lukose (2009), Jeffrey (2010b), Dyson (2014) and Ahuja and Ostermann (2015).

It becomes imperative to get a sense of what young people in India think of themselves and the world around them because our understanding of their concerns, sensibilities and aspirations is fairly limited. By widening the net of intellectual enquiry into a much-under-studied subject, this book attempts to fill a major gap in empirical research on the state of India's young people by exploring various social issues based on facts and intellectual reasoning.

This study is, in fact, a continuation of an earlier study on the attitudes, opinions and aspirations of India's youth conducted a decade ago in 2007. A decade is a long time to understand not just surface level social phenomena, but also to get a fair sense of the deeper, underlying changes unfolding in the society. It also provides a substantial analytical leeway to engage in cross-temporal comparisons, and to study the breaks and continuities with the past. If one were to glide over the vast panorama of India's economic, political and cultural landscape over the last decade, one is likely to be overwhelmed by the pace of transformation that the country seems to be going through. This study is based on a sample survey of 6122 respondents aged between 15 and 34 years across 19 major states of India. (For detailed information on the methodology, refer to Appendix I.)

While economic reform itself has proceeded at a sluggish pace, India's economy continues to register fairly high rates of growth, acquiring the tag of the world's fourth fastest growing economy, after Estonia, Uzbekistan and Nepal (Dutta, 2017). Politically, the last decade, especially its latter half, has been rather tumultuous with India witnessing a major anti-corruption movement that spawned the rise of a brand new political party, and a landmark national election in 2014 that fundamentally changed the nature competition. On the cultural front, there have been frequent clashes between the forces of conservatism and liberalism on various contentious issues such as women's rights, minority rights, LGBTQI (lesbian, gay, bisexual, transgender, transsexual, queer, questioning, intersex) rights/ decriminalising of homosexuality, censorship, freedom of expression and, more recently, on the issue of growing intolerance in society. On the lifestyle front, there has been a proliferation of the mall, multiplex and café/restaurant culture across Indian cities and towns which has radically changed the way urban Indians spend their money and leisure time. Similarly, Lukose (2009) examines the connections between globalised consumption practices, citizenship in public spaces, education and gender through the lenses of fashion, romance, politics, caste and language. Women's participation in public consumer spaces (and discourses) is marked by gender constraints. Participation in these spaces, thus, becomes a complex process located at the boundaries of private and public, masculine and feminine, and traditional and modern.

Lastly, tremendous advancements in the world of communications and networking technology in the last ten years have also drastically transformed the way we live, communicate and consume information. Our televisions have become thinner and our phones smarter. Further, a deeper penetration of the internet and the growth of social media have led to greater interconnectedness. However, these sophisticated tools of communication come with their own risks and challenges, having profound implications for individual privacy, social cohesion and governance.

Enchantment of the state

One of the key insights of the study lies in undimmed enchantment of the state, which remains the 'central repository of people's moral aspirations' (Kaviraj, 2005) despite the global onslaught of neoliberalism. With greater liberalisation and privatisation of the economy, the state's role as the provider of welfare tends to get more limited; it is expected that non-state actors will step in to fill the vacuum created by the state's withdrawal from its traditional domains. India presents a fascinating exception to this larger global trend; even after two and half decades of economic liberalisation, India's youth continue to look up to the state as their eternal benefactor – as a provider of education, employment and relief in times of distress. This enchantment manifests itself in myriad ways; it shows up as much in the agitations of debt-ridden farmers for a debt waiver as it does in various dominant castes making aggressive claims on the shrinking pool of public employment opportunities. The recent spate of agitations spearheaded by the Jats in Haryana, the Patels in Gujarat, the Kapus in Andhra and the Marathas in Maharashtra demanding quota benefits in government jobs reinforces the idea of the state as the ultimate provider. That these protests were born of a growing sense of frustration and disillusionment amongst the youth is understandable; what is more puzzling is the sheer romanticism that fuels such forms of social action, the firm conviction that their demands are legitimate and the expectation that the state will come to their rescue, despite its perceived failures on multiple fronts.

This revolution of rising expectations amongst the youth merits serious attention by governments, lest it degenerate into social unrest and large-scale political violence. Over the last decade, numerous countries and continents, irrespective of their youth bulge, have witnessed youth-driven protests. The commonality across international protests such as the Arab Spring in 2010–11 and the Occupy Wall Street Movement in 2011, and national events such as the India Against Corruption Movement of 2011, the wave of protests in the aftermath of the Delhi gang rape in late 2012 and the youth's engagement with politics during the birth of the Aam Aadmi Party (AAP) in 2013, has been the visible mobilisation and participation of young people mostly in their twenties. More recently, in the events that unfolded across prominent educational campuses such as Jawaharlal Nehru University (JNU), Hyderabad Central University, the Film and Television Institute of India, Jadavpur University and the Delhi University, not only were young people recognised as having played a vital and central, if not exclusive, role, their participation and angst somewhat debunked the myth of young people as being self-absorbed and depoliticised. Even though many of these protests have been painted as being ideological in nature, with students divided in opposing camps, they also point at a much deeper social problem of discontent and disillusionment due to exacerbated unemployment, scarcity of resources and reduced opportunities for upward social mobility. Across contexts, they reflect a common experience of precariousness.

This study confirms some of these trends. It found that amongst young employed Indians today, only a small fraction is employed in decent, well-paying professional jobs. A vast proportion of youth described themselves as either self-employed or engaged in low-paid jobs that do not guarantee a steady wage. Not surprisingly, the study found employment and jobs to be the top-most concern of young Indians. Nearly every fifth youth cited joblessness as the greatest problem confronting the country. The study also found anxiety with respect to jobs to be amongst the top five anxieties of the youth, irrespective of whether they were employed or not employed.

If a decade ago, the lack of employment opportunities was making most of the young Indians opt for self-employment, now it seems to be making them extend their years of education. Many amongst today's young generation are studying further either in order to delay their entry into the workforce or perhaps as means of 'time pass' (Jeffrey, 2010a). The idea of 'time pass' has lately gained currency in many of India's small towns, and offers a salient analytical construct to explain how 'over-educated' unemployed young men negotiate with their perceived joblessness and the uncertainty that looms over their lives. The Jat men in Jeffrey's pioneering study would often characterise their situation as 'passing time', while criticising the sense of ennui and aimlessness that typifies it. However, this waiting also serves a significant social purpose: an opportunity to acquire skills and mobilise politically. Unable to partake in the information technology (IT) revolution that swept through the more affluent English-speaking urban middle classes, the rich rural classes, in their attempt to not be excluded from the changing distribution of social and political power, turned to education in the hope of joining the regional bureaucracy to maintain their stronghold. However, the promise of a government job not being forthcoming results in the characteristic waiting that Jeffrey associates with the educated Jat youth of the region.

Given this obsession with accumulating degrees and delaying their entry into the workforce, it is not surprising that a third of the youth described themselves as students, on being asked about their occupation. Interestingly, the study shows that the proportion of youth who described their occupation as 'student' in 2016 was more than twice that recorded in the youth study conducted in 2007. While the fact that more and more youngsters are studying now is undoubtedly a promising sign, as it increases the possibility of a higher degree of skill formation amongst them and is indicative of a desire to move away from menial and low-paid work, what is rather intriguing is that the study also found self-reported unemployment to be much higher amongst young graduates than those with lower levels of education. In other words, it found that acquisition of greater education and skills by the youth did not necessarily guarantee gainful employment for them.

This may be attributed to three factors. One, there could be a demand–supply mismatch, or in other words, there are not enough jobs being generated for the millions of graduates entering the labour market every year. This includes youth belonging to communities that have traditionally not been highly educated, but are now beginning to make huge investments in education in order to achieve social and economic mobility. Two, some educated young people might be choosing to stay unemployed rather than work in jobs that they believe are not commensurate with their educational qualifications. And three, it is also highly possible that the sectors in which they are seeking jobs – services and manufacturing – do not find their education and skills to be well suited to the kind of jobs on offer. This basically boils down to the question of employability.

India's post-reform growth story has been much celebrated across the globe, but its growth trajectory has a major structural anomaly. While services and manufacturing have emerged as the biggest contributors to India's gross domestic product

(GDP), agriculture continues to be the single largest employer of the country's workforce. The study found the farm sector continuing to be a major employer of young Indians. One in every six, as opposed to one in every seven a decade ago, associated themselves with it, with many of them describing themselves as agricultural workers rather than farmers tilling their own land. This is completely at odds with the experience of many of the world's advanced economies, where the non-farm sector not only contributes a lion's share to GDP, but also employs a majority of the workforce. Despite registering much higher rates of growth than agriculture, India's manufacturing and service industries have not been able to absorb the surplus labour force in agriculture. This has led some analysts to suspect India's growth credentials, and has given rise to what many refer to as 'jobless growth'.

There is no gainsaying that while the Indian state no longer occupies the proverbial 'commanding heights of the economy', it continues to dominate certain sectors of it, despite the programme of economic liberalisation that it embarked on in early 1990s. Economic reform, as many would have thought and anticipated, has not been able to displace the romantic idea of the state from the core of public imagination. This is also evident from the clamour for government jobs amongst India's youth today. The study found that most young Indians continue to fancy a *sarkari naukri* (a government job), in fact, slightly more than they did a decade ago. In other words, for a majority of youth, an ideal job continues to be one that is located in the public sector as it offers them a sense of material security, permanence, stability and perhaps social status. This sentiment in favour of a government job cuts across localities, and even youngsters residing in big cities express a far greater preference for it than they did a decade back. This overwhelming preference for a government job perhaps explains the strong support that the study found for the continuation of job reservation for the Dalits, Adivasis and OBC (Other Backward Caste) communities, especially amongst youth belonging to these beneficiary communities. However, it is not clear whether there has been a decline or increase in the level of this support over the years, since the study did not collect information on reservations previously in 2007. What is clear from the study though is that a greater proportion of youth, barring those belonging to the upper castes, support rather than oppose the policy of reservations, and more so in the public sector.

Negotiating modernity

What is modernity and how are young Indians engaging with it? The study presents a nuanced picture of how the tradition–modernity dialectic is unfolding in Indian society. It eschews categorisation of India's youth into the conventional left–right straitjacket. This is so because the prevailing Western categories of liberal and conservative do not adequately explain the attitudinal nuances of India's young people. However, some scholars have treated tradition and modernity as being dichotomously related to each other, perhaps for purposes of heuristic convenience. In his critically acclaimed work *Mistaken Modernity* (2000), sociologist

Dipankar Gupta lamented about a superficial version of modernity amongst India's middle classes and elites. According to Gupta, the modernity of this particular class of Indians was characterised more by the adoption of Western consumer habits and lifestyles than by adherence to notions of equality and tolerance. Gupta had defined true modernity in terms of attitudes, especially those that come into play in social relations.

While Gupta's analysis offers rich sociological insights into how Indian middle classes have responded to modernisation, it succumbs to the same temptation that many Western scholars have failed to resist in their postulations on Indian modernity. Contesting the modernisation paradigm back in the late 1960s, Rudolph and Rudolph (1967) saw tradition and modernity as being 'dialectically, rather than dichotomously related'. Traditional societies, they argued, also have internal variations that carry with them the potential for deviations from dominant norms and structures. In other words, there are substantial grey areas between the domains of tradition and modernity that exist in many post-colonial societies and scholars need to adopt sensitive analytical frames to look at them. For instance, traditional institutions such as caste and kinship have engaged with modern democratic politics in ways few modernisation scholars could have possibly imagined. Many civic associations and 'paracommunities' in India present a unique blend of traditional and modern features in how they engage with political parties, build and sustain organisations and mobilise their co-ethnic members along vertical and horizontal networks.

The study found something very similar in the professed attitudes of India's youth. It is interesting to see how young people today are navigating their way in a rapidly changing environment over which they seem to have little control. Modern notions of dress and modern patterns of lifestyle and consumption seem to have acquired wide currency. According to Nakassis (2016), style comes up often in 'everyday talk about status, value and aesthetics'. Moreover, it is the keen practice of being cool and trying to fit in to that elite social group to sustain their individuality. The study found around two in five young Indians to be either highly or moderately style conscious, that is, they were found to be fond of wearing stylish clothes and shoes, keeping the latest mobile phones and visiting beauty parlours and salons. Meanwhile, as a response to new opportunities for consumption and entertainment in the form of an emerging café, multiplex and mall culture, there was a marked increase in the consumption and spending patterns of youth, particularly amongst those residing in cities. The study found that close to half the youth in big cities and about a third in smaller ones regularly watched movies in a cinema hall, regularly ate out at restaurants and cafés and regularly visited shopping malls. Nakassis (2016) in the third part of his book, on film, examined the relationship between film-making and youth culture. Brand, language and film are all sites of mass mediation. He argued that the film text is 'a contact zone and space of encounter' through which audiences and film-makers mutually orient towards the same types of detachable signs.

However, these modern lifestyle and consumption patterns co-exist with attitudes that are firmly rooted in traditional ways of thinking. There was a great deal of ambivalence in how India's youth looked at questions on individual liberty, equality and social justice. The study found youngsters to be holding fairly liberal views when it came to supporting education for women, attaining leadership roles and having the freedom to make sartorial choices. But the same set of people was also found to be conservative when it came to accepting a man and a woman as equals within the domain of the household. The idea that wives should always listen to their husbands seems to have been internalised by both men and women because of their socialisation. The study also found opinions to be highly polarised on whether it is right for women to work after marriage. About half of India's youth supported the proposition, while the other half was averse to it. Young married men who said they had a daughter/s were found to be as patriarchal, if not more, in their attitudes as those with sons.

Interestingly, having a friend from the opposite sex mellows down one's patriarchal beliefs. Mingling with the other gender tends to temper notions of patriarchy as one engages with and experiences the 'otherness of the other'. Two in every three young men who reported not having any close female friends were found to be patriarchal in their mindset, while a little less than 50 per cent of the young men who said they had close female friends were found to be patriarchal. The direction of causality could, of course, be the other way round as well, that is more patriarchal men being less likely to befriend women because of their misogynistic attitudes than those who are less patriarchal. However, some validation of the inter-group contact hypothesis was found in the study; that is, those with cross-group friendships were found to be more liberal and less prejudiced in their attitudes about other communities than those with same-group friendships. For instance, caste-based prejudice was found to be weaker amongst youth with cross-caste friendships. The proportion of those who had a problem if their neighbour belonged to a different caste was eight percentage points higher amongst those who did not have a close friend from another caste than those who had one.

What about the actual incidence of cross-group friendships? How likely are India's youth to have a close friend from another ethnic group? The study found a fairly large proportion of young Indians to have befriended people belonging to castes and religions other than their own. About four in five young Indians had a close friend from another caste, and about two in every three said they have close friends who do not belong to their own religion. There may have been an element of social desirability in the way they answered this question. Nonetheless, this is an important finding as the inter-group contact theory or the contact hypothesis (Allport, 1954) posits that inter-personal interactions and friendships between members of different groups help promote positive attitudes towards others and reduce prejudice. It has been argued that when friendships are intimate, people include aspects of their friends in their own self-concept (Aron et al., 1991). The basic argument of contact theory is that bias against a category of people can be reduced as one learns more about that category of people. So if a Hindu becomes close friends with a Muslim, then he/she might grow to appreciate Muslim culture because of his closeness and intimacy to the Muslim friend, and might develop positive feelings and attitudes toward Muslims as a group. The same process applies to all other groups – caste, gender, sexual orientation, etc.

Having a close friend from another religion also makes a difference, in fact a bigger one than that seen with respect to caste. The study showed that the youth who had close friends from another religion were over two times less likely to feel uneasy if their neighbour belonged to another religion than those with only co-religionists as close friends. Not just friendships, marriage outside of one's religion also matters. Married youth who had a spouse from another religion were 10 per cent less likely to feel uneasy if their neighbour belonged to a different religion than those whose spouse was from the same religion.

The study also found a correlation between inter-religion, inter-caste and cross-gender friendships amongst the youth and their insecurity about friendships in general. This can be said because anxiety about losing a friend was found to be much greater amongst those who had a friend from another religion, another caste and the opposite gender than those who did not. This pattern is not a one-off and was witnessed across religious groups, Hindu castes and communities, and amongst both men and women. Young Muslims, Hindus, Christians and Sikhs who had a close friend from a religion other than theirs showed much higher anxiety about 'losing a friend' than their co-religionists who did not have a close friend from another religion. Similarly, young Hindu upper castes, OBCs, Dalits and Adivasis having a close friend from another caste turned out to be more worried about 'losing a friend' than their counterparts who had no close friends from a caste other than theirs. To cite another example from the study, an inter-religion friendship was also found to matter in terms of anxiety amongst youth regarding riots and mob violence. Youth with close friends from another religion were found to be 10 per cent more anxious about riots breaking out in their city, town or village than youth who did not have any close friends from another religion.

While in a multicultural and diverse country such as India it is not surprising that the youth are entering into friendships that are not dictated by their communitarian identities, nonetheless, it is significant considering the unequal relationships amongst castes and the historical animosity amongst religious communities, particularly between Hindus and Muslims.

On the question of marriage, an overwhelming majority of the youth were still guided by traditional norms governing mate selection. While many more youngsters did not consider marriage to be the be all and end all in life, as compared to a decade ago, and many according to the study seemed to be delaying their age of marriage, their attitudes and practices with respect to inter-community marriages have largely remained unchanged. Although acceptance of inter-caste marriage has increased manifold, the reported outcome of inter-caste marriage was extremely low at only 4 per cent. Meanwhile, the reported outcome of inter-religious marriage was even lower at 3 per cent. Parent-arranged marriages are still the norm as over four in every five married youth described their marriage as such. Only one in ten youth said that they had a love marriage. Not surprisingly, this tiny minority of youth with self-arranged marriages was found to be far more liberal in attitudes regarding love and relationships than those with parent-arranged marriages. They were, for instance, twice as likely to approve of dating before marriage, live-in relationships and the celebration of Valentine's Day as youth with arranged marriages, or for that matter even unmarried youth.

Acceptance of homosexuality was also found to be quite low amongst the youth. Only one in every four approved of it either fully or partially. While this figure of approval might be considered by some to be promising given that there is social stigma around the issue and discussions about sexuality, particularly homosexuality, are usually looked down upon in Indian society, it is nevertheless very low compared to Western societies. Surprisingly, the study found acceptance of same-sex relationships to be much greater amongst those youths who were found to be highly religious in practice than those who reported being less religious or not religious at all. Moreover, acceptance of it was far greater amongst youth living in villages than those residing in big cities. This is extremely counterintuitive.

Anthony John Desantis, in his study *Philosophical Precursors to the Radical Enlightenment*, significantly deals with the core tenet of Enlightenment philosophy that undergirds all modern consciousness as a firm conviction that science and reason alone are the chief engines of human advancement. Modernity, thus, implies a departure from the sacred, faith-based, non-rational ways of thinking about the world to ones which are based on utility, calculation and science. However, what appears to be a contradiction between the sacred and the secular is also a persistent feature of modernity in many traditional societies because secularism is often viewed as a neutral or flat space that forbids religious opinion or interference in political questions – this issue is closely examined by Asad (2003). India is no exception to this. Findings of the study revealed that close to half of India's young population thinks that religion should get precedence over science when the two clash with each other. Intriguingly, it was not the least educated youth who were most likely to take this stance, but the most educated young Indians, its graduates, post-graduates and professionals. This presents an analytical puzzle for many scholars like Bauman (2000) who introduced the concept of 'liquid modernity', which suggests a rapidly changing order that undermines all notions of durability. It implies a sense of rootlessness to all forms of social construction. In the field of development, such a concept challenges the meaning of modernisation as an effort to establish long-lasting structures.

With the advent of modernisation, societies like India are witnessing an increasing nuclearisation of the joint family system and disruptions in intra-family dynamics, defined by Sandeep Nerlekar (2017) in his article which explains the politics within the four walls. The response of India's youth to the pressures of modernity has been tempered by the weight of tradition, so much so that mediating between the two has emerged as amongst youth's biggest concerns. It was found that youth across all age groups rated family problems as amongst their greatest worries. The pressure to maintain family traditions, customs and habits in the face of modernity is something that this generation is struggling to grapple with. The greatest anxieties about maintaining family traditions were found amongst the most religious youth. This is understandable; because religion is the wellspring of a society's morals, its customary practices and many of its conventions, those having a more religious upbringing are perhaps more likely to encounter difficulties in dealing with modernity.

The study also tried to measure prejudice and discriminatory attitudes amongst Indian youth, and on this front, the findings are not too alarming. After taking into consideration a whole host of questions that tapped into prejudice, only one in every five youth was found to have faced discriminated either highly or somewhat. As expected, prejudice amongst Indian youth was higher than average with respect to non-vegetarians, those who drink alcohol and live-in couples. Also rather surprisingly, not many youths reported having faced discrimination. Merely one in every six reported being victims of discrimination in the recent past, be it on the grounds of religion, caste, economic status, region or gender. The more educated youth were relatively more vocal on the question.

Engagement with politics

The youth in India are amongst the least engaged when it comes to participating in politics. This is reflected in their turnout during elections, which has been consistently below the national average since 1998. The study found that about half of the India's young voters (46 per cent) have no interest at all in politics, but interest is rising over time. This was evident in the 2014 Lok Sabha election, when turnout amongst the youth stood at an impressive 68 per cent, compared to the national average of 66 per cent. But what factors determine political participation amongst the youth? Political socialisation theory identifies the role of family as being instrumental to shaping political attitudes (Niemi and Sobieszek, 1977). Children are likely to have a high level of interest in politics if their parents also have high interest. This seems to hold in the context of the Indian youth; the study found that youth whose parents were interested in politics were more likely to be interested in politics. However, there is much more to political participation than just casting one's vote. Political parties require enormous amounts of human resources to reach out to the electorate, and they often rope in youngsters to undertake campaign activities such as door to door canvassing, distributing pamphlets, putting up posters/banners, organising and participating in rallies/road shows and giving donations. Surprisingly, the study found a very low proportion of India's youth engaging in such election-related campaigns. More than three quarters of the youth claimed to have never participated in any of these activities.

Low levels of interest in politics also find reflection in levels of party identification; over half of India's youth identified with some political party, but a substantial proportion did not (48 per cent). Party identification was found to be the greatest in eastern India and the least in the west. Also, it was extremely high amongst Muslims and Sikhs.

In terms of their political attitudes, a similar kind of polarisation can be witnessed to their stance on issues of culture and identity; there is certainly a conservative strain amongst them on certain issues. Take censorship of cinema, for instance, an issue that comes up from time to time. The growing trend of cinema censorship does not seem to bother young Indians much. Three out of every five young Indians agreed with the proposition that films that hurt religious sentiments should be banned. The study also found fairly widespread support for the continuation of the death penalty, with only about a third wanting it abolished. On the issue of India–Pakistan relations, while a majority was found to be in favour of improving relations with Pakistan, there was a significant chunk (about a third) that was opposed to any peace initiatives with the neighbouring country. That said, not all politically oriented questions elicited a conservative response. For instance, a majority of young people were of the opinion that student unions serve an important purpose and that they should not be banned. A fairly large proportion of youth also held the view that young Muslims are being falsely implicated in terrorism-related cases. Both these views are far from being conservative. However, it must be stressed that on both these questions and the one on Indo-Pakistan relations, there was a fairly large proportion of youth who stayed silent, choosing not to express their opinion. By contrast, on questions related to censorship of cinema and the death penalty, they were found to be far more vocal.

Structure

This book consists of nine chapters (including the Introduction) and each chapter discusses study findings that were touched upon, in some way or the other, on the three aspects mentioned in the title of the study – attitudes, aspirations and anxieties of India's youth. The first chapter is this Introduction. The second chapter explains the underlying principle behind the job profile, job preferences and career priorities of young Indians. The third chapter scrutinises the opinions of youngsters on the highly contentious policy of reservations in the employment and education sectors, and their behaviour towards the issue. The fourth chapter measures the degree of political participation amongst the youth and examines their attitudes regarding select political issues.

The fifth chapter shares the findings related to the social and cultural attitudes of youngsters, and attempts to place them within the tradition–modernity dialectic confronting Indian society. The sixth chapter offers a detailed outlook on the attitudes, preferences and practices of India's youth towards the institution of marriage.

The seventh chapter focuses on a variety of aspects related to the lifestyle and habits of the youth. The eighth chapter highlights their various anxieties and insecurities, and tries to ascertain their emotional state of mind. Finally, the last chapter attempts to understand and analyse experiences of discrimination in India. In most of these chapters, comparisons with the findings of the youth study conducted in 2007 have been given in order to highlight the changing patterns with respect to youth behaviour and attitudes. However, some of the questions that were asked in this study were not asked in 2007, thus making a comparative exercise impossible. We would like readers of this book to bear this in mind.

References

Ahuja, Amit and Ostermann, Susan (2015) Crossing caste boundaries in the modern Indian marriage market. *Studies in Comparative International Development*, 51(3): 365–387.

Allport, Gordon W. (1954) *The Nature of Prejudice*. Cambridge, MA: Addison-Wesley.

Aron, Arthur, Aron, Elaine N., Tudor, Michael and Nelson, Greg (1991) Close relationships as including other in the self. *Journal of Personality and Social Psychology*, 60(2): 241–253.

Asad, Talal (2003) *Formations of the Secular: Christianity, Islam, Modernity*. Stanford, CA: Stanford University Press.

Bauman, Zygmunt (2000) *Liquid Modernity*. Cambridge: Polity Press.

Desantis, Anthony John (2011) *Philosophical Precursors to the Radical Enlightenment: Vignettes on the Struggle Between Philosophy and Theology from the Greeks to Leibniz with Special Emphasis on Spinoza*. Graduate Theses and Dissertations. Available at: http://scholarcommons.usf.edu/etd/3067. Accessed on 19 December 2018.

Dutta, Prabhash K. (2017) India, not China, is among the fastest growing economies: World Bank. *India Today*. 17 July. Available at: http://indiatoday.intoday.in/story/india-china-fastest-growing-economies-world-bank/1/1004183.html. Accessed on 29 October 2017.

Dyson, Jane (2014) *Working Childhoods: Youth, Agency and the Environment in India*. Cambridge: Cambridge University Press.

Gupta, Dipankar (2000) *Mistaken Modernity: India Between Worlds*. New Delhi: Harper India.

Jeffrey, Craig (2010a) Timepass: youth, class, and time amongst unemployed young men in India. *American Ethnologist*, 37(3): 465–481.

Jeffrey, Craig (2010b) *Youth, Class and the Politics of Waiting in India*. Stanford, CA: Stanford University Press.

Kaviraj, Sudipta (2005) On the enchantment of the state: Indian thought on the role of the state in the narrative of modernity. *European Journal of Sociology*, 46(2): 263–296.

Lukose, R.A. (2009) *Liberalization's Children: Gender, Youth, and Consumer Citizenship in Globalizing India*. Durham, NC: Duke University Press.

Nakassis, C.V. (2016) *Doing Style: Youth and Mass Mediation in South India*. Chicago, IL: University of Chicago Press.

Nerlekar, Sandeep (2017) Disintegration of the joint family system, emergence of nuclear family. *Forbes India*. Available at: www.forbesindia.com/blog/beyond-the-numbers/disintegration-of-the-joint-family-system-emergence-of-nuclear-family/. Accessed on 28 October 2018.

Niemi, R.G. and Sobieszek, B.I. (1977) Political socialization. *Annual Review of Sociology*, 3(1): 209–233.

Rudolph, Lloyd and Rudolph, Susanne (1967) *The Modernity of Tradition: Political Development in India*. Bombay: Orient Longmans.

2

JOB PREFERENCES AND CAREER PRIORITIES

Shashwat Dhar

Two and a half decades after embarking on a programme of economic liberalisation, India's enchantment with the post-colonial state remains puzzlingly undiminished. Nowhere is this enchantment more striking than in young India's obsession with a *sarkari naukri* (government job). This shows up quite clearly in the study, with two out of every three young people in India conceding that they would choose a government job as their occupation, if they had a choice. Preference for a government job is the strongest among the most educated, particularly within the large segment of India's young graduates, who despite their educational qualifications, are struggling to find decent jobs. India's growth story, once celebrated across the globe, is now beginning to show signs of wearing off. Unemployment rates rose consistently from 4.7 per cent in 2012–13 to 5 per cent in 2015–16 (Ministry of Labour and Employment, 2016), even while India's annual gross domestic product (GDP) growth rate increased from 5.6 to 7.6 per cent in the same period (World Bank, 2016). India's manufacturing sector has just not grown fast enough to absorb its abundant reserves of surplus labour.

The problem has been further compounded by the huge volumes of stressed assets in India's banking system, and the resultant dip in private investment. While the ruling National Democratic Alliance (NDA) government has promulgated a slew of policy initiatives to revive manufacturing (Make in India) and create gainful employment (Skill India Mission), there are serious misgivings about the employ-ability of India's young graduates. India's youth are just not getting the kind of jobs they covet. Not surprisingly, a plurality of them (18 per cent) in the study rec-ognised unemployment as the single most important problem facing the country.

An analysis of the occupational profile of India's youth, which forms the first part of this chapter, reveals how occupational choices may be constrained by the historical baggage of belonging to a certain caste. It also sheds light on how India is still struggling to make the transition from a low-skill, low-productivity agricultural economy to a high-skill, high-productivity industrial economy. Farming continues to be the second most widely reported occupation among young Indians. While the gap between agriculture's contribution to India's GDP and its share of employment has narrowed in recent years, a substantial segment of India's population (about 40 per cent) still relies on agriculture as its principal source of income (Damodaran, 2014). Since employment growth has been largely sluggish in the organised sector, more young Indians are taking up jobs in the informal economy, further exposing them to the vagaries of the market. Uncertainty with respect to wage employment and the lack of quality jobs in the formal economy have swollen the ranks of the educated unemployed youth.

Scepticism about jobs, though quite strong, has not dimmed the aspirations of young Indians. Their occupational preferences speak a lot about their ambitions and what they wish to make of their lives. Their life goals and priorities and their desire for upward social mobility through migration are some of the issues that get addressed in the second part of the chapter.

Trends in occupational profile of India's youth

The occupational profile of India's youth seems to have undergone a major transformation over the last decade, with a third (32 per cent) of the country's youth reporting their main occupation as 'student'. This figure was up by a whopping 19 per cent since 2007, when a mere 13 per cent youth were reportedly pursuing their studies (Figure 2.1). Underlying these trends is an unprecedented boom in India's higher education sector, which has witnessed a rapid expansion since the 2000s (Varghese, 2015). Much of this expansion is accounted for by the proliferation of private universities, many of which offer degrees in technical and professional disciplines. However, the dismal quality of education and decrepit infrastructure in

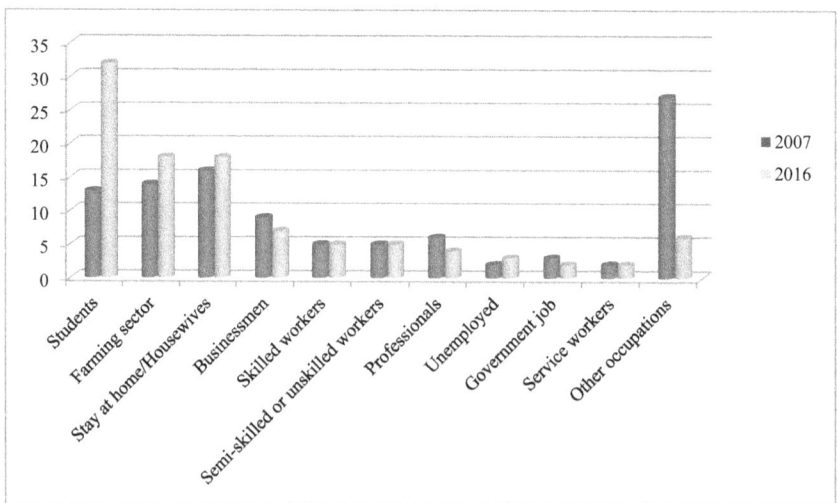

FIGURE 2.1 Trends in occupational profile of India's youth (%)

many of these self-financed private institutions makes it difficult for their students to find gainful employment upon graduation. Bardhan (2017) also attests to the looming crisis in India's higher education sector, arguing that the quantitative expansion of higher education in post-independence India has occurred at the expense of quality. While stressing the stark deficiencies in infrastructure (under-qualified faculty, poor computer and broadband connectivity, inadequate laboratory facilities, under-maintained classrooms and buildings), he also points to serious learning and cognitive deficits amongst graduate students, and laments how some politicians have reduced universities into 'degree-giving factories'.

Discounting the proportion of youth still studying, agriculture emerged as the single largest employer of India's youth. Considered to be the backbone of India's US$ 2 trillion economy, agriculture was found to employ about a fifth (18 per cent) of India's youth, up by four percentage points since 2007. About two-fifths (39 per cent) of these youth were agricultural workers, working on other people's lands to earn their wages.

Business was reported as the main occupation by only 7 per cent of the youth. Upon probing further, it was found that a significant proportion (40 per cent) of these young Indians run small shops and business establishments. A large segment of India's young population (18 per cent) consisted of those who stay at home. Many of them described themselves as housewives. The fact that this figure is up by two percentage points since 2007 confirms the trend of declining participation of women in the labour force (NSSO, 2011–12). The decline is mainly driven by rural India, where the percentage of women in the labour force plummeted from 33.3 per cent in 2004–5 to 25.3 per cent in 2011–12 (NSSO, 2011–12). The drop in labour force participation rates is most pronounced for young women.

A cross-sectional analysis of these findings lays bare the extent to which caste, educational attainment and occupational status overlap in Indian society. Compared to upper-caste youth, it was found that Dalit and Adivasi youth lag far behind when it comes to access to education. While over two-fifths (42 per cent) of upper-caste youth reported themselves as students, only about a quarter (25 per cent) of Dalit youth and a mere one-sixth (16 per cent) of Adivasi youth said they were pursuing their studies (Table 2.1). 'Other Backward Caste' (OBC)

TABLE 2.1 Caste and community-wise educational profile of India's youth (%)

	Graduate or above	High school pass	Primary pass	Non-literate
Hindu upper caste	69	24	4	3
Hindu peasant proprietor	55	37	7	1
Hindu upper OBC	49	36	9	6
Hindu lower OBC	50	36	9	4
Hindu Dalit	41	41	11	7
Hindu Adivasi	20	34	20	26
Muslim	40	37	15	8
Others	58	31	8	4

and Muslim youth figured somewhere in the middle, with about a third (33 per cent) of them reporting themselves as students.

Interestingly, the gap in educational attainment is highly conspicuous when analysed in terms of caste. Compared to 69 per cent of upper-caste youth, only 41 per cent of Dalits and 20 per cent of Adivasis were found to have completed college education (Table 2.2). This result finds strong support in the literature on educational inequality in India. Recent empirical work on the subject points out that there has been little improvement in caste-based inequality at the college level in India, despite the impressive history of affirmative action aimed at granting historically marginalised groups access to a college education (Desai and Kulkarni, 2008).

But what explains this asymmetry in access to tertiary education? Why is a young upper-caste person more likely to be studying compared to a young Dalit or Adivasi? The answer probably lies in what Deshpande (2006) calls the persistence of 'non-merit' inequalities in Indian society. In other words, it is not merit alone that shapes access to higher education institutions, but also two additional sets of resources as identified by Galanter (1984) – economic resources (for prior education, training, materials, freedom from work, etc.) and cultural resources (networks, contacts, confidence, guidance and information). Generally speaking, a young upper-caste person has far greater economic and cultural resources at his/her command than a young Dalit or Adivasi would. This makes the costs of higher education much less prohibitive for him/her.

Caste inequality also manifests itself in the occupational structure and more often than not, it ends up reinforcing embedded occupational hierarchies. The study shows that a much larger proportion of Dalit youth (9 per cent) was engaged in low-paid semi-skilled/unskilled work compared to youth from other communities (4 per cent). This is no surprise; Dalits or 'ex-untouchables' have historically been relegated to certain occupations, many of which are perceived to be repugnant and degrading by upper castes. Hence, it is common to find Dalits engaged in trades such as skinning dead cattle, manual scavenging, desalting/cleaning drains and culverts, etc. Likewise, an overwhelming majority of Adivasi youth (58 per cent) were found to be engaged in agriculture and allied activities such as cattle rearing, fishing, etc. By contrast, one sees a relatively higher proportion of upper-caste youth who reported themselves as professionals

TABLE 2.2 Education-wise occupational profile of India's youth (%)

	Professional	Government employment	Business	Service	Skilled	Semi- or unskilled	Farming	Students	Stay at home	Unemployed
Graduate+	7	4	8	2	4	3	7	42	12	4
High school pass	1	1	7	1	7	5	21	31	19	3
Primary pass	1	–	3	2	4	10	38	7	31	1
Non-literate	–	–	2	1	1	9	56	–	29	–

Note: The rest of the youth reported being in other occupations.

(6 per cent) and government employees (4 per cent), occupations which have traditionally been the preserve of the upper castes.

The study also looked at the growing problem of unemployment among India's youth. About 3.2 per cent of young Indians reported themselves as unemployed. Interestingly, the most educated among the youth are also most vulnerable to joblessness. It was found that self-reported unemployment rates go up with a rise in the levels of educational attainment, with graduates reporting the highest levels of unemployment at 4 per cent in the study.[1] Better educated youth have the luxury of delaying their entry into the workforce by being voluntarily unemployed. Hence, the incidence of unemployment is higher among them. This is also confirmed by findings of the National Sample Survey Office (NSSO) 64th round.

There are significant regional and inter-state variations in the volume of young people who reported themselves as unemployed. The study found a far greater concentration of unemployed youth in eastern India, most particularly in the states of Odisha and West Bengal. While some 8 per cent of Odisha's youth reported themselves as unemployed, the corresponding figure for West Bengal was a whopping 13 per cent. This is in stark contrast to the western and central states like Gujarat and Madhya Pradesh, where self-reported levels of joblessness were found to be much lower at 2 per cent and 1 per cent, respectively. This could be either because these states do not have a substantial proportion of highly educated youth (the study found this to be true for Madhya Pradesh, at least) and hence there is a low demand for white collar jobs, or it could be that these states have actually been able to provide better employment avenues to their youth.

Occupational preferences

The occupational preferences, as such, of India's young have demonstrated little change, though there are some noteworthy developments on this front. A close examination of the job preferences of young Indians helps explain why today's youth aspire for certain kinds of jobs and not others. In order to understand their job preferences, two questions on occupational choice were asked in the study. One, an open-ended question on the occupation they would have chosen for themselves if they had complete freedom to do so, and a closed question on which amongst the following jobs they would choose if given a choice: a government job, a private job or setting up one's own business/profession. Responses to the open-ended question indicate that even though a fifth (21 per cent) of the youth preferred their current job, about 16 per cent of them would choose a government job, if one includes the preferences of those who aspired to join the civil services, the police and the armed forces (Table 2.4). Amongst the most eager aspirants of a government job were people in the 15 to 22 age bracket, students and unemployed youth.

This fascination with a government job was seen even in the case of the closed question. It was found that an overwhelming majority of India's youth (65 per cent or almost two-thirds) would prefer a government job, if given a choice. Setting up one's own business came a distant second (19 per cent or one in every five), followed by a

TABLE 2.3 Job preferences of India's youth (open-ended question) (%)

Preferred occupation if one had the freedom to choose one

My current job	21
Government job	11
Teaching	7
One's own business	5
Science and engineering	3
Medicine and health	3
Police	2
Military	2
Literature, art, entertainment, creative fields	1
Civil services	1
Politics, activism, law	1
Farmer	1
Banking and accounting	1
Others	7
No response	34

Note: No response is very high since the question was asked in an open-ended way.

job in the private sector. Only 7 per cent or less than one in every ten of India's youth said they would like to go for a private job, though it remains unclear as to which industry or sector within the private sector they would prefer to work in.

A quick look at the time-series evidence on job preferences of India's youth shows that the appeal of a government job has remained undiminished over the last decade. In 2007, in response to the same closed question, 62 per cent of the youth said they would prefer a government job. In the 2016 study, this increased slightly to 65 per cent (Figure 2.2). That the demand for government jobs has

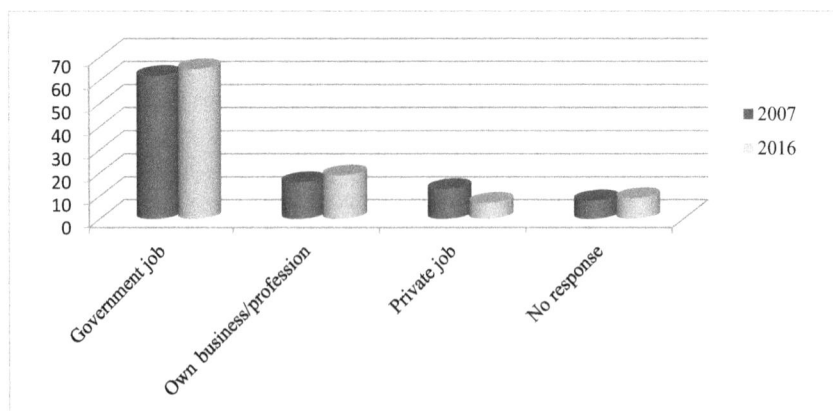

FIGURE 2.2 Job preferences of India's youth (closed question) (%)

Note: 2007 figures are from the CSDS-KAS Youth Study 2007.

gone up despite two and a half decades of pro-market reforms being in force says something about the economic ideology of young India. The dismantling of the dirigisme economy in the early 1990s may have opened up new avenues of growth and employment in the private sector, but it has not really effected a fundamental shift in how the Indian state has been conceptualised in the popular imagination. The ideas of nationalism and egalitarianism have become internalised in the Indian psyche; they still play a decisive role in shaping public opinion on the role of the state in managing the economy, alleviating poverty and promoting the larger good (Yadav, 2004). The state may no longer occupy the commanding heights of the economy, but for a vast majority of Indians, the state continues to be a gateway to their cherished dreams and aspirations.

The other noteworthy thing about these figures is the sharp fall in preference for private jobs, particularly amongst graduates. This marked shift may be attributed, among other things, to growing trend of young people setting up their own business ventures. The study shows that the preference to set up one's own business has grown over the last decade. Young Indians are finally taking the plunge into entrepreneurship and investing in start-ups in a big way (Pandya-Wagh, 2015). The idea of being in charge of one's own business and the sense of freedom it brings appeals to a lot of these youngsters. Another probable explanation for this shift perhaps lies in the growing attraction of a government job among today's youth. Young adults are increasingly investing their time in preparing for jobs in the public sector; evidence shows that a much larger proportion of Master of Business Administration (MBA) aspirants, who would have otherwise ended up working in the corporate sector, are now increasingly preparing for banking and other government exams (Patil, 2017).

India's job market is also witnessing a major demand–supply mismatch, mainly caused by a massive skill deficit in India's workforce. It is estimated that a mere 2.3 per cent of the workforce in India has undergone any formal vocational training, compared to 68 per cent in the UK, 75 per cent in Germany, 52 per cent in USA, 80 per cent in Japan and 96 per cent in South Korea (Wheebox, 2016). This skill deficit renders a vast section of India's graduates unfit for gainful employment in the private sector.

There is a rich body of ethnographic work that brings to light the rampant problem of unemployability amongst India's young graduates. In his classic study of unemployed young men in North India, Craig Jeffrey points to how the idea of studying is only a means of 'time pass', and that a lot of these young people recognise that accumulating more degrees is unlikely to increase their employability (Jeffrey, 2010). However, the failure to get salaried, middle class jobs leads these men to cultivate identities as unemployed, jobless youth, who simply remain in colleges as bachelors, passing time as a means to negotiate their perceived unemployment. Having grown up with the idea of serving the state, a large section of such youth continues to study and prepare for government exams in the faint hope of securing a government job someday.

But besides the romantic idea of 'serving the state', what is it about a government job that makes so many of India's young graduates hanker after it? The answer is a complex one. In a country where nine out of ten people are employed in the economy's informal sector, with a large majority of them having low earnings with limited or no social protection (IHD, 2014), the value of a government job cannot be overstated. The economic logic is overwhelming: a government job (if permanent) offers a long-term guarantee of job security and stability. Getting a regular monthly salary in a low-income country like India is no less than a luxury. However, the monetary benefits extend far beyond basic remuneration; a government employee is also entitled to a host of 'non-wage benefits' or perquisites that may have substantial monetary value (Nagaraj, 2014). Among other things, government employees (at least a significant fraction of them) get access to subsidised housing, schooling and healthcare services. They are also entitled to receive a regular post-retirement pension upon completing a certain stipulated period in service. The sociological logic is no less compelling: a government job is highly prized in India's matrimonial market; it is not uncommon to see matrimonial advertisements in India flaunt the bridegroom's 'permanent job' as a leverage to attract the best matches and in some cases, a hefty dowry (Madhavan, 2016).

While there is little evidence to show that a government job is less exacting than other occupations, it is commonly believed that it involves much less 'drudgery', has comfortable working hours and allows for abundant family time. This could be a major attraction, given that most Indians are deeply family-oriented people.

What shapes job preferences?

A person's job preferences are influenced and shaped by a variety of socio-economic factors. Parental influence and occupation, and even schooling for that matter, go a long way in shaping a person's occupational preferences. The study found that preference for a government job goes up significantly with greater parental influence on decisions about career/education. The occupation of the parent, particularly of the father, has a discernible effect on the child's occupational status/preferences. A far greater proportion of young people whose fathers were professionals, government employees, businessmen and skilled workers reported their occupational status as student (58, 48, 49 and 45 per cent, respectively) compared to those whose fathers were engaged in semi-skilled or unskilled work and farming and allied activities (29 and 25 per cent, respectively). Moreover, the latter two occupational categories reveal a far greater degree of inter-generational occupational continuity than all other occupations. This is no coincidence; it just reveals the extent to which occupational mobility is contingent on what the father does to earn a living. If the father is a farmer or an unskilled worker, the son or daughter is far less likely to be studying and acquiring the skills that enable them to move up the occupational hierarchy than somebody whose father is a high-end professional, a government employee or a skilled worker. This is indicative of low inter-generational occupational mobility in society.

Schooling, both in terms of public–private divide and the medium of instruction appears to have a clear relationship with job preferences. The study found that preference for a private job was 9 per cent higher amongst youth educated in private, English-medium schools compared to those who studied in government schools, where the language of instruction was vernacular.

Geographical location emerged as yet another salient factor that shapes job preferences. As Table 2.5 shows, a government job has a slightly stronger appeal in rural India, i.e. in its villages compared to its towns and big cities. While there are more takers for private jobs in urban India, even amongst urban youth, one can discern an increasing aversion to the private sector compared to about ten years ago. This situation presents a striking contrast to a time when young graduates from India's biggest metropolitan cities would display much alacrity to join large private corporations and multinational companies (MNCs) (Muralidharan, 2015). Today's youth seems very different in this respect; it does not really fancy the idea of working for a private firm, even if it means drawing a greater salary.

Keeping all other factors constant, a person's educational attainment is the best predictor of his/her occupational preferences. It was observed that with higher levels of education, preference for a government job goes up significantly and this was particularly true of graduates, three-quarters of whom said they would like to take up a government job, if given a choice (Table 2.4). Even those who were educated only up until high and primary school expressed an overwhelming preference for a government job. This is not unexpected; there are many low-level jobs in the public sector that do not require a high level of educational qualification or skill training. Cleaning staff, peons, drivers, cooks etc. may not be very educated, but may possess certain basic skills which make them eligible for government service.

Understandably, non-literate youth were the least likely to express a preference for a government job, but still a substantial portion of them too aspired for a government job, despite the fact they may not have the requisite qualifications to be eligible.

Career priorities of India's youth

A related question to job preferences of India's youth is the question of career priorities, which primarily deals with the goods that matter most to the youth when it comes to choosing an occupation. To understand these priorities, the study asked which one of various jobs the youth would give most priority to – a permanent job even if it means drawing a little less salary, a job with an opportunity to work

TABLE 2.4 Job preferences of India's youth by educational qualification (%)

	Government job		Private job		Own business	
	2007	*2016*	*2007*	*2016*	*2007*	*2016*
Graduate or above	54	73	25	9	19	16
High school pass	66	64	11	6	15	20
Primary pass	53	57	7	3	18	24
Non-literate	49	32	8	1	15	23

Note: The rest of the youth gave no response.

with people of their liking, a job with good income in which one does not have to worry about money, or a job that gives them a feeling of satisfaction? Findings indicated that a third of the country's youth accorded the greatest priority to having a permanent job, even if it means drawing a little less salary. Job satisfaction came a close second, followed by a good income (Figure 2.3).

A glance at the decennial trends in young peoples' job priorities reveals an interesting pattern. While security of employment continued to be on top of the priority list, a high paying job was much less preferred in 2016 than it was a decade back (almost 13 per cent less). Contrary to popular perception, this generation is also far less inclined to believe that money can buy happiness. In other words, it is less likely to believe that having a lot of money is important to remain happy in life. The importance ascribed to money declined from 79 per cent in 2007 to 60 per cent in 2016. This generation also placed a greater premium on job satisfaction, with 26 per cent of the youth according the top priority to job satisfaction compared to 19 per cent in 2007.

A cross-sectional picture of job priorities shows that geographical location has a marked effect on job choice. Moving away from villages to big cities, having a permanent job becomes less and less of a priority for India's youth and having a job with a good income assumes much greater importance. In villages, some 37 per cent of the youth accorded the highest priority to a stable and permanent job, compared to a mere 24 per cent in big cities. Likewise, about 20 per cent of youth in villages aspired to a job that pays them really well compared to 26 per cent of youth in big cities. This is understandable as the cost of living in a big city is exponentially higher than in a small town or a village. Also, with the kind of aspirational, consumption-driven lifestyle today's youth aspire to lead, having a good income becomes all the more important.

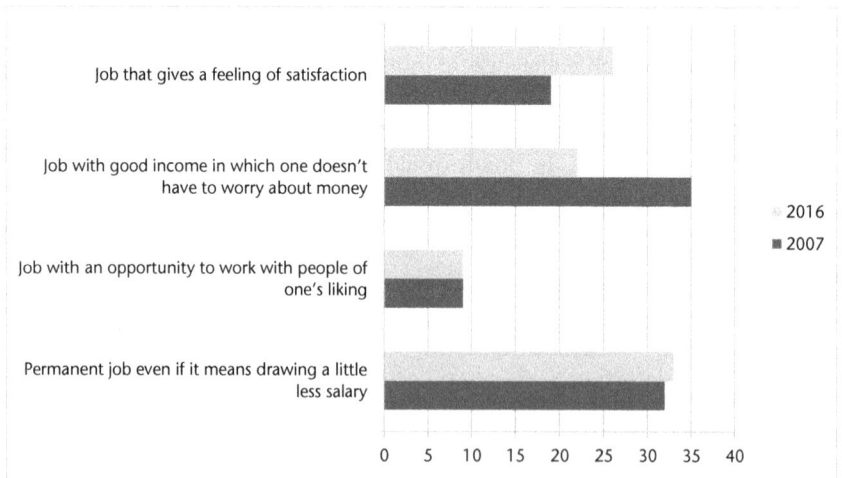

FIGURE 2.3 Career priorities of India's youth (%)

Note: The rest of the youth gave no response.

A person's educational attainment also appears to shape his/her career priorities, but only as far as the importance of work satisfaction is concerned. While youth across the extremes of the educational ladder were similarly positioned on the importance of a well-paying job, they differed significantly in the value they place on job satisfaction. Findings showed that job satisfaction mattered to only 11 per cent of non-literate youth, 16 per cent of primary pass youth, 19 per cent of those who had passed high school and a substantial 34 per cent of those who had a graduate degree. In other words, the more educated you are, the greater is the premium you place on finding satisfaction at work.

Aspiration to migrate for higher education and work

The last decade has witnessed a surge in the number of young Indians going abroad to pursue higher studies abroad. This has much to do with growing demand for quality education by a rapidly burgeoning middle class, which seems to be increasingly amenable to loosening its purse strings to provide the best education to its children. Given the dismal state of higher education in India (as reflected in the continually low rankings of Indian universities), kids from many well to do middle class households are looking beyond India's borders to satiate their desire for quality education and better job prospects which are believed to accompany it. However, only a few have the luxury to pursue such dreams and even fewer end up giving reality to those dreams. While it is true that more and more young Indians are going abroad to study and obtain work, findings showed that only one in every seven young people cherished dream to obtain higher education abroad or to find work in a foreign country. Around four in every five youth had no such ambition (Table 2.5).

There could be various reasons for this. One is finances. The prohibitive costs of studying in a foreign university, with its exorbitant tuition fees and high living expenses, ensure that a foreign education remains beyond the reach of most young Indians. This explains why youth from relatively well-off families were more eager to pursue their higher studies abroad. On being asked if they were thinking of obtaining higher education abroad, only about 14 per cent of the youth from poor families said they were contemplating going abroad for higher studies, compared to over a third (34 per cent) of the youth hailing from middle-class families and 27 per cent from rich families. The anticipated returns on investing in foreign education could be another deterrent, especially at a time when there is an acute job crunch in countries that have traditionally been popular destinations for Indians seeking better opportunities abroad.

TABLE 2.5 Aspirations of India's youth to study or work abroad (%)

Thinking of . . .	Yes	No
Obtaining higher education abroad	14	79
Working/finding a job abroad	15	81

Note: The rest of the youth gave no response.

Not surprisingly, a person's educational attainment and schooling were also found to be associated with his/her desire to go abroad for the said purposes. The more educated youth were also much keener to go abroad for higher education and work, with a fifth (20 per cent) of graduates aspiring to study in foreign universities and about the same proportion of graduates (22 per cent) considering the possibility of finding work abroad. Look at schooling, it is found that youth from private, English-medium schools were more likely to fancy the idea of going abroad to study and work, compared to those who had studied in non-English-medium, government schools. Of course, this has much to do with how educational attainment, schooling and economic status reinforce each other because the richer you are, the more likely it is that you will be more educated and also have studied in a private, English-medium school.

However, there is something else that matters more than one's economic condition and schooling in shaping a person's aspirations to go abroad – the density of one's kinship network, or what is called 'social capital' in academic parlance. The odds of going abroad to study and work increased phenomenally if the person had a kin or a close relative studying or working abroad. About 7 per cent of the youth said they had a family member or a close relative who is studying or has studied abroad, and amongst them the desire to study abroad was about 56 per cent. Similarly, 11 per cent or little over one in ten youth said they had a family member or close relative working abroad and amongst them the desire to work abroad was 54 per cent. This also explains why youth from Kerala, Punjab and Tamil Nadu showed a greater inclination to not just pursue their higher studies abroad (24, 24 and 20 per cent, respectively) but also to find a job in a foreign country (48, 32 and 24 per cent, respectively) compared to youth from other states. People from these states are known to have a substantial presence in India's vast diaspora.

Conclusion

Three broad conclusions can be safely drawn from the study. One, the occupational profile of today's youth has undergone a significant shift over the last decade. This change has been engendered by the massive rise in the number of young people pursuing their studies. Two, the aspiration for a government job remains undiminished since the last decade. In fact, with greater liberalisation and privatisation of the economy, the expectations from the state in terms of its perceived capacity to create jobs have only grown. As the government gets downsized and many of its services get outsourced to non-state actors in the years to come, there will be even greater competition for the fewer job opportunities that are available in the public sector. This has the potential to spurn social unrest and political violence. The agitations by Jats in Haryana, Patels in Gujarat, the Marathas in Maharashtra and the Kapus in Seemandhra are somewhat symptomatic of the underlying job crisis that is brewing in India. Three, since the jobs of the future are going to be extremely skill-intensive, one of the most challenging tasks before governments and policymakers is to bridge the massive skill deficit that has kept India from fully realising its demographic dividend. A skilled workforce is an asset that is surely worth investing in for a country that has some of the lowest rates of labour productivity in the world.

Note

1 Self-reported unemployment amongst youth in the 15–21-year-old age group is not factored in this analysis because a substantial proportion of young people in this age bracket are either in high school or are pursuing their undergraduate studies.

References

Bardhan, P. (2017) A new class act. *The Indian Express*, January 20.

Damodaran, H. (2014) Only 40 per cent of rural households dependent on farming as main income source: NSSO. *The Indian Express*, May 24.

Desai, S. and Kulkarni, V. (2008) Changing educational inequalities in India in the context of affirmative action. *Demography*, 45(2): 245–270.

Deshpande, S. (2006) Exclusive inequalities: merit, caste and discrimination in Indian higher education today. *Economic and Political Weekly*, 41(24): 2438–2444.

Galanter, M. (1984) *Competing Equalities: Law and the Backward Classes in India*. Berkeley, CA: University of California Press.

Institute for Human Development (IHD) (2018) *India Labour and Employment Report 2014: Workers in the Era of Globalization*. Delhi: Institute for Human Development.

Jeffrey, C. (2010) Timepass: youth, class, and time among unemployed young men in India. *American Ethnologist*, 37(3): 465–481.

Madhavan, N. (2016) Why Indian PhD and BTech holders love lowly government jobs. *Hindustan Times*, February 3.

Ministry of Labour and Employment (2016) *Report on Fifth Annual Employment: Unemployment Survey. Vol 1*. Chandigarh: Government of India.

Muralidharan, T. (2015) Why the craze for government jobs? *The Hindu*, November 15.

Nagaraj, R. (2014) *Public Sector Employment: What Has Changed?*, Working Paper. Mumbai: Indira Gandhi Institute of Development Research.

National Sample Survey Office (NSSO) (2011–12) *Employment and Unemployment*. 68th round. Government of India: Ministry of Statistics & Programme Implementation.

Pandya-Wagh, K. (2015) India's fast-growing start-up business scene. *BBC News*. Available at: www.bbc.com/news/business-33424303 (accessed on 24 October 2018).

Patil, A. (2017) Are government jobs stealing a march over Indian private sector in 2017? *Hindustan Times*, June 15.

Varghese, N.V. (2015) *Challenges of Massification of Higher Education in India*. Working Paper. Centre for Policy Research in Higher Education, National University of Educational Planning and Administration.

Wheebox (2016) *India Skills Report 2016*. Wheebox. Available at: https://wheebox.com/logo/ISR-2016-small.pdf (accessed on 1 December 2016).

World Bank (2016) GDP growth (annual %): 1961–2016. World Bank. Available at: https://data.worldbank.org/indicator/NY.GDP.MKTP.KD.ZG (accessed on 15 December 2016).

Yadav, Y. (2004) Economic reforms in the mirror of public opinion. *The Hindu*, June 13.

3

OPINION ON THE ISSUE OF RESERVATIONS

Arushi Gupta

The topic of reservations or affirmative action in India has been highly contentious and hotly debated. In India, reservation policies were adopted in the princely states and presidencies well before Independence in order to reduce caste-based inequalities and end discrimination faced by historically disadvantaged groups. They have not only continued since then but have also been extended further. Not only are reservations applied in the political domain in the form of reserved constituencies for Dalits (former 'untouchables' or Scheduled Castes) and Adivasis (indigenous people or Scheduled Tribes) in the Lok Sabha and the state Vidhan Sabhas, but also in the spheres of education and employment, and it is in these two spheres that they are highly contentious. It is mandatory for most of the government-run or controlled institutions (except for strategic areas) to have reservations in jobs and in admissions to higher educational institutions. Apart from Dalits and Adivasis, many states have also for long been providing reservations to 'Other Backward Castes' (OBCs) in public sector employment and higher educational institutions. Since the early 1990s they have been beneficiaries of employment reservations at the all India level, and since 2005, reservations have been extended to them (excluding the top layer or affluent sections amongst them) in central educational institutions of higher learning: 27 per cent of all available seats are reserved for OBCs, in addition to the 22.5 per cent reserved for Dalits and Adivasis.

Keeping in mind the system of reservations in India, it becomes pertinent to know whether we have reservations because of caste inequalities or because caste prejudice led to the reservation system in India, as explained by Satish Deshpande (2015) in *The Hindu*. Is there any defined category of the beneficiaries of reservations? These questions remain inseparable from the broader and ever-evolving debate on the reservation in India.

In very recent times there have been agitations by dominant agrarian castes such as Patidars in Gujarat, the Marathas in Maharashtra, Kapus in Andhra Pradesh and Telangana and Jats in Haryana, demanding inclusion in the OBC category on grounds of increasing socio-economic disadvantage. There is also a demand for extending reservation benefits to economically weaker sections within the general category. At present the Constitution provides reservation to only three social classes: Dalits, Adivasis and OBCs. Also, reservation policies do not apply to private enterprises and private educational institutions, not even for Dalits, Adivasis and OBCs. Suggestions for extending reservations to private sector employment have been met with strong resistance from many in the private sector.

The structure of Indian society is constructed on inequalities largely based on caste. The caste system in India is highly exclusionary and hierarchical. Marc Galanter in his 1992 book, *Competing Equalities: Law and the Backward Classes in India*, raises two important questions: can castes or communities be used to define the arena of 'backwardness'? Or does the ranking of the castes in the Indian society define backwardness?

It is presumed that backwardness can be measured either by caste or that there is a need to measure caste and community itself to define backwardness more accurately. In a very famous case of Chitralekhavs, state of Mysore, 1964, the Supreme Court laid down two important principles: first, 'the caste of a group of citizens may be a relevant circumstance in ascertaining their social backwardness' and second, though caste is important to determine social backwardness of a citizen, 'it cannot be the sole dominant test', as explained by Bhagwan Das (2000). Caste remains an important criterion to identify the backward communities, but it is the economic backwardness that should define the reservations for the communities. Thus, it becomes necessary to abolish caste completely.

Reservations in India are provided to the deprived sections that have suffered the most historically, lie at bottom of the caste hierarchy and are considered to be untouchables, impure and polluting. Dalits, Adivasis, OBCs and in some states the backward castes amongst the Muslim community fall within the paradigm of reservations. For the longest period in history they have been denied civil, educational, cultural and religious rights. Further, they have suffered racial ostracisation and residential segregation as well as social isolation, in contrast to the upper castes studied by Thorat and Senapati (2007). There exists another category comprising Muslims, Sikhs, Christians, Parsis, Jains and Buddhists who are constitutionally recognised as a minority community and have suffered from caste-based discrimination in jobs and educational institutions.

Broadly speaking, the reservation debate comprises two diametric arguments, the argument of merit and the compensatory principle. Contrary to the merit argument which opposes reservations, the compensatory principle regards the merit argument to be hegemonic and recognises the need to uphold the principle of justice laid in the Constitution as well as to maintain equity in society. However, Patel (2008) describes how the compensatory principle has been criticised on various grounds: class–caste relations, reverse discrimination and the inclination towards primordial loyalties amongst others.

The opinion of the youth is of prime importance as reservations in government jobs and educational institutions are one of the major roadblocks to their progress. This remainder of this chapter heavily draws on the Centre for the Study of Developing Societies (CSDS) study and tries to capture views of Indian youth on reservations for reserved categories in government and private jobs and government educational institutions. The study attempted to analyse the opinion of the Indian youth on the existing reservations for Dalits, Adivasis and OBCs in government jobs and in government educational institutions. In addition, the opinion of youth was also sought on the proposal for extending reservations for Dalits, Adivasis and OBCs to private jobs, and to backward Muslims in government jobs. Opinions were also sought on the emerging demands of the dominant farming communities to be included in the OBC category quota. Broadly, the argument seems to be based on two different grounds: one, complete refusal to revamp the policy of reservations or to extend the reservations list and two, the futility of continuing with this policy on caste grounds, a view held by anti-reservationists.

Opinion on government jobs and educational institutions

The backward castes suffer from substantial inequalities in employment and educational institutions. It is to be noted that the reservations were not provided to correct economic inequalities but rather to eliminate the monopoly of the upper castes in government jobs and educational institutes in order to create a just and equal society. In the government sector, the employment rate for the OBCs in central services in 2015 was merely 12 per cent, as analysed by Prabhakari (2015) in his article highlighting the Mandal Commission Report. In educational institutes, the condition is worse where more than 50 per cent of the teaching seats are lying vacant for Dalits and Adivasis, as reported by Singh (2016). To rectify the situation, 15 per cent of the seats are reserved for Dalits in government educational institutes and government jobs, 7.5 per cent of the seats are reserved for Adivasis and 27 per cent for OBCs.

It is important to note that reservations are provided in government jobs, government educational institutions and not in the private sector. The reservations in the government sector are further expanded to government housing schemes, government space for shops and commercial activities etc. Other than this, the communities are also provided with several relaxation schemes to compete for government jobs such as: relaxation of minimum age to enter government service, relaxation of fees, separate interviews for Dalits/Adivasis and a provision for pre-examination training. Given the absence of backward communities from the upper ranks of government jobs, reservation in promotion was also specified. Article 15(4) of the Indian Constitution allows the reservation of seats for socially and educationally backward classes, Dalits and Adivasis in educational institutes including, technical, medical and engineering colleges under the control of central and state governments. Further Article 16(4), permits the state to make reservations for the backward communities who in their opinion are not adequately represented in appointments to public services. Moreover, Thorat and Senapati (2007) in their study also discuss scholarships and special hostel facilities, concessions that are also provided to the backward communities.

It has been widely argued that the reservations in the government educational institutes as well as government jobs constitute an advantage of the backward communities. In order to provide a level playing field, reservations should be provided in educational institutes and not in jobs. Contrary to this, Ashwini Deshpande (2015) has argued that job appointments are not based on a fair process and preference is given to an upper caste member, even though a lower caste member is equally qualified.

Given this backdrop, when the youth were asked about their opinion on reservations for the reserved categories, the preference was more for government jobs than government educational institutions. The preference was greater for reservations for Dalits and Adivasis than for OBCs in both government jobs and educational institutions.

Opinion on Dalit-Adivasi quota in government jobs and educational institutions

Since caste-based inequalities are the basis for providing reservations in India, any analysis of this issue must be done in terms of caste. The study, in fact, shows that the caste of the person makes a huge difference to his/her opinion on the issue of reservation. On support for reservation for Dalits and Adivasis in government jobs, youth belonging to the Dalit and Adivasi communities (the beneficiary groups) were (not surprisingly) found to be more in support than youth from other communities: 71 per cent of the Dalit youth and 60 per cent of the Adivasi youth said they supported reservation for Dalits and Adivasis in government jobs (Table 3.1). A majority of Muslim youth (50 per cent) and a plurality of OBC youth (44 per cent) were also found to be in support of it. The fairly strong support for Dalit-Adivasi reservation amongst OBC youth can be explained by the fact that OBCs themselves are beneficiaries of reservation and hence might be averse to opposing reservations for others. With respect to Muslims, the high support for Dalit-Adivasi reservation could be due to the desire for reservation benefits amongst many Muslims (as seen later in this chapter). Meanwhile, the lowest outright support for Dalit and Adivasi reservation in government jobs was found amongst upper caste youth (30 per cent).

A similar pattern was also found with respect to support for reservation for Dalits and Adivasis in educational institutions; that is, the Dalit and Adivasi youth were most supportive of it and Hindu upper caste youth were most opposed to it. Meanwhile, on comparing the support for both types of reservations (in government jobs and in educational institutions), the study found slightly greater approval for the former amongst all communities. The difference is greatest amongst Adivasi youth (60 per cent for jobs as opposed to 52 per cent for education), followed by Dalit youth (71 per cent as opposed to 67 per cent) (Tables 3.1 and 3.2).

TABLE 3.1 Opinion of India's youth on Dalit-Adivasi reservation in government jobs (%)

	Complete support	Conditional support	Oppose	No response
Overall	**48**	**6**	**26**	**18**
Hindu upper caste	30	10	43	18
Hindu OBC	44	8	27	21
Hindu Dalit	71	6	12	12
Hindu Adivasi	60	3	11	27
Muslim	50	7	25	18

Note: Conditional support means those who said there should only be a Dalit quota or only be an Adivasi quota, or that a quota should be in place but the proportion should be less.

TABLE 3.2 Opinion of India's youth on Dalit-Adivasi reservation in government educational institutions (%)

	Complete support	Conditional support	Oppose	No response
Overall	**46**	**9**	**28**	**18**
Hindu upper caste	28	10	46	17
Hindu OBC	42	10	28	21
Hindu Dalit	67	7	14	13
Hindu Adivasi	52	5	13	31
Muslim	49	7	25	19

Note: Conditional support means those who said there should only be a Dalit quota or only be an Adivasi quota, or that a quota should be in place but the proportion should be less.

Even though a majority of Dalit and Adivasi youngsters supported reservation in government jobs and/or educational institutions for their communities, there exist differences in opinion amongst them based on their economic status. For instance, Dalit youth from poor and lower economic strata were far more supportive (74 per cent) of existing reservation provisions for them in government jobs as compared to middle class or rich Dalit youth (65 per cent). Amongst Adivasis too, a similar pattern was found (62 per cent of poor and lower economic strata supported reservations in government jobs as compared to 58 per cent of upper and middle class Adivasi youth). A similar pattern was observed in support for reservations in educational institutions. A 7 per cent difference was seen amongst the Adivasi youth from poor and lower class (54 per cent) as compared to youth from upper and middle class (47 per cent). Amongst the Dalits the difference was of 6 percentage points (69 per cent from lower and poor economic strata and 63 per cent from upper and middle class). The data, therefore, validate that the Dalits and Adivasis are not a homogenous group and consists of various castes or *jatis* (subcastes) within them, as a result of which some groups are able to benefit from the reservation policy while others are not. An elite or a top layer emerges, leading to a confrontation in the reservation system. In the *Indra Sawhney vs. Union of India* case, 1992, the same issue was raised and the Supreme Court was asked to define 'social backwardness'. As a result, the Court upheld 50 per cent of the quotas and laid down 11 indicators to define 'backwardness'. Further, the nine-member committee ascertained that the top layer can only be used to describe OBCs and not Dalits/Adivasis. While, this case made it clear that reservations will be provided to the historically disadvantaged communities, another judgment, in *Ashok Kumar vs. Union of India*, 2008, specified that reservations should be provided on the basis of economic conditions to strengthen the principle of secularism con-tributing to the building of a casteless society.

Educational attainment does not seem to make much of a difference, at least with respect to Dalits. Both non-literate Dalit youth and highly educated Dalit youth were found to be equally supportive of reservation policies for their community. Amongst Adivasis, however, education does matter. Support for Dalit-Adivasi reservations amongst them, be it for government jobs or for gov-ernment educational institutions, rose with educational qualification. While only 48 per cent of non-literate Adivasi youth were supportive of a quota for Dalits-Adivasis in government jobs, amongst those who had completed graduation or a higher degree, the support was much higher at 65 per cent. Similarly, only about a third of non-literate Adivasis were found to support reservation for their com-munity in government-run educational institutions, compared to nearly three in every five well-educated Adivasi youth. It is believed that reservation in education for the backward community acts as a springboard for good and well-paying jobs. But in many parts of the world, this has been proven wrong. For instance, Pierre Bourdieu and Jean-Claude Passeron (1977) provide evidence of French society, where education often leads to dominant class structures. It is often perceived that education is provided to the wealthy and, in turn, they have access to affluent jobs. Thomas Weisskopf (2004) studied various data sources across various educational institutes and reflected that in the absence of reservations it becomes difficult for backward communities to attain education, leading to jobs and often promotions.

Opinion on OBC quota in government jobs and educational institutions

Just as the youth were asked about their view on the existing Dalit-Adivasi quotas, they were also asked about what they thought about the 27 per cent quota for OBC communities. The overall support for the latter was found to be only slightly less than the overall support for the former. About 45 per cent of the youth were in support of OBC reservation, be it in government jobs or government educational institutions (Tables 3.3 and 3.4). This is just a few per cent less than overall youth support for Dalit-Adivasi quotas.

There are, however, significant differences in opinion amongst the Dalit-Adivasi youth and OBC youth. In the case of Dalit-Adivasi quotas, the study found the beneficiary groups (Dalits and Adivasis) to be more supportive of reservations than the non-beneficiary communities. In the case of OBC reservations, however, the study finds that beneficiary community, i.e. OBC youth, both from the dominant section and the lower section, to be less supportive of reservation for their community as compared to Dalit and Muslim youth. While only about 46 per cent of upper OBC youth gave complete support to the existing provision of reservations to OBCs in government jobs and 47 per cent in educational institutions and 43 per cent of lower OBC youth gave complete support to the existing provision of reservations to OBCs in both, the support amongst Dalits and Muslims was much higher at around 63 per cent and 53 per cent, respectively. On disaggregating Muslim responses in terms of castes, the study further notes that complete support for OBC reservation to be greater amongst Muslim OBCs (about 61 per cent) than Muslim upper castes (about 45 per cent). This does not come as a surprise as some Muslim communities in some states have been included in the OBC category and hence are eligible for reservation under the OBC quota.

While analysing the opinions of the Hindu OBC community through the prism of economic class, one common pattern emerged. Hindu OBCs from the lower and poor economic strata were more likely to approve of reservation for OBCs in government jobs and government educational institutions than OBCs belonging to upper and middle classes or the top layer. This pattern by class holds even upon disaggregating the larger OBC community into upper OBCs and lower OBCs.

TABLE 3.3 Opinion of India's youth on OBC reservation in government jobs (%)

	Complete support	Conditional support	Oppose	No response
Overall	45	5	30	19
Hindu upper caste	29	7	48	17
Hindu upper OBC	46	7	26	21
Hindu lower OBC	43	4	31	22
Hindu Dalit	63	4	20	14
Hindu Adivasi	32	2	26	41
Muslim	53	6	23	18

Note: Conditional support means those who said there should be a lower quota.

TABLE 3.4 Opinion of India's youth on OBC reservation in government educational institutions (%)

	Complete support	Conditional support	Oppose	No response
Overall	45	6	30	20
Hindu upper caste	29	7	45	18
Hindu upper OBC	47	6	25	22
Hindu lower OBC	43	5	30	22
Hindu Dalit	62	4	20	14
Hindu Adivasi	28	3	28	41
Muslim	52	6	23	19

Note: Conditional support means those who said there should be a lower quota.

Opinion on proposed reservations in private sector jobs

Post-liberalisation, outsourcing and privatisation have decreased the number of jobs in the government sector and increased job opportunities in the private sector. This has led to increasing demands for the extension of caste-based reservations to private sector employment. Reserving jobs in the private sector was part of the National Common Minimum Programme of the United Progressive Alliance (UPA) I government and it initiated a national dialogue with political parties and industry leaders in 2004 to see how this could be implemented. However, the proposal met with strong resistance from the corporate sector, and since then no significant headway has been made on this issue.

The issue of reservation in private sector jobs continues to stimulate debate because of the question on whether reservations should be provided only to the Dalits and Adivasis or also to OBCs. OBCs lack uniformity across states and hence, it was decided by the Supreme Court to exclude the OBCs with higher incomes but it failed to yield any result, as shown by Thimmaiah (2005). Recently, the *Hindustan Times* (2016) has showed that the National Commission for Backward Classes has put forward the demand for the reservations for Dalits, Adivasis and OBCs in the private sector with special emphasis on a 27 per cent reservation for OBCs in cooperative and philanthropic organisations.

The study attempted to gauge the opinion of young Indians on this aspect of reservation. Indian youth were asked whether they supported or opposed extending reservation to private sector jobs for the Dalit-Adivasi and OBC communities. On the Dalit-Adivasi reservation in private sector jobs, the youth response was split down the middle: 38 per cent supported the idea and 38 per cent opposed it. About 3 per cent gave it partial support and the rest did not respond (Table 3.5). However, on the question of reservation for OBCs in private sector employment, the proportion of those opposed to it was greater than those in support of it. A little over two in every five youth (42 per cent) opposed the idea of introducing quotas for OBCs in private sector jobs, and only one in every three (35 per cent) supported it (Table 3.6).

These findings, when viewed comparatively, highlight two things. First, that there is slightly greater support amongst the youth to the idea of having quotas for Dalits and Adivasis in private sector jobs than for the idea of a quota for OBCs in the private sector. And second, that there is less support amongst the youth for the idea of private sector quotas than public sector quotas. While 48 per cent and 45 per cent were found to be in full support of reservations for Dalits-Adivasis and OBCs in public sector jobs respectively, the figures dropped to 38 per cent and 35 per cent respectively with regard to private sector quotas for the same communities. This overall pattern holds for Dalits-Adivasis and OBCs as well; that is, youth belonging to these communities were also less likely to support the idea of quotas in private sector jobs for themselves than they were to support the existing provision of quotas in public sector jobs.

TABLE 3.5 Opinion of India's youth on the idea of quotas for Dalits and Adivasis in private sector jobs (%)

	Fully support	*Conditional support*	*Oppose*	*No response*
Overall	**38**	**3**	**38**	**22**
Hindu upper caste	19	2	59	20
Hindu OBC	38	2	36	24
Hindu Dalit	57	3	25	15
Hindu Adivasi	38	2	18	41
Muslim	39	2	38	22

Note: Conditional support means those who said there should be a quota only for Dalits or only for Adivasis.

TABLE 3.6 Opinion of India's youth on the idea of quotas for OBCs in private sector jobs (%)

	Support	*Oppose*	*No response*
Overall	**35**	**42**	**23**
Hindu upper caste	18	61	21
Hindu upper OBC	39	36	25
Hindu lower OBC	36	39	26
Hindu Dalit	50	33	17
Hindu Adivasis	25	33	42
Muslim	39	39	23

Once again, disaggregating the Dalit-Adivasi and OBC responses by economic class seems to suggest that it is youth belonging to the lower section of the society amongst all these communities that show greater support for reserving seats in private sector jobs than those who are economically better-off. For instance, every four in ten and every six in ten Adivasi youth and Dalit youth respectively from lower and poor economic strata preferred reservations in private jobs for Dalits and Adivasis. The pattern is similar amongst the OBCs also, where the support is greatest amongst the youth from lower and poorer economic class.

Opinion of youth on proposed reservations for Muslims in government jobs

Muslims constitute 14.2 per cent of the population of India and is the second largest religious community, as revealed in the 2011 Census. It is widely believed that the Muslim community is an egalitarian community and there exists no distinction between castes. Providing reservations to Muslims is considered unconstitutional because reservations in India are not provided on an individual basis but rather provided to the group/individuals belonging to a deprived/disadvantaged caste community. J.H. Hutton, Census commissioner in 1931 wrote,

Caste was in the air, and neither the followers of Islam nor of Christianity could escape the infection of caste; even the change of religion does not destroy the caste system, for Muslims who do not recognise it as valid are found to observe it in practice and there are many Muslim castes as well as Hindus.

(cited in Krishnan, 2012b)

Within Muslims, there exist *zats* or *biradaris* which are considered to be socially and educationally backward communities. As Ashgar Ali Engineer (1991) has pointed out, it was the shift in the artisan and occupational castes to Islam along with their traditional social status that gave birth to the low castes in Muslims. Similarly, Krishnan (2012a) has explained that people of various castes belonging to professions such as carpenters, weavers, gardeners, barbers etc. who converted to Islam were looked down upon by the rest of the Muslim community. Demands for reservations for Muslims in public sector jobs have been gaining momentum ever since the publication of the Sachar Committee report in 2006 and the Justice Ranganath Mishra Commission report in 2009. While the former presented a dismal picture of discrimination being faced by Muslims in employment, the latter recommended giving a 10 per cent reservation to Muslims in central and state government jobs on the grounds of their socio-economic backwardness. This issue of extending reservations beyond caste has been highly controversial and has hit legal roadblocks, with courts overruling the decisions of some state governments in this regard.

In the study, the opinion of youngsters on this contested issue was also obtained. They were asked if reservations should be implemented for backward Muslims in government jobs. Overall, only about one in every three or 35 per cent of the youth supported the idea of reserving seats for backward Muslims in government jobs. Two in every five (41 per cent) were opposed to it and about a quarter (24 per cent) did not respond to the question (Table 3.7). The figure in support for Muslim reservation (35 per cent) is less in comparison to the support shown by the Indian youth to questions related to reservations for Dalit-Adivasi and OBC youth in government jobs (48 and 45 per cent, respectively).

The idea of reservations for Muslims in government jobs found greatest support amongst Muslim youth, not surprisingly. Three in every five Muslim youth (60 per cent) in the study fully supported the idea and one in every five (21 per cent) was opposed to it. About 20 per cent did not answer the question. The second highest support for the idea was witnessed amongst Dalit youth at 49 per cent. In fact, other than Muslim youth, Dalit youth was the only other category amongst whom support for the idea of Muslim reservation was found to be greater than opposition to it. Amongst youth belonging to all other communities, including OBCs, opposition to it was higher than support for it.

Interestingly, the support for Muslim reservation amongst Muslim youth in terms of economic stratification was more amongst the upper and middle classes (64 per cent) than those belonging to the lower economic strata (55 per cent).

TABLE 3.7 Opinion of India's youth on the idea of quotas for backward Muslims in government jobs (%)

	Support	Oppose	No response
Overall	**35**	**41**	**24**
Hindu upper caste	19	59	22
Hindu OBC	32	41	27
Hindu Dalit	49	31	19
Hindu Adivasi	21	36	43
Muslim	60	21	20

This pattern is opposite to the one witnessed amongst lower and upper sections of Dalit-Adivasi and OBC youth on questions related to Dalit-Adivasi and OBC reservations (discussed earlier).

Opinion on the demand of non-OBC farming communities to be included within the OBC quota

Another significant issue with respect to reservations on which youth opinion seems necessary is related to the demand of many farming/peasant communities (who are neither strictly upper caste nor OBCs) to be included in the OBC category and thus be eligible for reservations. Such demands have come from Patidars in Gujarat, Jats in Haryana, Kapus in Andhra Pradesh and Telangana and Marathas in Maharashtra.

The study found youth to be more opposed to this demand than in support. While every fourth youth (26 per cent) was found to be in favour of inclusion of such communities within the OBC category, about one in every third (34 per cent) was averse to the idea. One in every ten gave conditional support to the idea; that is, they were in favour of inclusion but only after increasing the existing OBC quota beyond 27 per cent.

There were differences in opinion based on the social group to which the youth belong. Amongst OBC groups (the community most likely to be affected by the inclusion of non-OBC communities within the OBC fold), youth belonging to dominant or upper OBC groups were far more supportive of the demand than youth from the lower OBC communities. Amongst Dalit youth too, support for it was greater than the overall average (Table 3.8). Interestingly, youth belonging to the beneficiary groups or the group demanding this reservation, were not found to be much in support of the demand. Only about one in every four youth from the dominant non-OBC farming castes approved of it and two in every five were found to be opposed to it. There is, however, a class dimension to this. The poorest sections amongst these dominant farming communities supported the demand (42 per cent) much more than the privileged amongst them (15 per cent).

TABLE 3.8 Opinion of India's youth on the demand of non-OBC farming communities to be included in the OBC category (%)

	Fully support	Support but only after increasing existing OBC quota	Oppose	No response
Overall	**26**	**10**	**34**	**30**
Hindu upper caste	18	6	53	23
Hindu dominant farming castes	23	11	41	24
Hindu upper OBC	32	11	30	28
Hindu lower OBC	26	10	33	31
Hindu Dalit	33	11	30	27
Hindu Adivasi	13	5	17	64
Muslim	26	11	30	33

The broader picture

Taking into account the opinion on reservation as discussed above (barring the issue of the demand of non-OBC farming castes), an Index of Attitude Towards Reservation was constructed (see Appendix II to find out how the index was constructed) in order to understand the broader and more holistic sentiment regarding reservation amongst India's youth. The results indicated a polarised situation. While 37 per cent of the youth were found to be strongly in support of the idea of reservation, 35 per cent were strongly opposed to it. About 13 per cent were moderately in support of reservations, and 16 per cent were low in their support. The polarity on the issue was found to be the strongest amongst youth residing in big cities, where 38 per cent were strongly in favour of reservations and 37 per cent strongly opposed to it. Youth in smaller cities were more likely to oppose the idea of reservations than support it. Meanwhile, it was opposite amongst youth in villages; they were more likely to support than oppose.

In terms of age, opposition to reservations was the strongest in the youngest bracket, i.e. 15 to 17 year olds (39 per cent) followed by the oldest, i.e. 30 to 34 year olds (37 per cent). Meanwhile, opposition to reservation was the weakest amongst the youth aged between 18 and 25 years of age (33 per cent). In fact, nearly two in every five of them were strongly in favour of it. Educational attainment makes a huge difference to a young person's perception of reservations. The more educated the youth, the more likely they are to support it. While 38 per cent of youth who had completed college education were found to be strongly in support of reservations in general, the figure of high support amongst non-literate youth was six per cent less at 32 per cent.

As discussed earlier with respect to specific opinions of the youth, the economic background of a person matters quite a lot on how this issue is perceived. Youth from the lower section of the society were found to be most supportive of reservations followed by those from the middle-income categories. Upper class youth were least supportive of it. In terms of caste, Dalit and Muslim youth were found to be most in favour of reservations and upper caste youth most opposed to them. The view amongst OBC youth was polarised – both extreme support and extreme opposition to reservations was seen amongst them. Meanwhile, Adivasi youth come across as being opposed to reservations in the Reservation Index because a high proportion of them did not answer many of the questions related to the issue.

Interestingly, a correlation between caste discrimination and support for reservation can be observed. About 9 per cent of the youth reported having faced discrimination on the basis of caste and strong support for reservations amongst them was about 45 per cent, which is much higher than the overall average of 37 per cent. Meanwhile, having a discriminatory or non-discriminatory attitude towards other communities also makes a difference to one's opinion on reservation. Only 17 per cent of youth who were found to be very discriminatory in their attitudes were strongly in favour of reservations. The support was more than two times higher at 42 per cent amongst those who were found to be not at all discriminatory in their attitudes towards others.

To sum up, the study has found fairly strong support amongst India's youth for existing reservations for Dalit-Adivasi and OBCs in government jobs and educational institutions. A greater proportion amongst all castes and communities, barring Hindu upper castes, were found to be in support of these quotas than opposed to it. This pattern of greater support than opposition can also be seen with respect to extending reservations to Dalits and Adivasis in private sector jobs; however, the degree of support for this idea is less than that offered to existing public sector reservations. The idea of extending reservations to OBCs in private sector jobs, however, does not find widespread support. The same is true for the proposal of extending reservations to Muslims in government jobs. This idea found approval only amongst Muslim youth and to some extent Dalit youth. Meanwhile, the economic background of a young person belonging to a beneficiary group seems to matter in how they view the issue of reservations for their community. Youth belonging to economically well-off sections within Dalits-Adivasis, OBCs and the dominant farming castes were found to be slightly more opposed to reservations for their community than those who are less well-off within these communities. Only on the question of Muslim reservation is this pattern not seen. Muslim youth belonging to the upper and middle classes were more approving of the idea of extending reservations to Muslims (on the grounds of backwardness) than their co-religionists from the lower class, perhaps because some amongst the latter category are already benefitting from reservations as part of the OBC quota in various states.

Finally, even as the overall Reservation Index as well as the youth's opinions suggest more support than opposition for the idea of reservations, there is a desire amongst the youth to go beyond caste as the only basis of reservations. Many were found to be in favour of the idea having reservations only on the basis of economic status. When asked whether reservations should be only on the basis of caste or only on the basis of economic status or whether they should be scrapped altogether, two in every five youth (40 per cent) preferred to have economic status as the criterion. While one in every seven said it should continue to be on the basis of caste, about one in every ten wanted both caste and economic status to be the basis. Only 17 per cent wanted the entire policy of reservation to be scrapped altogether. The desire for having economic status as the basis for reservation was also found amongst those youth who showed high support for reservation in the overall Reservation Index. Nearly half of them were of the opinion that reservations should be on economic basis instead of caste. This sentiment in favour of the economic criterion was seen amongst youth across all castes and communities, including those from reservation beneficiary groups like OBCs and Dalits. Dalit youth, however, were also found to be the most resistant to the proposition of doing away with caste as the criterion compared to youth from other communities.

References

Bhandari, Dalveer (2008) *Judgment Summary III, Outlook.* Available at: www.outlookindia. com/website/story/judgment-summary-iii/237169 (accessed 14 May 2018).

Bourdieu, Pierre and Passeron, Jean-Claude (1977) *Reproduction in Education, Society and Culture.* New Delhi: Sage Publications.

Das, Bhagwan (2000) Moments on the history of reservation. *Economic and Political Weekly,* 34(43,44): 3831–3834.

Deshpande, Ashwini (2015) From formal to substantive equality, Seminar paper. Available at: www.india-seminar.com/2015/672/672_ashwini_deshpande.htm (accessed 26 October 2016).

Deshpande, Ashwini and Newman, Katherine (2007) Where the path leads: the role of caste in post university employment expectations. *Economic and Political Weekly,* 42: 4133–4140.

Deshpande, Satish (2015) Reservations are not just about quotas. *The Hindu.* Available at at: www.thehindu.com/opinion/lead/reservations-are-not-just-about-quotas/ article7036459.ece (accessed 8 February 2018).

Engineer, Ashgar Ali (1991) Remaking Indian Muslim identity. *Economic and Political Weekly,* 26(16): 1036–1038. Available at: www.jstor.org/stable/4397952 (accessed 8 February 2018).

Galanter, Marc (1992) *Competing Equalities: Law and the Backward Caste in India.* Delhi: Oxford University Press.

Hindustan Times, The (2016) Govt. wants OBC quota in private sector, 9 February 2016. Available at: www.hindustantimes.com/india/government-panel-wants-obc-quotas-in-private-sector/story-RmRRgStR9M8IoTBEgRjQHK.html (accessed 25 April 2018).

Jodhka, Surinder and Newman, Katherine (2007) In the name of globalization: meritocracy, productivity, and the hidden language of caste. *Economic and Political Weekly,* 42: 4125–4132.

Krishnan, P.S. (2012a) Reservations for Muslims in India: a step for inclusive development. *Economic and Political Weekly,* 47(33).

Krishnan, P.S. (2012b) A fair deal for Muslims. *Frontline,* 29(4). Available at: www.frontline. in/static/html/fl2904/stories/20120309290409000.htm (accessed 22 November 2016).

Krishnan, P.S. (2017) Quotas are for justice, not to plug job holes. *The Indian Express,* January 3. Available at: http://indianexpress.com/article/opinion/columns/sc-st-reservation-quota-jobs-patidars-marathas-jats-4456243/ (accessed 10 February 2017).

National Commission for Religious and Linguistic Minorities (2009) *Ranganath Misra Report*. Indian American Muslim Council. Available at: https://iamc.com/reports/2009/12/report-of-the-national-commission-for-religious-and-linguistic-minorities-ranganath-misra-report/ (accessed 22 November 2016).

Patel, Tulsi (2008) Stigma goes backstage: reservation in jobs and education. *Sociological Bulletin*, 57(1): 97–114.

Prabhakari, Siddharth (2015) 20 years after Mandal, less than 12% OBCs in govt jobs, *The Times of India*. Available at: http://timesofindia.indiatimes.com/india/20-years-after-Mandal-less-than-12-OBCs-in-central-govt-jobs/articleshow/50328073.cms (accessed 6 December 2016).

Sachar Committee (2006) *Report*, PRS India. Available at: www.prsindia.org/administrator/uploads/general/1242304423~~Summary%20of%20Sachar%20Committee%20Report.pdf (accessed 22 November 2016).

Sachchidananda (1990) Welcome policy. *Seminar*, 375: 18–21.

Shah, A.M. (1991) Job reservations and efficiency. *Economic and Political Weekly*, 26: 1732–1734.

Singh, Maanvender (2016) Reservations amidst the din of 'Development'. *Economic and Political Weekly*, 52(38).

Thimmaiah, G. (2005) Implications of reservations in private sector. *Economic and Political Weekly*, 40(8): 745–750.

Thorat, Sukhadeo and Senapati, Chittaranjan (2007) *Reservations in Employment, Education and Legislature: Status and Emerging Issues*, Working Paper. Indian Institute of Dalit Studies.

Weisskoph, Thomas (2004) *Impact of Reservations on Admissions to Higher Education in India*. EPW. Available at: www.epw.in/journal/2004/39/special-articles/impact-reservation-admissions-higher-education-india.html (accessed 22 November 2016).

4

POLITICAL ENGAGEMENT AND POLITICAL ATTITUDES OF INDIAN YOUTH

Jyoti Mishra and Pranav Gupta

The political system is an integral part of any society and citizens' participation in politics is an essential characteristic of a strong political system. There is a systematic process through which citizens take part in politics such as voting in elections, participation in civic movements and policy-making process, etc. However, their participation in the political process varies. Some take active part in politics and political activities whereas others are not that active. This phenomenon of political participation was widely analyzed and theorized from the perspective of political behavior. Scholars of political behavior have tried to classify citizens in various groups measuring their level (degree) of participation. Lord Byrce had provided a stratum of citizens based on their level of participation in *Modern Democracies* (Byrce 1921). Based on this edifice, other scholars like Stein Rokkan (1962), Grabeil Almond and Sydney Verba (1963) and Lester Milbrath (1965) extended this theory using empirical methods. The nature and range of themes of these studies were different while defining political participation. Some studies only focused on voting behavior (Gosnell 1930) whereas other studies used a range of political and community-based activities for measuring political participation (Almond and Verba 1963; Milbrath 1965). One of the noteworthy classifications was done by Almond and Verba in their book using the comparative method, *The Civic Culture: Political Attitudes and Democracy in Five Nations* (Almond and Verba 1963). Later, Milbrath (1965) extensively defined political participation using empirical data and suggested possible ways and reasons for participation in political activities. The thrust of these classifications was to divide people into active and inactive citizens.

Studying political participation and partisanship among the youth is extremely important. Numerous scholars have concluded that the "impressionable years" of early adulthood – late teens to mid- or late twenties, are a critical period of the lifecycle for the formation of political opinion and socialization. Attitudes tend to become fairly stable after early adulthood and political events during this period are more likely to be remembered and influential (Stoker and Bass 2013)

The motivation to participate in political activities depends on various factors such as political stimuli (interest in politics and political discussion), social identity (religion, sex, locality and caste) and personal attributes (age, class, level of education, media exposure). Consistently, these factors have played a significant role in positioning citizens on the stratum of political participation. For instance, people with relatively less interest in politics tend to be less active in politics. Similarly, social identity also explains the extent of political participation. People placed at the lower strata of social hierarchy participate less in politics and political activities. However, a common point in these studies has been that youth are less active in politics. Nevertheless, the young population of society is seen as a conductor of social change. If we take India's case, we notice that some landmark political events and social movements, which have shaped India over the last seven decades, have either started from the country's campuses or have been led by youth leaders. It is difficult to imagine any change in the status quo without support amongst the youth.

Hence, if one seeks to understand the advent of social and political transformations, it is necessary to examine political participation of the youth and their position on contentious political issues and progressive beliefs. Are the youth are interested in engaging with the state or not? Active political participation indicates continued engagement with the state, rather than disillusionment, and can be considered as a positive appraisal for electoral democracy. Through the existing theories of political behavior, this chapter examines the level of political participation of Indian youth and unveils the reason for uneven patterns of political participation among them.

The chapter is broadly divided into four sections. First, it explores the engagement of the youth with mainstream electoral politics. This includes interest in politics, voting in elections, party identification and participation in election campaigns. Second, it examines participation in protests and demonstrations amongst the youth. What drives youngsters to participate in protests? Third, in the context of recent claims over rising intolerance, it ascertains the position of the Indian youth on the issue. Do they concur with the view that personal liberty is increasingly being curbed? Is there support for some progressive beliefs at least amongst the youth? Finally, it looks at how the youth prioritize amongst multiple overlapping identities that all Indians hold.

Youth and mainstream politics

Interest in politics

Political interest is one of the most important dimensions of political behavior. Higher interest in politics may be associated with greater political engagement and better quality of decision making. The study found that around half of the Indian youth (51 percent) had an interest in politics in varying degrees. It is worrying to note that a large proportion of the youth – close to half of them (46 percent) had no interest in politics at all (Table 4.1). At the same time, it is encouraging to note that there has been a slow but continuous rise in interest in politics amongst the youth. In 1996, only 37 percent youth had an interest in politics, which has increased by 14 percent over the years. In the last seven years, there has been a significant increase in interest in politics (Figure 4.1).

Interest in politics amongst the youth seems to be positively related to education. The proportion of youth interested in politics was 31 percentage points higher amongst college-educated youth (56 percent) as compared to non-literate youth (25 percent). Also, young men were more likely to be interested in politics (55 percent) as compared to young women (42 percent).

Contrary to popular perception, youth in the cities were almost as interested or disinterested as youth from small towns and villages. In fact, youngsters residing in tier two cities were most likely to show an interest in politics. For instance, 42 percent of the youth residing in big cities (mostly state capitals excluding metros) were found to be interested in politics. Less than a third of the rural youth (31 percent)

TABLE 4.1 Relationship between India's youth and their interest in politics based on location (%)

	Interest in politics	Little interest in politics	No interest in politics at all
Overall	**32**	**18**	**46**
Biggest cities	28	16	53
Big cities	42	20	37
Small cities and towns	33	19	44
Villages	31	19	45

Note: The rest of the youth gave no response.

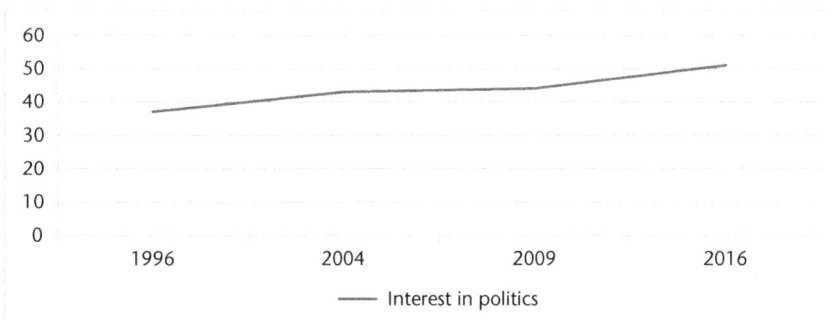

FIGURE 4.1 Youth's interest in politics 1996–2016 (%)

Note: These figures are only for the 18–34-year-old age group. This had to be done in order to ensure comparability with past studies. Figures for 1996, 2004 and 2009 are from the National Election Study (NES) conducted by CSDS during India's national elections. The question was however not asked in NES 2014.

were interested in politics. Interest was least amongst youth from the metros/biggest cities of the country, where more than half of the youth (53 percent) said that they had no interest at all in politics (Table 4.1). Economic status also seems to be associated with interest in politics. More than one third (37 percent) of youth from upper-class households had an interest in politics, as compared to only around a quarter (26 percent) from poor families.

Theories of political socialization suggest that family plays a great role in shaping the political attitudes of young ones (Niemi 1974). Children are likely to have a high level of interest in politics if their parents also have a high interest. This seems to hold in the context of the Indian youth too, as one finds an association between an individual and her parents' interest in politics. Youth whose parents were interested in politics were more likely to be interested in politics than youth whose parents did not have any interest at all in politics. It was found that amongst youth who said that their mother took an interest in politics, 59 percent said they took an interest in politics. Meanwhile, amongst those who said that they their father took an interest in politics, more than half (52 percent) reported being interested in politics. This information must be considered with caution as parental interest was not self-reported; rather it was the youth's perception about their parents' interest in politics.

How individuals prefer to engage in politics may differ. They may hold a very strong opinion on an issue and decide to participate in a civic movement or protest, campaign for a leader/party, contest an election or merely go out and vote regularly. A rise in political participation amongst any section of the society is always positive as it indicates greater engagement with the state.

How is Indian youth's engagement with the state and mainstream politics? Has there been a change in political participation amongst the youth as compared to earlier? Can the youth be considered to be aloof from mainstream politics?

Voting

Evidence from across the world suggests that youth are less likely vote in elections as compared to older age groups (Levine and Lopez 2002; Resnick and Casale 2011) Increasing voter turnout amongst youngsters has been an important focus of the Election Commission of India (ECI). The ECI regularly initiates voter awareness campaigns aimed at young voters. Also, special effort is made to enrol first time voters. In India, there seems to be a divergent trend as age does not seem to be associated with likelihood of voting. Turnout amongst the youth has been similar to the overall turnout across elections (Table 4.2). In fact, in the 2014 Lok Sabha election, turnout amongst the youth exceeded the overall turnout (Kumar 2014).

In this study, youth were asked whether they had voted in any election. More than half of the eligible voters (54 percent) said that they had voted in every election and close to one fifth (20 percent) said that they had voted in most elections. Only around a tenth of the youth said that they had never voted in any election. As compared to 2007, there has been an increase in self-reported participation in

TABLE 4.2 Turnout amongst 18–34-year-old voters (%)

Year of election	Youth	Overall turnout
1996	57	58
1998	63	62
1999	60	60
2004	58	58
2009	57	58
2014	69	66

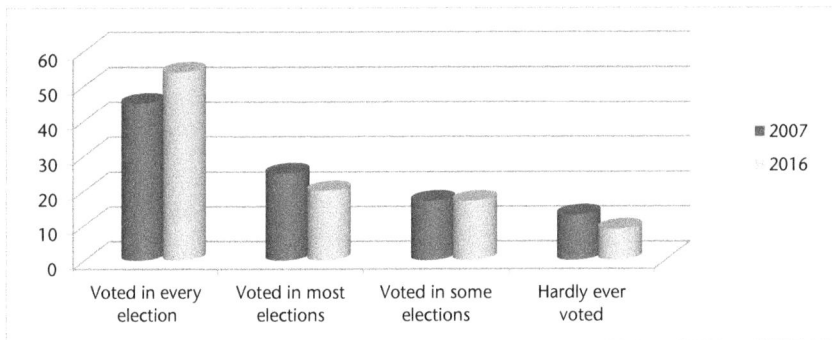

FIGURE 4.2 Voting amongst 18–34-year-old youth (%)

voting – a 4 percent decline in non-voters and a 9 percent increase in those who said they had voted in every election. The findings indicate that there has been a rise in electoral participation amongst the youth and a substantial proportion of them regularly cast their vote (Figure 4.2).

A relatively higher voter turnout amongst the poor, marginalized social groups and less educated is a common phenomenon in Indian elections (Yadav 1999; Kumar 2009; Banerjee 2014). This is considered to be paradoxical as these sections have lower resources, greater opportunity costs and less information. This paradox seems to be prevalent even amongst the youth. It is found that youth from marginalized social groups like Dalits, Adivasis and backward castes are slightly more likely to be regular voters as compared to upper-caste youth.

Participation in campaign activities

Electoral participation includes a broad set of activities apart from voting in an election or contesting an election. Many individuals work as vote mobilizers for parties and participate in campaign activities (Chhibber and Ostermann 2014). Also, many citizens attend campaign events like rallies and road shows organized by parties before elections. Limited participation of the youth was found in campaign activities of political parties. Less than a fifth of the youth had attended an election meeting

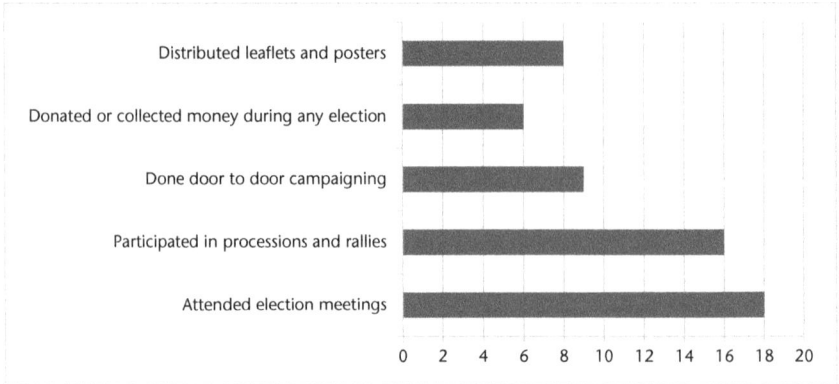

FIGURE 4.3 Participation in election campaign-related activities (%)

Note: Timespan given to the youth was the 'last ten years'.

(18 percent) or a rally (16 percent). Participation in campaign activities was much lower as slightly less than a tenth of the youth had done door-to-door campaigning (9 percent) or distribution of leaflet and posters (8 percent) (Figure 4.3).

Using these multiple activities, an Index of Electoral Participation was constructed (see Appendix I for details). It is worth mentioning that more than three-quarters of the youth (73 percent) had never participated in any of these activities. One-fifth of them had taken part in a few of these activities. Only a small fraction of the youth (5 percent) had actively participated in these activities – been involved in at least four of them (Table 4.3). High participation indicates the section of the youth which either work full time with a political party or are highly active volunteers. It is interesting to note that participation in campaign related activities has remained almost unchanged over the last decade.

Socio-economic variables such as level of education and economic class are positively related to participation in campaign-related activities as these activities involve opportunity costs in terms of both time and money (Table 4.4). However, the study also found that groups within the youth who were more likely to participate in campaign-related activities were relatively less likely to vote. For instance,

TABLE 4.3 Level of participation amongst 18–34-year-old youth in electoral activities (%)

Year of election	No participation	Low participation	Moderate participation	High participation
1999	68	20	5	7
2004	66	23	5	6
2009	73	12	8	7
2014	71	21	5	3
2016*	73	18	4	5

Note: *Figures are taken from the youth study in 2016. For other years, data from National Election Studies (NES) have been used.

TABLE 4.4 Youth electoral participation by socio-economic background of the youth (%)

	Vote regularly	*Participate in campaign activities*
Overall	**74**	**25**
Biggest cities	78	18
Big cities	69	31
Smaller cities	69	28
Villages	74	27
18 to 21 years	62	19
22 to 25 years	75	30
26 to 29 years	80	30
30 to 34 years	83	30
Graduate or above	72	29
High school pass	69	24
Primary pass	80	21
Non-literate	86	23
Hindu upper caste	73	25
Hindu upper OBC	74	26
Hindu lower OBC	78	20
Hindu Dalit	75	23
Hindu Adivasi	79	16

Note: 'Vote regularly' includes those who have voted in all elections or most elections. 'Participation in campaign activities' includes those whose participation is high, moderate or low. These are youth who would have participated in at least one campaign activity mentioned in Figure 4.3.

while the relatively higher-educated youth were more likely to participate in campaign activities during an election, they were less likely to regularly vote in elections. This is also evident when a comparison is drawn based on locality. A greater proportion of youth living in the largest cities were found to be voting regularly, as compared to youth from small cities and rural areas. However, when it came to taking part in campaign activities, they were the least likely to do so. Less than a fifth of youngsters in the metro participated in campaign activities. Similarly, a higher proportion of lower Other Backward Caste (OBC), Dalit and Adivasi youth voted regularly, as compared to youth from other social groups but participation in campaign activities was relatively lower amongst these groups.

Party identification amongst the youth

Political parties and leaders often make youth-centric appeals, claiming to represent the interests of this demographic group. There is a belief amongst many that youngsters form an independent political constituency which often votes across caste lines. Political parties and incumbent governments try to lure this segment through targeted policies and schemes.

The study examined party identification amongst the youth by asking them which political party they liked the most.[1] The study found that only around half of the Indian youth (52 percent) identified with any party.[2] One-fifth

(20 percent) of the youth said that they liked the Bharatiya Janata Party (BJP). Support for the Congress was exactly half as compared to the BJP – 10 percent. Further, the parties were categorized based on their central political ideology/ agenda. Four percent of the youth were fond of socialist parties (JDU, JDS, RJD, INLD, BJD, and SP), 2 percent liked left parties (CPM and CPI), 2 percent preferred Dalit parties (BSP, RPI-A, LJP, and VCK), and another 2 percent preferred parties whose founding principle was combating corruption (AAP and Loksatta); 11 percent of the youth were found to prefer other regional parties, these include parties like the AIADMK, DMK, Shiv Sena, TRS, TDP, SAD, NCP, AITC etc. (Figure 4.4).

There is a substantial proportion of youngsters who did not like any specific political party. Lack of party identification should not be interpreted as either disillusionment with all political parties in the country or apathy toward politics at large. The study found that even around half of those youngsters who did not like any party (48 percent) said that the current political parties should be able to solve problems of the country. Some of these youngsters may not consider themselves to be aligned with a single party despite taking active interest in politics. They could be swing voters who shift between parties across elections based on their preferences.

There are sharp differences in party identification between regions. Party identification amongst the youth was relatively higher in the eastern part of the country where less than four out of ten youth (37 percent) were not fond of any party. It was least in western region, where more than half of the youth (54 percent) did not consider themselves to be close to any party. Support for the BJP was the highest amongst the north Indian youth, where 30 percent of the youth said that they were close to the BJP. The gap between the BJP and the Congress was least in eastern India where, 19 percent of the youth supported the BJP and 11 supported the Congress.

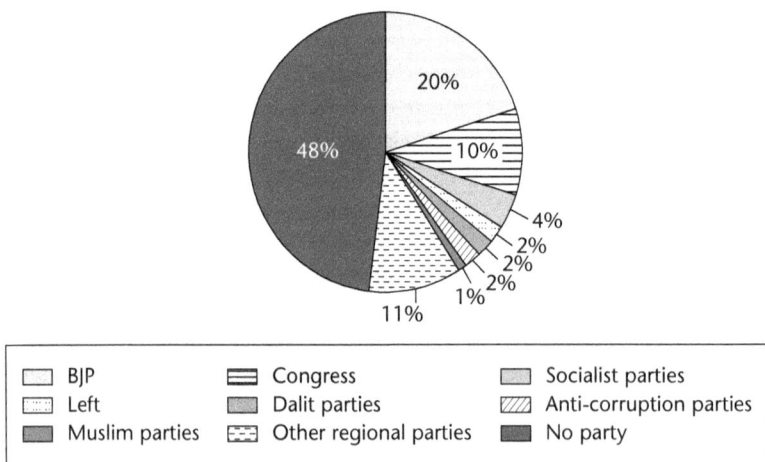

FIGURE 4.4 Political party preference/identification of India's youth (%)

TABLE 4.5 Party identification by socio-economic background of the youth (%)

	BJP	Congress	Others	No party
Overall	20	10	22	48
15–17 years	20	7	29	54
18–25 years	19	10	23	48
26–34 years	20	10	26	44
South India	9	8	32	51
East India	19	11	33	37
North India	30	8	15	47
West India	22	11	13	54
Big cities	20	9	21	50
Smaller cities	14	8	24	54
Villages	23	10	24	43
Hindu upper castes	27	4	18	51
Hindu OBC	24	7	24	45
Hindu Dalit	14	10	25	51
Hindu Adivasi	20	16	10	54

Party identification seems to be relatively higher in rural areas, where only 43 percent of the youth were politically unaligned (Table 4.5). The trends in party identification among the youth seem to reflect the overall trends in Indian politics. Support for the BJP seems to be coming from the metros and the villages. There was a 9 percent difference in support for the BJP between small cities and villages. A community-wise analysis of party preferences reveals that party identification is much higher amongst Muslims and Sikhs. Only around four out of ten youth amongst these groups were not aligned to a political party. Support for the BJP comes essentially from the party's core constituency – upper castes and a section of Hindu OBCs. But, even amongst Dalits and Adivasis, a greater proportion of youth considered themselves to be close to the BJP as compared to the Congress. There is sectional support for the Congress amongst the youth. The party seems to have greater support amongst Adivasis and Muslims. Close to a quarter of Muslim youth (24 percent) said that they supported the Congress party.

Youth in protests and demonstrations

Mass protests in various universities across the country after Rohith Vemula, a PhD scholar at Hyderabad Central University committed suicide, protests following the arrest of student leaders from the Jawaharlal Nehru University charged with sedition, Dalit movement in Gujarat after flogging of Dalits in Una district, the movement for demanding reservation for Patels, the protests organized by the Bhim Army after violence against Dalits in Uttar Pradesh's Saharanpur district are just a few examples of large movements, campaigns or protests held over the last few years which have been led by young leaders and have witnessed mass participation by the youth. These are some recent instances of Indian youth's engagement with politics outside mainstream electoral politics. Protests and demonstrations are considered as an important political activity, as on most occasions they are either in opposition to or support of a state policy/action or demanding state intervention on an issue.

In the present study, a sixth of the Indian youth (15 percent) said that they had participated in a protest or a demonstration in the last two years. The level of youth participation in protests increased substantially between 2011 and 2013, but there was a sharp decline in 2016. The level of participation currently is similar to the 2011 study. In 2011, only 12 percent of youth said that they had taken part in a protest or demonstration. This increased to 24 percent in 2013, according to the State of Democracy in South Asia Study 2013. The study was conducted soon after the Anna Hazare-led 'anti-corruption' movement, which had witnessed massive youth mobilization. In the current study, there has been a significant decline in participation in protests and demonstrations, as compared to 2013. Comparisons should be considered with caution due to differences in sampling frame and methodology.

The study found that participation in protests and demonstrations amongst the youth is relatively higher amongst some occupational groups. More than a quarter of youngsters engaged in business (27 percent) said that they had participated in a protest in the last two years. Professionals, government employees and skilled and service workers were also relatively more likely to take part in protests. Participation seems to be relatively lower amongst those engaged in agriculture (14 percent) and unskilled labor (17 percent). Only a small fraction of students took part in protests and demonstrations according to the study. Less than a sixth of students said that they had participated in a protest in the last two years.

Numerous factors may impede/facilitate participation in public activities like protests. These include the opportunity cost of participation, social factors and associational activity. A combination of these factors may explain the occupational category-wise trends in participation. Agricultural workers and unskilled laborers are concentrated in the informal sector of the economy which has limited formal associational activity. While there are farmer organizations in the agriculture sector, there are very few bodies which exclusively work for agricultural laborers or marginal farmers. Also, most individuals in these sectors work as daily wage laborers. Thus, they have a high opportunity cost of political participation as it leads to a direct loss of income. High participation in protests amongst professionals, government employees and skilled workers can be attributed to multiple factors. Relatively better economic well-being provides them with adequate resources for participating in political activities. Also, these occupational groups have stronger collective bodies. For instance, many professions have an apex union which represents them and organizes protests.

A substantial proportion of the youth seems to be participating in associational activities. Participation in activities of student unions/organizations is almost comparable to mainstream political bodies. More than a quarter (26 percent) of the youth said that they had participated in activities organized by a student organization in the last two years. Not participating in activities of student unions should not be considered as disillusionment with student politics or unions at large. Only a quarter of the youth (25 percent) supported a ban on student unions. A large number of the youngsters (46 percent) believed that they protect the rights and interests of students. This sentiment was even stronger amongst college students from both government colleges (55 percent) and private colleges (61 percent). Support for organized student unions is natural because they are the most vocal bodies for student rights. Also, the presence of student unions from across the ideological spectrum provides space to all students. There was high participation in activities of farmer organizations (23 percent) and trade unions (20 percent) as well. Expectedly, it was found that associational activity does translate into participation in protests and demonstrations. More than a quarter of the youth (27 percent) associated with at least one of these four – political parties, student unions/organizations, trade unions and farmer organizations – had taken part in a protest/demonstration. By contrast, less than a tenth (7 percent) of those without any associational activity had taken part in a protest.

Freedom of expression and rising intolerance

At the time of this study, there was a raging public debate on freedom of speech and expression in the country. The constitution of India guarantees "a freedom of speech and expression" as a fundamental right (Part III, article 19 (1)). This right is not absolute and is subject to reasonable restrictions. What is protected under the right and what could be termed as a 'reasonable restriction' has been at the crux of numerous protests which have occurred over the past year. The larger question is can something be said/done if it hurts the sentiments of another individual? What personal habits/statements could be termed as 'other regarding actions'? This contestation over what may be termed as an 'other regarding action' causing genuine harm has been the principal contestation in numerous controversies like the Jawaharlal Nehru University episode, various incidents of mob lynching, the ban on consumption of beef, and censorship of books and movies etc. Numerous public intellectuals have claimed that liberal 'voices' were being throttled in the public discourse and there was a sense of fear amongst those who wished to publicly counter orthodox views. Findings from the study suggest that the reality is neither as alarming as some may believe nor as tranquil as others may claim. Around half of the youth (53 percent) said that, in the last two years, they had never hesitated in stating their views on a political issue. Yet, there are reasons to worry as around a quarter of the youth (23 percent) said that they had hesitated in expressing their opinion on a political issue.

Does the Indian youth also believe that people in the country have become less tolerant about listening to contrarian views? More than half of the Indian youth (53 percent) felt that people have become less tolerant about listening to views of others (Table 4.6). This indicates that the popular claim about rising intolerance in the country is also shared by many youngsters. Personal experiences tend to shape the perception of individuals. It can be seen that youth who claimed that they had

TABLE 4.6 Opinion on rising intolerance amongst youth by socio-economic
background (%)

	People of India have become less tolerant
Overall	53
Graduate or above	63
High school pass	49
Primary pass	38
Non-literate	26
Big cities	62
Small cities	58
Villages	48
High news media exposure	64
Moderate news media exposure	62
Low news media exposure	43
Hindu	51
Muslim	65
Christian	58
Sikh	70

hesitated in expressing their opinion on political issues were slightly more likely to believe that tolerance had decreased. Almost six out of ten (59 percent) youth who had hesitated agreed that people had become less tolerant, as compared to only around half (53 percent) of those who had never felt hesitant. These figures should be considered with caution as the study was conducted soon after the protests in Jawaharlal Nehru University and the civil movement on intolerance. Thus, the figures may be biased upwards due to a higher recall.

Is this discussion over rising intolerance in India restricted to certain sections of society? Broadly, it is the highly educated youth, living in cities, who seem to believe that people in the country have become less tolerant as compared to earlier. It is worrying to find that youth from religious minorities like Muslims and Sikhs were more likely to agree that people have become less tolerant. Exposure to news media also seems to be playing a critical role, as only around four out of ten youngsters (43 percent) with low exposure believed so as compared to almost two-thirds (64 percent) of those with high exposure. These figures should be considered with caution due to high no response rates amongst some groups (Table 4.6).

The study also ascertained the youth's opinion on contentious issues which have been at the center-stage of the ongoing debate over liberty and progressive beliefs, namely, the banning of movies which hurt religious sentiments, beef consumption and the death penalty. It was found that six out of ten youth (60 percent) supported banning movies which hurt religious sentiments. Close to half of the youth (46 percent) objected to allowing beef consumption. Around half of the youth (49 percent) supported the status quo on capital punishment. These figures clearly indicate that most youngsters do not share the belief of liberals on many contentious issues.

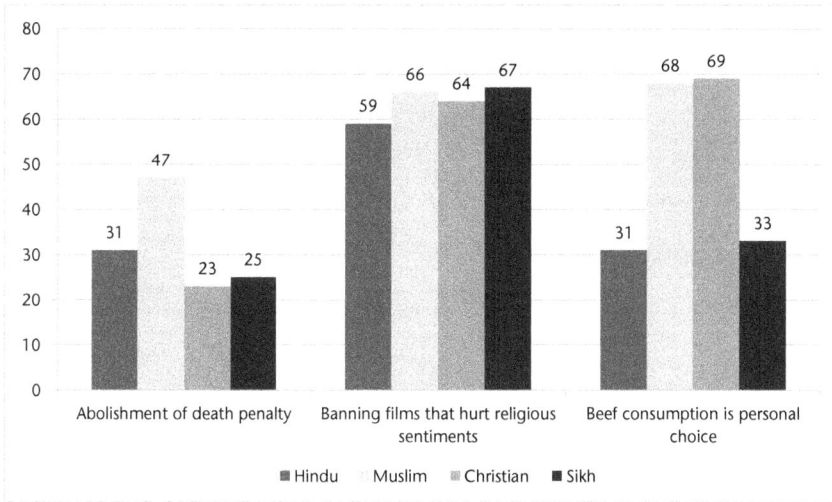

FIGURE 4.5   Opinion of different religious groups on some contentious political issues (%)

Sharp differences are found in opinion on these issues based on religion. Muslim youngsters were largely in favor of abolishing the death penalty, while Sikh and Christian youth were least supportive of abolishing it. Hindu youth were slightly less likely than others to support a ban on films which hurt religious sentiments (59 percent). Amongst other religious groups, there was almost equivalent support. Expectedly, there are stark differences on the issue of beef consumption. This may be motivated by personal habits, as consumption of beef is quite prevalent amongst Muslims and Christians. More than two-thirds of Muslim (68 percent) youth considered beef consumption to be a personal choice and opposed any objection to it. By contrast, only 31 percent of the Hindu youth and 33 percent of the Sikh youth seemed to concur with this view. A plurality of Hindu and Sikh youth seemed to oppose beef consumption (Figure 4.5). However, amongst Hindus, whether one is a vegetarian or a non-vegetarian made a significant difference in their opinion on this issue. Non-vegetarian Hindu youth were twice as likely as vegetarian Hindu youth to support consumption of beef, 40 percent as opposed to 20 percent.

Interestingly, opinion of the youth who like the BJP is similar to the average Indian youth on most matters except consumption of beef. Kishore (2017) has shown that on matters like abolishment of the death penalty, false implication of Muslim youth in terror cases, and rising intolerance, BJP supporters are as liberal or conservative as the average young person.

How does one resolve this evident paradox between the overall perception of the youth on various contentious issues and their views on intolerance and freedom of expression? The average youngster does not hold a progressive position like liberals on many contentious issues. But neither does she disagree with their claim about rising intolerance and curbs on freedom of expression. Not surprisingly, the average person stands away from either end of the ideological spectrum (Table 4.7).

TABLE 4.7 Opinion on some contentious political issues by youth's party identification (%)

	Abolishment of the death penalty	Films that hurt religious sentiments should be banned	Beef consumption is personal choice, nobody should have an objection
Left supporters	35	37	90
Other parties' supporters	38	39	50
Congress supporters	39	40	41
Aam Aadmi Party supporters	32	43	35
BJP supporters	30	35	23

Nation, religion, region, or caste?

In the context of the political attitude of youngsters, it is important to understand whether the Indian youth is centripetal or centrifugal[3] in their attitude and outlook towards the country. A centripetal attitude unifies people and enhances support for the state and its institutions, whereas a centrifugal attitude tends to divide a state on various grounds such as regionalism, caste, and religion.

The study asked the youth how proud they were of the various identities held by them. They were asked to rank multiple identities – state, caste, religious, and national identity – based on how proud were they about holding them. Only around half of the youth (51 percent) said that they were most proud of being Indian. Almost an equal proportion of youth preferred other identities like caste (13 percent), religion (14 percent), and region (11 percent).

Are certain religious groups more/less likely to belong to a specific category amongst these? Slightly more than half of the Hindus (52 percent) were most proud of being Indian. Caste seems to be the second preferred option as a sixth (15 percent) of Hindu youth ranked it in the first position. Muslim youth were slightly less likely to prefer national identity as their primary choice. Around four out of ten Muslim youth (42 percent) gave being Indian as their most preferred option. They were relatively more likely to consider their religious identity to be most important. Around a quarter of the Muslim youth (25 percent) placed their religious identity in the first position. Caste identity seems to be relevant for Muslim youth also, as around a third of them placed it as their first or second most preferred identity. Sikh youth were also relatively less likely to give primacy to their national identity. Amongst them, regional identity seemed to be quite important while caste was the least relevant (Table 4.8).

TABLE 4.8 Identity preference by religion (%)

	National identity	Religion	Caste	Region
Overall	51	14	13	11
Hindu	52	12	15	11
Muslim	42	25	13	8
Christians	55	17	10	12
Sikh	43	18	3	21

Disaggregating further, it is observed that the level of religiosity matters amongst Muslim youth. Increased religiosity seems to be associated with a greater likelihood of placing religion in the first position. Less than a tenth of Muslim youth (6 percent) with low religiosity placed religion in the first position. While around three out of ten (29 percent) high religiosity Muslim youth placed it as their first choice. Religiosity seems to be a factor only amongst Muslims.

This self-perception of identities amongst Muslims could be linked to a perception about the manner in which the state treats minorities and whether the state treats them on a par with other religious groups or makes distinctions. In the study, close to half of all the youth seem to believe that Muslim youth are being falsely implicated in terror-related cases (45 percent). Less than a third of the youth disagreed with this statement. Do the overall figures reflect a cross-community belief or is it solely because of an overwhelming sentiment amongst Muslims? Support for this belief amongst youth was found from all religious groups; though there were sharp variations in the level of support. Around four out of ten Hindu youth (42 percent) agreed with it, while around a third disagreed (32 percent). Close to seven out of ten Muslim youngsters (71 percent) agreed with it and there was limited disagreement. Christians were the only social group who were divided on this issue. The proportion of Christian youth who agreed with this view (40 percent) was almost equivalent to those who disagreed (43 percent) with it (Table 4.9). Individual incidents of hate crime or instances of religious prejudice may have a miniscule impact on public perception, but over time, repeated occurrence of such events at regular intervals is detrimental and may lead to fear amongst communities.

Regional identity is also important in the country, as evident from the fact that around a tenth of the youth (11 percent) considered it to be their primary identity. Like other sectional identities, regionalism also could deter national integration and social harmony on occasion. In many states, there have been concentrated movements and protests against the undeterred entry of migrants. Supporters of such movements argue that the undeterred entry of 'outsiders' leads to a dilution of regional culture and reduces economic opportunities for locals. An idea of 'son of the soil' has come to the forefront as many people believe preference should be given in employment to locals over migrants.

TABLE 4.9 Opinion on the issue that Muslim youth are falsely implicated in terror cases by religion (%)

	Agree that Muslim youth are falsely implicated	Disagree that Muslim youth are falsely implicated	No opinion
Overall	**45**	**31**	**24**
Hindu	42	32	26
Muslim	71	16	13
Christian	40	43	17
Sikh	51	33	16

TABLE 4.10 Preference for jobs to locals over migrants in the big cities by locality (%)

	Support preference for locals in jobs	Do not support preference for locals in jobs
Overall	**63**	**22**
Big cities	68	23
Smaller cities	52	30
Villages	66	18

There are demands for affirmative action for locals in education and employment. Youth in the study were asked whether locals should be preferred over people from other states for jobs. Close to two-thirds of the youth (63 percent) seemed to agree with this. This sentiment is not restricted to the metros only, as even youth from villages seem to believe this. Around two-thirds of the youth from large cities (68 percent) and villages (66 percent) supported the idea of 'son of the soil' (Table 4.10).

Why does the youth support such provisions? At first sight, this may seem to be merely an outcome of prejudice against outsiders. A rough comparison can be made between these beliefs and the growing anti-immigrant attitude in the West in recent years. The essential demand is reducing opportunities for non-natives. Alongside prejudice, these sentiments are also due to concerns about lack of economic opportunities. Rising inequality, unemployment and lowering real incomes have been identified as contributing factors for events like Brexit and the victory of Donald Trump. Rather than looking at these events merely through lenses of nationalism and racism, one should also recognize economic anxiety as a factor behind them (Romei 2016; Casselman 2017). Economic anxiety, especially concern about unemployment, seems to be an important reason behind supporting such provisions amongst the Indian youth as well. This is supported by the fact that even those who had no qualms about having a neighbor from a different state support special provisions for locals in equal measure. Unemployment is a major concern for the youth today (as indicated in Chapter 2) and they are likely to support any step which increases opportunities for them. Data also indicate that youth who have high anxiety levels about their job and employment are more likely to support the idea of the 'son of soil'.

Conclusion

Overall, it seems that the youth rarely behaves like a distinct political category. Differences based on other social cleavages like religion, class etc. remain present even amongst the Indian youth and influence their political behavior and opinion. Participation of the youth in politics may not be as high as we would like it to be, but it cannot be dismissed as being low either. The popular claim about youth apathy towards politics does not seem to be supported by empirical evidence.

Contrary to the binaries that dominate the popular media discourse on most issues, the youth hold a nuanced opinion. It is positive to note that the youth maintain an active engagement with politics, including mainstream electoral politics.

Notes

1 Figures for these questions indicate party preferences at the time of the study in April–May 2016.
2 This category includes youths who either mentioned the name of an independent candidate, 'none of the above', 'I do not like any party', 'I like all parties' or did not give any response.
3 While defining political culture, Arend Lijphart (1977) classifies attitudes into centripetal and centrifugal forces.

References

Almond, G.A. and Verba, S. (1963) *The Civic Culture: Political Attitudes and Democracy in Five Nations*. Princeton, NJ: Princeton University Press.
Banerjee, Mukulika (2014) *Why India Votes?* New Delhi: Routledge.
Byrce, Lord (1921) *Modern Democracies*. New York: Macmillan.
Casselman, Ben (2017) Stop Saying Trump's Win Had Nothing to Do with Economics. Available at: https://fivethirtyeight.com/features/stop-saying-trumps-win-had-nothing-to-do-with-economics/ (accessed on 12/8/2017).
Chhibber, Pradeep and Ostermann, Susan L. (2014) The BJP's Fragile Mandate: Modi and Vote Mobilizers in the 2014 General Elections. *Studies in Indian Politics*, 2(2): 137–151.
Gosnell, H. (1930) *Why Europe Votes*. Chicago, IL: University of Chicago Press.
Kishore, Roshan (2017) Has the Rise of BJP Made India's Youth Less Liberal? Live Mint. Available at: www.livemint.com/Politics/R0eujsnVtHNdxwgtf3uDxM/Has-BJPs-rise-made-Indias-youth-less-liberal.html (accessed on 19/8/2017).
Kumar, Sanjay (2009) Patterns of Political Participation: Trends and Perspective. *Economic and Political Weekly*, 44(39): 47–51.
Kumar, Sanjay (2014) The Youth Vote Made a Difference for the Victory of the BJP. *Panjab University Research Journal Social Sciences*, 22(2): 45–57.
Levine, Peter and Lopez, Mark Hugo (2002) *Youth Voter Turnout Has Declined by Any Measure*. The Center for Information & Research on Civic Learning & Engagement Fact Sheet.
Lijphart, Arend (1977) *Democracy in Plural Societies: A Comparative Explanation*. New Haven, CT: Yale University Press.
Milbrath, Lester W. (1965) *Political Participation: How and Why Do People Get Involved in Politics?* Chicago, IL: Rand McNally & Company.
Niemi, Richard G. (1974) *How Family Members Perceive Each Other: Political and Social Attitudes in Two Generations*. New Haven, CT: Yale University Press.
Resnick, Danielle and Casale, Daniela (2011) *The Political Participation of Africa's Youth: Turnout, Partisanship, and Protest*. Working Paper No. 56. World Institute for Development Economics Research, South Africa.
Rokkan, Stein (1962) *Approaches to the Study of Political Participation: Introduction*. Bergen: Chr. Michelsen Institute.

Romei, Valentine (2016) The Economic Factors Behind the Vote for Brexit. Available at: http://blogs.ft.com/ftdata/2016/06/30/the-economic-factors-behind-the-vote-for-brexit/?mhq5j=e1 (accessed on 12/8/2017).

Sampat, Kinjal and Mishra, Jyoti (2014) Interest in Politics and Political Participation, in Sanjay Kumar (ed.) *Indian Youth and Electoral Politics: An Emerging Engagement*. Delhi: Sage.

Stoker, Laura and Bass, Jackie (2013) Political Socialization: Ongoing Questions and New Directions, in Robert Y. Shapiro and Lawrence R. Jacobs (eds) *Oxford Handbook of American Public Opinion and the Media*. Oxford: Oxford University Press.

Tingsten, H. (1936) *Political Behaviour*. London: P.S. King.

Yadav, Yogendra (1999) Electoral Politics in the Time of Change: India's Third Electoral System, 1989–99. *Economic and Political Weekly*, 34(34/35): 2393–2399.

5

SOCIAL AND CULTURAL ATTITUDES OF INDIAN YOUTH

Souradeep Banerjee

Unlike Western democracies, neither social conservatism nor social liberalism predominantly defines Indian society. India encompasses a wide range of social and psychological dispositions, norms and structures which makes it difficult to be categorised as liberal or conservative. The great Indologist A.K. Ramanujan (1989) in his seminal essay 'Is there an Indian Way of Thinking', had aptly described the Indian mind as a 'brain with two lobes'. Cited as a puzzle for Western scholars and intellectuals, who believed in the dichotomy of modernity and tradition, Indian thinking has been characterised by features both modern and traditional.

Thus, scholars who have been able to identify this so-called uniqueness of the Indian identity have broken down the binary of liberal and conservative and argued that in India, traditional social structures and norms have taken a new, modern avatar and in a similar fashion, modernity in the form of economic and technological changes has also affected traditional structures and norms as much as they have equally affected the former (Rudolph & Rudolph, 1967). Hence, one experiences difficulty in explaining the character of Indian society as either liberal or conservative.

Much in consonance with the predominant characterisation of Indian society, the study similarly argues that it is difficult to place the Indian youth within the extreme categories of social liberal or social conservative. However, it can be argued that there are shades of liberalism and conservatism prevalent amongst Indian youth on certain social and cultural issues and not on others. For the purpose of understanding the social-cultural attitudes of the Indian youth, a social-cultural index was created (see Appendix I to find out how the index was constructed) which captures attitudes and perceptions on questions of what is defined as social liberal and social conservative. A social liberal is defined as one who believes in individual freedom and stands for social justice. A social conservative is one who stands for preservation of traditional beliefs. This chapter, based on the findings of the index, attempts to encompass the following: the notion of patriarchy which assesses the attitude of Indian youth, both boys and girls, toward women, their rights and aspirations; views on homosexuals; attitudes toward others, defined by their eating and drinking habits, caste, religion, nationality, marriage etc.

The chapter will assess these particular shades of liberalism and conservatism in three sections. The first section explores the notion of patriarchy in Indian society by assessing the attitudes of young Indians towards women and some issues concerning them. The second section looks at how Indian youth perceive homosexuality, as well as their attitudes towards marriage, live-in relationships and dating in general. The third section examines discriminatory attitudes of young Indians towards others with respect to caste, religion, region, race and dietary preferences. The fourth and final part discusses the overall liberal and/or conservative position of the Indian youth, taking into account the aforementioned aspects.

Attitude of India's youth toward women

The attitude towards women forms a crucial component of social and cultural attitudes. Like all other societies, India has been described as a patriarchal society but one has to look for nuances and details to get the complete picture. On the question of attitude toward women, the findings of the study indicate the dichotomy of '*Ghaire-Baire*' (Chatterjee, 1989). While, on one hand one observes a modest liberal attitude amongst youth towards women acquiring higher education, attaining leadership roles and having the freedom to wear what they want; on the other hand, one also observes that men display strong resistance towards women acquiring an equal position vis-à-vis men within the household. A majority of the youngsters (51 per cent) agreed (strongly or somewhat) with the proposition that wives should always listen to their husbands. Two in every five (40 per cent) disagreed with it and about one in every ten (9 per cent) did not answer the question (Table 5.1). Moreover, two-fifths of the youth (41 per cent) were also in agreement with the proposition that it is not right for women to do a job after marriage. Interestingly, a fairly high proportion of young women also held such conservative views. About one in every three young women were of the opinion that women should not work after marriage and over two out of every five of them favoured the idea of an obedient wife. This social internalisation of patriarchal norms explains their widespread persistence.

TABLE 5.1 Attitudes of India's youth on women-related issues (%)

Attitudes toward women	Agree	Disagree	No opinion
Not right for women to work after marriage	41	50	9
Men are better leaders than women	42	45	13
Higher education is more important for boys than girls	37	52	11
Wives should always listen to their husbands	51	40	9
Girls should not wear jeans	38	51	12

TABLE 5.2 Patriarchal attitudes by locality (%)

Locality	Very patriarchal	Somewhat patriarchal	Not very patriarchal	Not at all patriarchal
Big cities	15	22	36	27
Small cities	24	28	26	22
Villages	28	31	28	13

Going by these findings, the study attempted to empirically capture the attitude of Indian youth toward women through a patriarchy index. By the aforementioned parameters, 24 per cent of Indian youth were found to be very patriarchal and 18 per cent of youth were found to be the least patriarchal. However, the others were found to be somewhere in the middle: 29 per cent were somewhat patriarchal in their views and another 29 per cent were less patriarchal.

There are differences on the basis of locality. Youth from villages were found to have greater notions of patriarchy than youth from cities and big cities. The patriarchal attitude of youth declines with an increase in urbanity. Within urban areas, youth in big cities were found to be less patriarchal than youth from small cities (Table 5.2).

Notions of patriarchy differ across religions. Out of all the religious communities, Muslim youth were found to be the most patriarchal (61 per cent) followed by Hindu youth (53 per cent). In comparison, Sikh and Christian youth were found to be less patriarchal (31 per cent and 28 per cent, respectively). There are also differences amongst various Hindu communities. Youth from the Hindu Adivasi community were found to be the most patriarchal (70 per cent) followed by the lower Other Backward Caste (OBC) youth (58 per cent).

The study also highlights differences in notions of patriarchy amongst various regions of the country. Indian youth from the western and central region (33 per cent) were found to be the most patriarchal followed by youth from the northern region of the country (27 per cent). However, those from the eastern (17 per cent) and southern region (17 per cent) were found to be less patriarchal. Such a divergence in the notion of patriarchy between the two regions of the country is an outcome of the divergent kinship systems that define the northern and southern part of the country: the West Asian system in north India and the egalitarian East Asian system in the south (Dyson & Moore, 1983). This also explains the increased participation of girls in both schools and the labour force in the southern region (Kambhapati & Rajan, 2008).

Higher levels of education attainment weakens the support for patriarchy. It can be deduced from the study that the more educated, the less patriarchal one is likely to be. As per findings of the study, youth who were non-literate or had studied only up until primary school were found to be far more patriarchal (77 per cent and 66 per cent, respectively) than those who had only completed high school or attained higher education (59 per cent and 41 per cent, respectively).

Exposure to media plays an important role in the portrayal of women and women's issues. According to conventional theory and other studies, the strong

TABLE 5.3 Patriarchal attitudes by degree of media exposure (%)

Degree of news media exposure	Very patriarchal	Somewhat patriarchal	Not very patriarchal	Not at all patriarchal
High exposure	20	27	28	24
Medium Exposure	16	29	34	21
Low exposure	24	30	30	16
No exposure	40	27	23	11

TABLE 5.4 Patriarchal attitudes by friends of the opposite gender (%)

Friends from the opposite gender	Very patriarchal	Somewhat patriarchal	Not very patriarchal	Not at all patriarchal
Men who have female friends	21	25	30	23
Men who do not have female friends	29	34	27	11

presence of media is said to reinforce stereotypical notions of men and women. However, beyond providing entertainment, media increases the availability of information and exposure to diverse ways of life. In a predominantly rural country like India, television media is the primary source of information for households to receive information (Jensen & Oster, 2008). Such studies highlight the power of media in highlighting women's issues such as the dowry system, women's education, sanitation issues etc. (Jensen & Oster, 2008). The study's findings agree with the second argument. Youth who had no exposure to news media were found to be very patriarchal, while,youth who were highly exposed to news media were found to be less patriarchal (Table 5.3).

Interestingly, mingling with the other gender reduces notions of patriarchy as one experiences the otherness of the other gender. If youth had friends from opposite genders, the notion of patriarchy reduced, for both men and women (Table 5.4). However, one should be cautious though as the relationship could also be in the opposite direction. It could be that young men holding patriarchal may be averse towards being friends with persons from the opposite gender.

Attitudes of India's youth toward homosexuals

Contemporary Indian society is predominantly resistant to the idea of same-sex relationships which are still criminalised under Section 377 of the Indian Penal Code, a colonial-era provision. In 2009, the Delhi High Court declared parts of the Section unconstitutional as they violated basic human rights; however, its verdict was later overturned by the Supreme Court in 2013. The matter is now under review. Homosexuality is primarily a taboo topic for a majority of Indians, even though the Indian ethos towards sexual difference has been historically tolerant.

Hindu epics are replete with half-man and half-woman characters, ancient temple structures across India depict homosexual acts (Tharoor, 2016) and homoerotically inclined men are 'continuously visible' in medieval history (Vanita & Kidwai, 2000). However, in the twenty-first century, the majority of the Indian youth is not comfortable with the idea of a love affair between two men or two women. The findings of the study indicate that three in every five youth (61 per cent) considered a love affair between two men as wrong, one in every ten (10 per cent) considered it somewhat right and only one in every seven (14 per cent) considered it right. Similarly, with respect to a love affair between two women, 61 per cent of youth considered it to be wrong, 12 per cent considered it somewhat right and only 14 per cent saw nothing wrong with it.

Age makes a difference on how homosexuality is perceived by the youth. The youngest category (15–17 year olds) was more approving of homosexuality than the older youth. Interestingly, urbanity reduces approval for homosexuality (Table 5.5). Youth living in big cities were found to be less approving of homosexuality (21 per cent) than those living in smaller cities (27 per cent) and villages (29 per cent).

Numerous studies argue that religious beliefs play an important role in shaping one's attitude towards homosexuality. A Pew Research Centre survey conducted in 39 countries in 2013, for instance, found a strong relationship between a country's religiosity and opinions about homosexuality (Pew, 2013). However, in India, unlike the West, religiosity does not seem to play a significant role in determining attitudes towards homosexuality. If anything, it finds that those who are more religious (in practice) are more likely to be accepting of homosexuality. The higher the religiosity amongst the Indian youth, the greater is their acceptance of homosexuality. According to the study, only about 19 per cent of Indian youth with a low level of religiosity approved of a love affair between two men affair. In comparison, approval of homosexuality rose to about 30 per cent amongst youth who were highly religious.

TABLE 5.5 Youth's attitude towards homosexuality by age and religiosity (%)

	Approve of love affair between two men	Approve of love affair between two women
Youth (Overall)	25	24
15–17 years	31	30
18–21 years	24	23
22–25 years	27	27
26–29 years	26	26
30–34 years	21	20
Highly religious	30	29
Somewhat religious	25	24
Not very religious	23	22
Not religious at all	19	19

Attitudes toward marriage, live-in relationships and dating

The study also found young people to be fairly conservative on issues of marriage, live-in relationships and dating. Over half of the youth (52 per cent) were of the opinion that it was important in life to get married. Only 33 per cent disagreed and the rest gave no opinion on the matter. Meanwhile, around a third of the Indian youth (36 per cent) considered inter-caste marriage to be completely wrong. About a quarter (23 per cent) saw it as being partially right, and only a third fully approved of it. Close to half (45 per cent) were found to be completely opposed to inter-religious marriages and only 28 per cent were in complete support of them. Two-thirds (67 per cent) did not approve of live-in relationships. Over half (53 per cent) were opposed to dating before marriage, with only about one in every seven approving of it. Two in every five (40 per cent) were opposed to the celebration of Valentine's Day. More discussion on some of these attitudes can be found in the following chapter on marriage. These figures should be considered to be a low as there may be under-reporting of approval due to the social taboos attached to many of these activities.

Discriminatory attitudes of India's youth

Discrimination is a strong marker of social and cultural attitudes. An Indian is often described as 'Homo Hierarchus'[1] or a hierarchical man. The stratified and hierarchical society gives rise to several forms of discriminatory attitudes and practices which have become so ubiquitous in social and cultural attitudes that they often go unnoticed and unrealised.

The study captures such discriminatory attitudes of the Indian youth through a discriminatory index, characterised by the discrimination of the other (in this case their neighbour) on the basis of their eating and drinking habits, membership of other castes, religions or races, marriage type etc.

Discrimination on grounds of caste, religion and race

Though untouchability as a form of caste discrimination has receded in large parts of the country, invisible forms of discrimination persist and continue. Several studies show that caste discrimination exists in the housing market as landlords refuse to rent out their apartments to people belonging to the lower castes. The study confirms such findings: 81 per cent of the youth said that they had no problem with their neighbour belonging to a different caste and 13 per cent of the youth were found to have reservations.

Amongst various caste groups, it is youth from the Hindu Adivasi community (18 per cent) followed by youth from the Hindu OBC community (15 per cent) that were most likely to have expressed reservations if their neighbours were from a different caste. Though Adivasis are known to have more egalitarian social practices, it is the onset of modernisation along with '*sanskritisation*' which seems to have made both of them discriminate on the grounds of caste, especially those brought up under the Hindu fold (Srinivas, 1997; Xaxa, 2005). However, inter-mixing of people with other castes does liberalise attitudes of people toward them. Interestingly, youth who had friends from another caste were less likely to have a problem if their neighbours belong to another caste: 79 per cent of the youth were likely to have a close friend from another caste and only one in every ten of them (13 per cent) were likely to have a problem in having someone from a different caste as their neighbour (Table 5.6). Meanwhile, close to one-fifth of the young-sters (19 per cent) revealed that they did not have a close friend from a different caste and amongst them two in every five (22 per cent) were found to be opposed to having a neighbour from a caste other than theirs.

In a deeply unequal society such as India, discrimination also exists on the grounds of religion. For instance, discrimination in the housing market is even more pronounced for members of minority communities with surnames that are easily recognisable. Along similar lines, the study also captured this discrimina-tory tendency of religion being a significant fault line. According to the study, a significant 15 per cent (about one in every seven) of youth were likely to be uncomfortable with having a neighbour from a different religion (Table 5.6). Amongst various religious communities, Hindu youth were the most likely to be uncomfortable with having a non-Hindu as their neighbour (16 per cent). However, once again, as seen with respect to caste, socialising outside one's own religious sphere has a liberating effect on discriminatory attitudes. Youth who had close friends from another religion (two in every three reported as having one) were less likely to feel uneasy (10 per cent) than youth with only co-religionists as close friends (25 per cent). Similarly, married youth who had a spouse from another religion were less likely to feel uneasy if their neighbour belonged to a dif-ferent religion than theirs. Less than a tenth (7 per cent) of the youth whose spouse was from a different religion said they would have reservations, compared to one in every six (17 per cent) of those whose spouse was from the same religion.

Discrimination on the basis of skin colour generally associated with Western coun-tries is prevalent in India. In recent times, several people from different countries of Africa have migrated and settled in different parts of India in search of job and educa-tional opportunities: 63 per cent of India's youth were likely to have no discomfort if their neighbours were Africans and 17 per cent of India's youth were likely to have dis-comfort for the same. Discrimination toward Africans is a reflection of the pan-Indian preference for fair skin and the denigration of those people who have a dark complex-ion. In Indian society, fair skin is something desirable and is closer to purity and dark skin is associated with dirt and hence applies to untouchables (Kakar & Kakar, 2007).

Discrimination toward people from other states

Increased internal migration in the last few decades has produced strong 'nativist' and parochial feelings in several parts of the country. Events across the globe, especially the refugee crisis in Europe, are fostering xenophobic feelings not just in developing countries but also in advanced industrial countries. There is a perpetual fear of the 'other' coming and snatching away one's resources and job opportunities. The study, too, attempted to capture such emotions amongst India's youth: 71 per cent of India's youth was found to be comfortable if their neighbours were from a different state, while 14 per cent of youth expressed discomfort with the same. Interestingly, it was the youth from the western and central region of the country, followed by youth from the eastern region, who were more likely to be uncomfortable: 18 per cent of youth from the western and central region and 16 per cent of youth from the eastern region were found to be uncomfortable.

Discrimination on the basis of marriage

In Indian society, marriage is seen as a sacred union and a girl and a boy staying together outside marriage is looked at with contempt. One third of Indian youth (33 per cent) were likely to have objections if a boy and girl live together outside marriage and 44 per cent were likely to have no problems for the same. Live-in relationships are becoming common and widespread in metropolitan cities and small cities and face less resistance in urban areas. The findings of the study indicate that 37 per cent of Indian youth residing in villages were likely to have reservations about a boy and a girl living together outside marriage, while 28 per cent of youth in cities and same proportion of youth in big cities were likely to have reservations.

Discrimination on eating and drinking habits

Food that we eat and that is cooked in our kitchens is a marker of social identity and thus, also a source of contention and conflict: 72 per cent of Indian youth were likely to have no reservations with their neighbours consuming non-vegetarian food, while 23 per cent of youth were likely to have a problem. On this issue, amongst religious communities, Hindu youth (26 per cent) expressed the highest reservation when it came to their neighbours consuming non-vegetarian food and youth from the Christian community expressed the least reservation (4 per cent). In India, food has been a contested sphere and is reflective of caste hierarchies present and perpetuated. Certain kinds of food, especially non-vegetarian food (*tamasic*) are associated with the consumption habits of the lower castes and are derided by the upper castes, whose food habits are largely associated with vegetarianism (*sattvic*) (Kakar & Kakar, 2007).

One often hears of newspaper reports wherein people are denied accommodation in certain exclusive neighbourhoods of big, metropolitan cities and are discriminated on the basis of their eating habits. Amongst Hindus, youth from the upper castes were mostly found to have problems if their neighbours consumed non-vegetarian food. Over a quarter of them (26 per cent) said it would cause discomfort to them. Along with upper castes, youth from the OBC community, who over the years have attempted to ape the social and cultural practices of the upper castes as a process of '*sankritisation*', were equally resistant (26 per cent) to their neighbours eating non-vegetarian food. The study also found most upper caste youth and OBC youth to

TABLE 5.6 Measuring prejudices amongst India's youth (%)

	Will be fine if they are my neighbours	Will be uneasy if they are my neighbours	Might be uneasy if they are my neighbours	No response
People who cook non-vegetarian food	72	23	4	2
People from another caste	81	13	5	2
People who drink alcohol	42	47	9	3
People from another religion	75	15	7	3
People from Africa	63	17	9	11
People from another state	71	14	9	6
Boy and girl living together outside marriage	44	33	14	9

be pure vegetarians who do not even consume eggs (47 per cent and 30 per cent, respectively). In the study, 30 per cent of all the youth reported themselves as being pure vegetarians and nearly half of them (47 per cent) said they would have problems with a neighbour who consumes non-vegetarian food.

In recent times, several political parties have campaigned for the prohibition of the sale and consumption of alcohol in India. Perceived to be a socially desirable issue, 47 per cent of India's youth expressed a problem with their neighbours drinking alcohol. Women are more likely to have a problem than men: 51 per cent of women were likely to have a problem compared to 44 per cent of men. This also explains why in many states, policies on prohibition have been implemented keeping women voters in mind.

However, there are cultural variations in drinking patterns across religions, castes and localities. Amongst religious communities, Muslim youth (49 per cent) and Hindu youth (48 per cent) were more likely to have a problem with their neighbours drinking alcohol. Amongst Hindus, it was youth from the Hindu upper caste communities (53 per cent) that had expressed the highest reservation followed by youth from the OBC groups (49 per cent).

There is also a divide on the basis of locality. Youth residing in villages were more likely to have a problem with their neighbours drinking alcohol than youth residing in cities and big cities. Even amongst cities, youth residing in big cities were found to have comparatively less problem with their neighbours consuming alcohol. Youth residing in villages were more likely to have a problem with their neighbours drinking alcohol (50 per cent) than youth residing in small cities (44 per cent) and big cities (42 per cent).

Overall discriminatory attitudes of India's youth

The discriminatory attitudes and prejudices mentioned above led to the construction of an overall discriminatory index (see Appendix I to find out how the

TABLE 5.7 Discriminatory attitudes by locality (%)

Locality	Very discriminatory	Somewhat discriminatory	Not very discriminatory	Not at all discriminatory
Big cities	5	6	23	66
Cities	6	10	24	60
Villages	11	12	26	51

index was constructed), which empirically measures the discriminatory attitudes amongst Indian youth. On the basis of this index, one can say only one in ten (9 per cent) Indian youth is very discriminatory, another one in ten (10 per cent) is somewhat discriminatory, about a quarter (25 per cent) are discriminatory at a low level and 56 per cent not discriminatory at all. However, given the diverse profile of India's youth there are bound to be several differences on the basis of locality, religion, caste and gender. There is a big rural–urban divide when it comes to the youth bearing a discriminatory attitude. Youth residing in India's villages were found to be more discriminatory than youth residing in cities and big cities. A higher rate of urbanisation has played a role in the reduction in discriminatory attitudes; though discrimination might exist in other invisible forms (Table 5.7).

Amongst all religious communities, Hindu youth were found to be more discriminatory than youth belonging to other religions. According to the study, one in every five (20 per cent) Hindu youth was discriminatory (highly and somewhat combined), followed by Muslim youth at 15 per cent, Sikh youth at 9 per cent and Christian youth at just 4 per cent. In other words, Hindu youth were found to be four times more prejudiced than Christian youth and two times more discriminatory than Sikh youth.

The study also points out the class differences in prevailing discriminatory attitudes. Youth from the upper, richer sections were found to be more discriminatory compared to youth from the lower economic classes. The tendency to be discriminatory was found to be 20 per cent amongst upper class and middle class youth, 19 per cent amongst lower class youth and 17 per cent amongst youth from the poorest economic background.

No significant gender differences on the question of discriminatory attitudes could be noticed. If anything, young women were found to be slightly more discriminatory than young men, 20 per cent to 18 per cent.

Discrimination stems from prejudices and education plays a significant role in breaking this connection between prejudice and discrimination. It is argued that education liberalises discriminatory attitudes amongst the youth as they are not socialised in a certain culture of prevailing prejudices. The study corroborates this argument somewhat but not entirely. This is because even though youth who had completed college education were found to be the least discriminatory in the study (16 per cent), interestingly youth who had only studied up to primary and matriculation were found to be more discriminatory than youth who were non-literate (about 22 per cent as opposed to 18 per cent).

Are India's youth liberal or conservative?

Our central argument, much in adherence to the social and cultural traits of Indian society, is that majority of the Indian youth do not fall into the extreme categories of conservative or liberal, but rather are characterised as somewhat liberal and somewhat conservative, expressing their liberal and conservative positions on certain issues and not on others. To empirically measure overall social and cultural attitudes, a mega index was created (see Appendix I to find out how the index was constructed), which includes all the attitudinal variables discussed above. On the basis of this index and the study, one finds that only one in every ten youth (11 per cent) can be described as being very conservative and one in every seven (14 per cent) can be described as being very liberal; 37 per cent were somewhat conservative and 38 per cent were somewhat liberal. By combining the somewhat conservative and somewhat liberal categories, about three in every four youth (75 per cent) can be described as having moderate social attitudes that are neither extremely conservative nor extremely liberal.

There are differences owing to the diversity and complexities prevalent in Indian society. Beginning with locality, there are urban–rural differences in defining the social and cultural attitudes of the Indian youth. Youth residing in villages were mostly found to be conservative and somewhat conservative; youth residing in cities and big cities were found to be somewhat liberal and liberal (Table 5.8).

Differences in social and cultural attitudes exist on the basis of religion. Hindu youth were found to be the most conservative and Muslim youth were found to be somewhat conservative. On the contrary, Christian youth were found to be the most socially liberal (Table 5.9).

Within religious groups, there are differences amongst various castes and communities. Youth who belong to the Hindu Adivasi community were found to be

TABLE 5.8 Liberal and conservative attitude by locality (%)

Locality	Socially very conservative	Somewhat conservative	Somewhat liberal	Socially very liberal
Big cities	5	26	46	23
Cities	8	33	38	21
Villages	16	40	35	9

TABLE 5.9 Liberal and conservative attitude by religion (%)

Religion	Socially very conservative	Somewhat conservative	Somewhat liberal	Socially very liberal
Hindu	12	37	37	14
Muslim	9	43	37	12
Christian	2	21	54	23
Sikh	5	25	55	15
Others	8	31	45	16

the most socially conservative – 30 per cent of Adivasi youth had the most socially conservative responses in the study. This can be explained by the fact that Adivasis who have been integrated into the Hindu fold tend to emulate the social and cultural practices of the upper castes.

Differences in social and cultural attitudes on the basis of religion also indicate the influence of scientific thinking amongst Indian youth. The two have not been compatible and are known to have divergent approaches. Scientific thinking is said to make individuals more rational and increase one's acceptance of others; others have critiqued this notion. But Indian youth who have been influenced by science tend to be more socially liberal than those youth influenced by religion: 21 per cent of youth influenced by science were likely to be socially liberal compared to 14 per cent of youth influenced by religion who were likely to be socially liberal.

Education is often recognised as an agent of social change. Apart from religious practices and caste ethos, socialisation of the Indian youth takes place through the education that they have received. Education shapes youth's liberal disposition. The findings of the study indicate that the more educated the youth are, the more socially liberal they are likely to be. Two-thirds (65 per cent) of the youth who had attained higher education (graduation or beyond) were found to be either very or moderately liberal. This figure dropped to 46 per cent amongst high school pass youth, 30 per cent amongst youth who had studied only until primary level, and 23 per cent amongst non-literate youth.

People often emphasise the importance of not just education but English medium education as they think that the medium of English enables a person to come in contact with Western education which is associated with a scientific outlook and liberal values. English has also become a symbol of social empowerment and is often cited as a tool to dispel narrow-mindedness and parochialism. However, contrary to this perception, according to the findings of the study, one can argue that the language in which the youth receive education makes no difference. Youth from both English and vernacular medium backgrounds were found to be equally liberal (strongly and somewhat): 55 per cent amongst each. No difference between the two could be seen even in the extreme category of highly liberal: 15 per cent each.

As mentioned before, political and economic processes also shape social and cultural attitudes. In theoretical terms, politics is the autonomous intervening variable that drives other social processes. The decade of the 1990s marked a sharp break with the past as the country embarked on a process of economic liberalisation coupled with the political processes of '*Mandalisation*' and the rise of communalism. Such big changes were followed by further changes, with the emergence of the technological revolution which brought about massive shifts in the realms of technology and communication, media and social media in the twenty-first century.

To begin with, studying the impact of these processes on the shaping of social and cultural processes of the Indian youth would require us to differentiate the youth across three generations: pre-liberalisation (1980s), post-liberalisation (1990s) and the youth born in the twenty-first century. There is a clear pattern across the three generations. There is a striking resemblance in the social and cultural attitudes of Indian youth of the 1980s and the youth who were born in the twenty-first century. The Indian youth who were born in the pre-liberalisation era and the youth who grew up during the technological revolution were found to be socially conservative and somewhat conservative. But youth who were born in the decade of 1990s or the liberalisation period were found to be socially liberal (Table 5.10).

The so-called advances made in technology and communication have also increased the exposure of Indian youth to both media and social media. In the twenty-first century, mass media have a significant influence in modern culture; the media shape social and cultural attitudes and create what is called a 'mediated culture'. What influence does news media have on Indian youth? The findings of the study indicate that there is clear relationship: the more exposed youth are to the media, the more liberal they are likely to be. Thus, Indian youth who had no exposure to news media were found to be socially conservative and somewhat conservative. Alternatively, youth who had moderate and high exposure to news media were found to be socially liberal and somewhat liberal (Table 5.11).

With news media, the proliferation of social media in the form of Facebook, Whatsapp etc. has a great influence on the lives of Indian youth. The usage of social media seems to have an impact on perception of social issues. Nearly three in every four youth (72 per cent) who had high exposure to social media were found to be socially liberal (strongly and somewhat). Alternatively, only 38 per cent of youth who were not exposed to social media at all were found to be socially pro-gressive. In other words, liberalism amongst the youth seems to increase alongside an increase in consumption of social media.

The rapid development in transport and communication has increased indi-vidual mobility. Mobility beyond one's village and one's state to one's country

TABLE 5.10 Liberal and conservative attitude by generations of India's youth (%)

Generations of Indian youth	Socially very conservative	Somewhat conservative	Somewhat liberal	Socially very liberal
Pre-liberalisation (born in the 1980s)	13	41	34	12
Born in the 1990s	9	32	41	17
Born at the start of the 20th century	14	42	34	10

TABLE 5.11 Liberal and conservative attitude by media exposure (%)

Exposure to media	Socially very conservative	Somewhat conservative	Somewhat liberal	Socially very liberal
High exposure	6	25	47	22
Medium exposure	10	31	42	17
Low exposure	12	42	35	10
No exposure	20	51	23	6

has a big influence on people's minds as they meet new people and interact with diverse cultures. Such interactions make one more acceptable of 'otherness', which is an indicator of a liberal mind. The study captured such mobility through a travel index (see Appendix I to find out how the index was constructed), which empirically measures the geographical boundary of India's youth mobility. According to the findings of the study, about one in every ten youth had not yet travelled outside their village/town/city and amongst them 57 per cent were found to be socially conservative. This dropped to 43 per cent amongst those who had travelled either outside their village/town/city or their state or the country.

In conclusion, an examination of the social and cultural attitudes of the Indian youth in this chapter helps us understand why the youth does not fit into the prototype Western categories of liberal and conservative. By delving deeper into issues of their attitude toward women and discriminatory attitudes and prejudices, one gains an understanding of certain liberal and conservative attitudes. On the question of patriarchy, the distinction between the public and the private spheres which used to characterise the gendered division of labour in Indian society has reduced. Youth have become more liberal toward women getting educated, women taking up a job after marriage, women attaining leadership roles, yet, the majority of youth continue to believe that within the household a woman's positions is subordinate to her male companion (her husband). On the question of discriminatory attitudes and prejudices, the majority of Indian youth continue to be liberal and are less discriminatory toward the so-called 'other' in terms of another religion, caste, food habits, colour of the skin, on account of marriage, barring youth from certain communities and ethnic groups. The rising tide of conservatism and xenophobic attitudes is perceived to be a threat to liberals and liberal attitudes. But the Indian youth, much in consonance with the ethos of the larger Indian society, continues to express shades of both liberalism and conservatism. Nonetheless, in this 'Global Age of Anger', the millennials (Indian youth born in the twenty-first century), much like their compatriots across the world, express far more conservative attitudes than the previous generation.

Note

1 The term 'Homo Hierarchicus' is owed to Louis Dumont's treatise (1972) on the caste system. The Indian man/woman is often characterised as a hierarchical being based on the notion of purity and pollution.

References

Chatterjee, Partha (1989) Colonialism, Nationalism & Colonized Women: The Contest in India, *American Ethnologist*, 16(4): 622–633.

Dyson, Tim & Mick Moore (1983) On Kinship Structure, Female Autonomy, and Demographic Behavior in India, *Population Development Review*, 9(1): 35–60.

Dumont, Louis (1972) *Homo Hierarchicus: The Caste System and Its Implications*. Chicago, IL: University of Chicago Press.

Jensen, Robert & Emily Oster (2008) The Power of TV: Cable Television and Women's Status in India, *Quarterly Journal of Economics*, 124(3): 1057–1094.

Kakar, Sudhir & Katharina Kakar (2007) *The Indians: Portrait of a People*. Delhi: Viking, Penguin.

Kambhapati, Uma & Raji Rajan (2008) The Nowhere Children: Patriarchy and the Role of Girls in India's Rural Economy, *Journal of Development Studies*, 44(9): 1309–1341.

Pew (2013) *The Global Divide on Homosexuality*. Pew Research Centre. Available at: www.pewglobal.org/2013/06/04/the-global-divide-on-homosexuality/ (accessed on 15 January 2017).

Ramanujan, A.K. (1989) Is There an Indian Way of Thinking? *Contributions to Indian Sociology*, 23(41).

Srinivas, M.N. (1997) *Caste: Its Twentieth Century Avatar*. Delhi: Viking, Penguin.

Susanne, Rudolph & Lloyd Rudolph (1967) *The Modernity of Tradition*. Chicago, IL: University of Chicago Press.

Tharoor, Shashi (2016) *Overcoming India's Official Homophobia*, Project Syndicate. Available at: www.project-syndicate.org/commentary/overcoming-india-s-official-homophobia-by-shashi-tharoor-2016-04?barrier=accessreg (accessed on 11 December 2016).

Vanita, Ruth & S. Kidwai (eds) (2000) *Same-Sex Love in India: Readings in Indian Literature*. New York: St Martin's Press.

Xaxa, Virginus (2005) Politics of Language, Religion and Identity: Tribes in India, *Economic and Political Weekly*, 14(13): 1363–1370.

6

MARITAL PRACTICES AMONGST THE YOUNG IN INDIA

Continuities and transformation

Asmita Aasaavari

Marriage and family are preeminent institutions in the lives of people in most societies. In recent decades, demographic trends, intra- and inter-country migration and industrialization have brought about myriad changes in the institution of marriage and family structures around the globe. These changes have manifested in, *inter alia*, young people marrying late, couples having fewer children and more married women engaging in paid work outside home. In some societies, the shortage of female spouses has led to a significant rise in the number of transnational, cross-border and cross-culture marriages, with distinct social implications.

In the Indian subcontinent, marriage as a social institution has remained nearly universal and socially compulsory. Marriage is articulated not solely as the union of two individuals but also as the establishment of a tie between two social groups such as families, households, lineages or clans. Sometimes marriage reiterates an already existing tie between them. Driven by economic and socio-cultural factors, spouse selection is managed by parents and extended kin more often than by prospective spouses. Increased modernization and globalization, urbanization, expansion of education and employment opportunities for women have affected spouse selection, marriage preferences and desires. They have contributed to the changing patterns of marriages, most notably in paving the way for inter-caste and self-choice[1] marriages (colloquially known as love marriages). This suggests a possibility that these developments would pit parental control in spouse selection against increasing individualism and preferences on the part of youth.

Given these concerns, this chapter assesses whether marriage as a social institution has undergone changes in India. To understand how and why such changes take place and their consequences is an important area of sociological research. In an attempt to understand marital choice and related behaviors of the young, the chapter focuses on both married and unmarried persons across locality, gender, caste-class groups and religious communities. It intends to explore whether arranged marriages, which tend to be hegemonic and culturally privileged, are being replaced by self-choice marriages. Specifically, it also examines if there has been an increase in inter-caste and inter-religious marriages, and whether the likelihood of self-arranged marriages increases with higher levels of educational attainment. Most importantly, in an increasingly globalizing India, do decisions around marriage continue to be a family affair only, operating within and influenced by considerations of caste, gotra[2] or economic class?

While the chapter draws upon survey findings, it recognizes that marriage arrangements in India do not necessarily fall into neat binary categories of 'arranged' and 'self-choice/love'. Rather, they need to be viewed as a process that involves varying degrees of participation from the prospective couples and their kin.

Marital choice in India

There is considerable heterogeneity within the Indian subcontinent with respect to marriage practices. Geographically, the most notable difference is the divide between the North and South (Karve 1965; Dyson and Moore 1983; Kolenda 1987). While cross-cousin marriage, i.e., marriage among blood relatives, is an accepted norm in South India; it is prohibited in North India which follows the principle of caste endogamy and gotra exogamy, i.e. marrying within the caste group but outside the gotra group. The kinship system in the North, particularly amongst Hindus is strongly tied to arranged marriage, which sustains the patrilineal and patrilocal family system and the caste system. Despite variation in kinship patterns across northern and southern India, a significant number of marriages are either arranged in nature or carry hallmarks of it. In arranged marriages, couples are neither expected nor encouraged to form relationships before they are married, although such attachments are expected to develop afterwards. They support the caste system by ensuring that spouses are of the same caste and the kinship system by prioritizing the older generation's decisions and broader kinship ties over that of the marital couple (Gore 1965; Mody 2008).

Many studies on India suggest that the institution of arranged marriage may be on the decline (Allendorf and Pandian 2016). Apparent growth in what are colloquially known as 'love marriages' is described in ethnographic studies from Haryana (Chowdhry 2007), Delhi (Mody 2008), West Bengal (Allendorf 2013), Ladakh (Aengst 2014), Gujarat (Netting 2010) and Andhra Pradesh (Still 2011). In summarizing a collection of marriage ethnographies, Kaur and Palriwala (2014) conclude that "the articulated rules of partner selection have become muddled with the espousal of new 'modern' values of 'love' and 'choice.'" Further, in keeping with the developmental idealism theory, Uberoi (2006) notes that it is widely anticipated that arranged marriage will inevitably decline with India's modernization. However, other studies indicate that the predominance of arranged marriage persists. In an ethnographic study from Tamil Nadu, Fuller and Narasimhan (2008) suggest that while the potential for interpersonal compatibility is now taken into account by parents while choosing spouses, the broader practice of arranged marriage remains intact.

The steadily growing body of scholarship on marriage and kinship, mostly ethnographies, has captured the changes in and the complexity of marriage in contemporary India. However, measures of spouse choice and related behaviors are not routinely included in nationally representative surveys. Therefore, it is difficult to evaluate the extent of marital change in India. Moreover, the literature on kinship and marriage has not intersected adequately with the scholarly work on the preferences and desires of youth. In this light, the article makes a valuable contribution to the rapidly accumulating scholarship on kinship and marriage practices in India. The attitudes and experiences of young people will enrich our sociological understanding of the prevalent socio-cultural norms around intimacy and love, parental authority, negotiation within the family and are likely to reflect the centrality (or lack thereof) of the institution of marriage.

The chapter is organized as follows. By focusing on the cohort of married youth, the first section assesses the association between marriage-related preferences and variables such as education, age, gender, caste etc. The second section examines the group of unmarried youth and discusses their marital choices in terms of arranged and self-choice marriages. The third section examines whether the gender of the child is likely to play a positive influence by sensitizing married youth towards issues of gender equity.

Importance attached to marriage seems to have declined

Comparing the 2016 survey with the 2007 study, in the last decade the proportion of young married adults has decreased by eight percentage points: in 2007 a little over half of the youth (54 percent) were married. In 2016, this reduced to 46 percent (Figure 6.1 here). This reduction is driven by young men. While 48 percent of 15–34-year-old men were found to be married in the 2007 study, in the 2016 study the share of young married men dropped to 39 percent (Table 6.1).

The sharpest drop in the proportion of married youth was in the age category of 21 to 25 years followed by 26 to 29 years (Table 6.1). Interestingly, the proportion

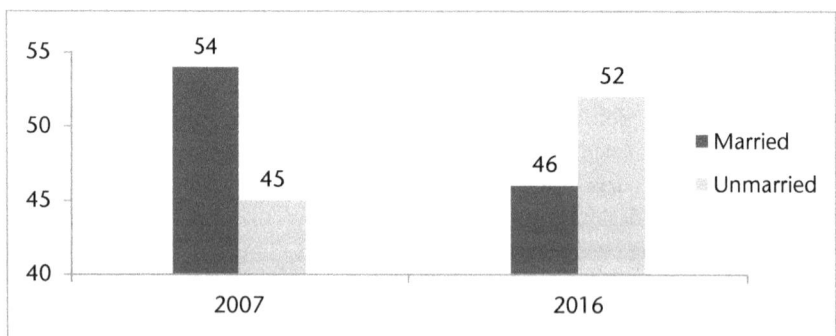

FIGURE 6.1   Proportion of married youth over the last decade (%)

TABLE 6.1 Proportion of married youth by age and gender (%)

Age group	Married overall		Married men		Married women	
	2007	2016	2007	2016	2007	2016
Overall	54	46	48	39	61	59
15–17 years	5	5	5	4	4	6
18–20 years	18	16	11	9	27	28
21–25 years	56	40	44	30	71	53
26–29 years	78	72	70	64	87	84
30–34 years	90	90	88	88	94	94

of youth marrying before the legally permissible age remained similar. The older youth (26 to 34 year olds) were more likely to be married than younger youth, but even amongst them (particularly 26 to 29 year olds) there was a decline in the proportion of those who were married. This indicates that roughly, in relative terms, the age of getting married has risen.

While the decline in the proportion of married youth is visible across localities, it is more prominent in rural areas than in urban areas. In 2007, in rural areas over three-fifths (61 percent) of the 15 to 34 year olds were married. In 2016, this had dropped by 9 percent to 52 percent. In urban areas, there has been a six-point decline in the proportion of married youth, from 46 percent to 40 percent in the last decade (Figure 6.2). Juxtaposing these findings with the widely held belief that in India in urban areas norms around marriage, upward mobility etc. are likely to be more relaxed, the findings reveal that the decline in the percentage of married youth has been most prominent in rural areas. This may be viewed as an encouraging sign of changing attitudes as far as delaying the decision to get married is concerned.

In both localities, urban and rural, young men were less likely to get married than young women. Moreover, in both localities, there was a sharper decline in the proportion of young married men over the last decade than in the proportion of young married women. In rural areas, the share of young married men fell from 54 percent 2007 to 44 percent in 2016. Similarly, in urban areas, 41 percent of young

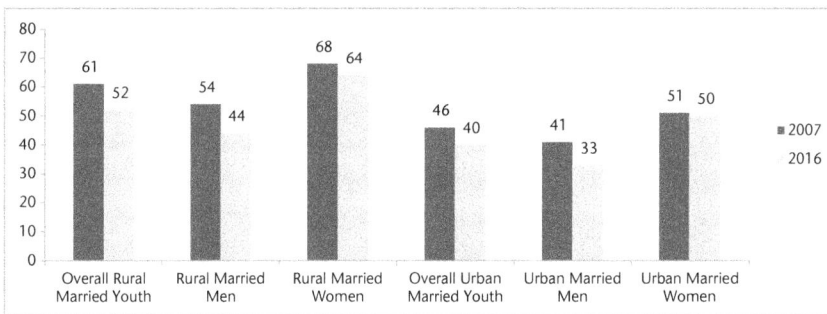

FIGURE 6.2 Proportion of married youth by locality (%)

men were married in 2007 which decreased to 33 percent in 2016 (Figure 6.2). Meanwhile, the decadal decline in the proportion of young married women in rural and urban areas was 4 and 1 percent respectively. This finding is also corroborated by ethnographic studies which suggest that men have greater choice and agency over their marriage than women in India (Caldwell et al. 1983; Allendorf 2013; Allendorf and Pandian 2016).

Expectedly, a higher share of young men were more likely to be unmarried than women. That is, the former were more likely to be able to delay the pressure of getting married. This is also supported by the prevalent customs of marriage and the associated notions of purity and pollution wherein there is greater pressure from and desire amongst families to control women's sexuality by getting them married at a socially appropriate age (Dube 2001). The same does not hold true for men.

One possible explanation for the postponement of marriage and an increase in the percentage of unmarried youth can be attributed to the increase in the level of educational attainment resulting in greater bargaining power within the family as well as the gradual change in public attitudes. The demands of the modern knowledge-based economy entail placing greater focus on one's career and aspiring for fast paced professional mobility. However, this pressure and exercise of greater individual agency has worked more in favor of young unmarried men than young unmarried women. Unlike a decade back, youth are marrying later in life now. Increasing opportunities to pursue higher education, prioritizing professional growth and concerns of financial security are likely to have contributed to a greater proportion of unmarried youth.

Education is an important claim to modernity and is likely to impact spouse choice by opening possibilities and avenues for meeting potential mates. Being able to seek higher education pushes back marriage timelines. With successive levels of education, the percentage of married youth decreases, i.e. non-literates are more likely to be married than those who are high school pass or graduates because education helps individuals attain greater levels of individuation and lessen familial control. In the 2007 study, 45 percent of those who were college educated reported being married. A decade later, this figure had reduced by ten percentage points to 35 percent (Figure 6.3).

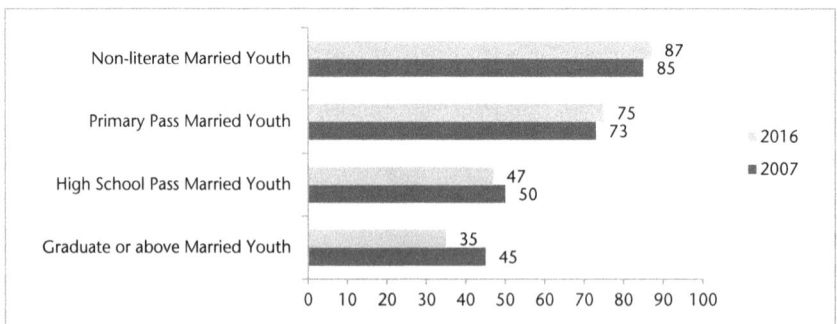

FIGURE 6.3 Proportion of married youth by education (%)

Arranged marriage or self-choice marriage?

In India, the type of marriage individuals opt for is indicative of the level of influence played by their family, prevalent norms and peer group influence in the process of mate selection. In arranged marriages, parents customarily choose a spouse based on the caste, religion and socio-economic standing of the prospective spouse and her or his family. In contrast, in self-choice marriages, young people choose their own spouse on the basis of individual compatibility or affection, usually gained through interactions before marriage (Allendorf and Pandian 2016). Thus, preference for arranged marriage needs to be conceptualized as not merely limited to spouse choice. It also signals the continued importance of caste, religion, socio-economic class and other aspects of the status of prospective spouses and their family.

Preference for marriage type amongst married youth reveals interesting variations across locality, caste, religion and education. The study found 84 percent of married youth as having had an arranged marriage, compared to a meager 6 percent who opted for self-choice marriage. The fact that such a small fraction of marriages were self-choice i.e. based on love, clearly shows that one institution that globalization, liberalization and other economic forces have been unable to weaken is that of arranged marriage. The acceptance and reported incidence of arranged marriage continues to be extremely high in twenty-first century India. Over 80 percent of the marriages in big cities, small cities and villages were arranged in nature and youth in big cities were most likely to have had a self-choice marriage (Table 6.2).

TABLE 6.2 Marriage type by locality, education and caste/religious community (%)

	Arranged marriage	Self-choice marriage	Love-cum-arranged marriage	No response
Overall	84	6	4	6
By locality				
Big cities	81	9	6	4
Smaller cities	87	7	4	2
Villages	83	5	4	8
Graduate or above	78	9	5	8
High school pass	86	5	4	6
Primary pass	88	4	4	5
Non-literate	92	3	2	3
By caste and religion				
Hindu upper caste	86	6	3	6
Hindu OBC	81	6	6	7
Hindu Dalit	82	10	3	6
Hindu Adivasi	91	1	2	6
Muslim	87	7	3	3
Christian	75	12	4	10
Sikh	90	3	3	5

Level of autonomy in partner choice is directly related to education. Access to education means that individuals have greater ability and confidence to take decisions independently, and increased opportunities to meet potential partners in educational institutions and/or workplaces. This is also supported by the findings of the study: self-choice marriage was most prevalent amongst those who were graduates or above (9 percent), arranged marriage was most prevalent amongst those who were non-literates (92 percent), followed by primary pass (88 percent) and high school pass (86 percent).

Inter-caste marriage

Owing to the compulsions of democratic politics, there has been increased interaction between those at the opposite ends of the caste hierarchy. Members of groups categorized as lower caste have been successful in pushing for affirmative action legislation with the support of upper caste members. However, this does not signal the demise of caste hierarchy (Ahuja and Ostermann 2015). The relationship between marriage and caste is complex as marriage is arguably one of the most central social practices in India that implicates the caste system. Individuals choose to marry within their own caste as it guarantees the reproduction of caste from one generation to another. The fact that caste continues to govern relations in the private sphere is supported by how the incidence of inter-caste marriage is low despite an increase in its acceptability. The study found that only 4 percent of the youth had an inter-caste marriage, but its social acceptance (those who did not see anything wrong with inter-caste marriages) was much higher at 55 percent. Trends in acceptance of inter-caste marriage show changes in the expected direction. It has increased by 24 percentage points, from 31 percent in 2007 to 55 percent in 2016 (Table 6.3).

This raises a valid question on whether social outcomes reflect people's actual preferences and whether they can be the sole indicator of social attitudes. The low percentage of inter-caste marriages might not necessarily imply low interest in such marriages, but may in fact be indicative of a gap in the social approval and the outcome of inter-caste marriages. The low outcome of inter-caste marriage (just 4 percent) indicates that even though previously unequal groups have become equal economically and socially, they remain distinct by subscribing to the socially accepted norm of caste endogamy (Table 6.4).

TABLE 6.3 Youth opinion on inter-caste marriage (%)

	2007	*2016*
Right	31	55
Wrong	64	36

Note: The rest of the youth gave no response. No response indicates that they did not wish to answer the question.

TABLE 6.4 Proportion of inter-caste and inter-religious marriages (%)

Type of marriage amongst married youth	
Intra-caste marriage	92
Inter-caste marriage	4
Intra-religious marriages	98
Inter-religious marriages	2

Note: In the case of inter- and intra-caste marriages, the rest of the youth gave no response (4 percent). No response was zero for inter- and intra-religious marriages.

TABLE 6.5 Relation between marriage type and caste of spouse (%)

	Spouse is from another caste	*Spouse is from the same caste*
Those who had a self-choice marriage	34	63
Those who had an arranged marriage	1	97
Those whose marriage was love cum arranged	13	83

Note: The rest of the youth gave no response.

Nearly one-third of those who had a self-choice marriage were found to have married someone outside their caste. Alternatively, 97 percent of arranged marriages were within the caste (Table 6.5).

Not just in practice, but in attitudes too, the study found that married youth who had an arranged marriage displayed more resistance towards the idea of an inter-caste marriage and inter-religious marriage than those whose marriage had been self-arranged (Table 6.6). Religion is a bigger fault line than caste. Overall, the acceptance for inter-religious marriage was much less than that for caste. Married youth, both with arranged marriage and self-choice marriage, were more likely to be against a woman and a man living together outside marriage, however if we compare the responses of the self-choice marriage cohort and the

TABLE 6.6 Opinion of youth on inter-caste/inter-religious marriage, homosexuality, dating etc. by marriage type (%)

		Inter-caste marriage	*Inter-religious marriage*	*Live-in before marriage*	*Dating before marriage*	*Celebrating Valentine's day*	*Love affair between women*	*Love affair between men*
Those who had a self-choice marriage	Consider it to be right	72	69	34	53	60	32	32
	Consider it to be wrong	15	28	62	42	30	57	57
Those who had an arranged marriage	Consider it to be right	43	35	15	25	30	23	23
	Consider it to be wrong	48	57	76	66	54	64	64

Note: The rest of the youth gave no response.

arranged marriage cohort, the former appear to be slightly more broadminded about it. On the question of homosexuality too, those with an arranged marriage were more likely to oppose it than those who had a self-choice marriage (Table 6.6).

The widespread inclination towards arranged marriage among married youth can be attributed to three factors. First, it reflects the continuing hold of caste in everyday life and in marriage markets specifically. Second, it points towards the continuing importance of parental authority, kin involvement in spouse selection and the inclination to operate closer to tradition and convention. Third, arranged marriages are seen as robust and long lasting, with greater chances of parental support being extended to the couple in times of marital distress. Given the perceived lack of parental support in self-choice marriages, they are considered inferior, conflict ridden and less successful (Grover 2007).

Furthermore, family and community honor is a cherished ideal amongst Hindus, Sikhs and Muslims and the onus of protecting it falls invariably on women. Spouse selection without parental consent is therefore viewed as inappropriate behavior, resulting in punishment, shame and honor killings (Chowdhry 2007). Therefore, from the perspective of young women, rejecting arranged marriage and opting for love marriage is accompanied by a fear of denigrating the family's reputation. By taking responsibility for their own marital choice (i.e. by opting for self-choice marriage), young women fear that they might not be able to extensively draw upon kin support or shelter.

Marital preferences of unmarried youth

Like the married youth, amongst the unmarried too, preference for arranged marriage was high with five in ten of the young unmarried cohort opting for it. Preference for self-choice marriage accounted for 12 percent and roughly one-fifth (19 percent) had not made up their mind on the kind of marriage they would like to enter into and if at all they would like to get married (Table 6.7). About one in ten (10 percent) preferred love-cum-arranged marriage – an intermediate category between parent-arranged and self-arranged marriage of 'self-selecting spouse with parental involvement.' In this type of marriage, while young adults do not wish their parents to select their spouses for them without the former's approval, the cultural environment and societal norms do not support Western style dating either (Lessinger 2002; Medora 2003). Therefore, selecting a spouse with the involvement of parents serves as a convenient middle ground.

In cities, the search for partners differs from villages and is often less likely to be mediated by caste networks. The relative anonymity of an individual's identity in cities makes it difficult for rules of purity and pollution to be observed; thus, individuals have greater freedom to exercise their choice in mate selection. Since the perceived threat of violence when marriage-related social norms are transgressed is relatively stronger in villages and smaller cities than in metropolitan cities

TABLE 6.7 Marital preference of unmarried young people (%)

	Prefer self-choice marriage	Prefer arranged marriage	Prefer love-cum-arranged marriage	Undecided
Overall	12	50	10	19
Big cities	13	40	15	21
Smaller cities	12	51	11	18
Villages	11	55	6	19
Graduate or above	12	48	12	20
High school pass	11	52	8	18
Primary pass	4	55	4	21
Non-literate	4	83	0	9
Hindu upper caste	12	49	11	20
Hindu OBC	9	55	9	18
Hindu Dalit	14	46	8	20
Hindu Adivasi	9	62	7	17
Muslim	15	44	12	22
Other castes	14	39	14	18
15–17 years	10	52	8	19
18–21 years	12	47	10	21
22–25 years	12	50	12	17
26–29 years	14	55	12	15
30–34 years	5	51	10	19

Note: The rest of the youth gave no response. Undecided refers to those who have not yet made up their mind on the kind of marriage they would like to opt for and/or if at all they want to get married.

(Chowdhry 2007), this explains why unmarried youth in small cities and villages display highest preference for arranged marriage (Table 6.7). Those who were more educated seemed more willing to opt for self-choice marriage (12 percent). Non-literate single youth were found to be more likely to prefer arranged marriage (83 percent).

Amongst all castes, unmarried Hindu Adivasi youth display the highest preference for arranged marriage (62 percent), whereas unmarried Muslim and Dalit youth had the highest preference for self-choice marriage (15 and 14 percent, respectively). This finding contrasts with the oft-cited norms pertaining to marriage in tribal communities in India, which are more favorable towards self-choice marriages than other caste and religious communities. Ethnographic accounts indicate that marriage in tribal societies is choice based and women have greater freedom in personal spheres such as pre-marital sex, divorce and remarriage (Xaxa 2004). Even among Hindus, women belonging to 'lower' socio-economic classes are known to enjoy greater freedom than upper caste Hindus. The highest proportion of unmarried youth inclined towards arranged marriage was found among 26 to 29 year olds (Table 6.7). The preference of this age cohort for self-choice marriage was also the strongest (14 percent).

The study also found information on the opinion of Indian youth on the importance of getting married in life. Time series data on this question show a noticeable

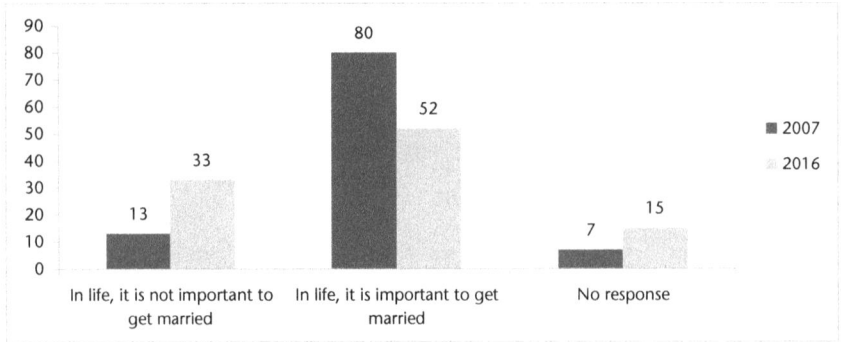

FIGURE 6.4   Change in perception about marriage (%)

TABLE 6.8   Change in perception about marriage by locality (%)

	In life, it is not important to get married		*In life, it is important to get married*	
	2007	*2016*	*2007*	*2016*
Rural	12	33	80	51
Urban	14	31	82	55

Note: The rest of the youth gave no response.

shift in favor of opting to not marry. While one third agreed, more than half (52 percent) disagreed. Compared to a decade ago, young people appeared to be over two times more likely to be open to the idea of not marrying. Young people were in fact found to be two times less opinionated on the question in the 2016 study than they were a decade ago in the 2007 study (Figure 6.4).

Amongst rural youth, agreement on this question (i.e. it is not important to get married in life) was found to be nearly three times greater as compared to 2007 (Table 6.8). Amongst urban youth it was two times more. Those who are primary pass, high school pass and graduate and above were found to be over twice as likely to express this sentiment as they were a decade back; 22 to 29 year olds were three times more likely to agree than they were a decade back.

Life partner consideration

The wave of industrialization and globalization in India has had a profound impact on culture, lifestyle and dietary preferences. Indian youth's beliefs and attitudes towards marriage and the qualities they seek in their life partner have undergone transformation, more so because in India, marriage is considered a lifelong partnership.

Over the decades, the impact of education, economic diffusion, rapidly changing socio-economic and cultural values, and gender roles in private and public realms have resulted in a much greater influx of women in the workforce. There has also been heightened awareness of sexual harassment forcing people to re-evaluate assumptions about men and women. As a result, not only would there be greater cultural acceptance of unmarried and married women's engagement with paid work outside home but also a new focus in marriage markets and socio-cultural values of mate preference wherein unmarried women's careers would be given due importance, if not equal to those of their male counterparts. Certain socio-cultural values such as physical features and skin color of potential spouse, and personality traits such as simplicity and an understanding and respectful nature, are often considered indispensable and kept in mind while selecting a marriage partner. Therefore, such cultural values are likely to remain constant and impervious to changes in rest of the society, given their large-scale social acceptability and desirability across different cohorts.

The study asked young people to state the important considerations that they would keep in mind while choosing a life partner. Amongst married youth, those who had a love marriage were much more likely to cite love as an important consideration than those who had an arranged marriage or love-cum-arranged marriage. Earlier analysis in this chapter has shown that 97 percent of arranged marriages were endogamous in nature (within castes) and caste has been an important factor that often overrides other aspects in marriage markets. In complete contrast, an analysis of considerations that are sought in a potential life partner amongst married youth suggests that those who had an arranged marriage did not cite caste, religion, region as their most important consideration while choosing a life partner. Those who had a love marriage (11 percent) were more likely to give primacy to the profession and salary, looks and skin color (10 percent) of their spouse than those who had an arranged marriage. On other parameters such as being educated, being understanding and respectful, having a good nature and a simple personality, there were no marked differences between those who had a love marriage and those who had an arranged marriage. Regardless of type of marriage, married youth expect their potential spouse to be good natured and simple (amongst those with love marriage – 15 percent, arranged marriage – 13 percent and both types of marriage – 16 percent), understanding and respect-ful (love marriage –9 percent, arranged marriage – 6 percent and both types of marriage – 8 percent). Nine percent of those who had a love marriage expected their partner to be traditional, cultured and have moral values, as opposed to 5 percent of those who had an arranged marriage (Table 6.9).

No response in this question was strikingly high (49 percent). Disaggregating the no response figures by background variables reveals that amongst the married youth, those who had an arranged marriage and love-cum-arranged marriage were more likely to not have given an answer to this question (54 and 51 percent respectively) than those who had a love marriage (33 percent). Young women were more likely not to have provided an answer to this question than men. More than half the youth in villages (53 percent) did not have an opinion in this question, followed by small and big cities (47 and 45 percent respectively).

TABLE 6.9 Qualities sought by young people in marriage partners (%)

	All youth, married or single	Those with an arranged marriage	Those with a love marriage	Those with love-cum-arranged marriage	Unmarried youth
Good nature and simple personality	14	13	15	16	15
Educational qualification	8	3	2	8	11
Understanding and respectful	6	6	9	8	6
Looks/skin color	5	4	10	2	6
Traditional, cultured, moral	5	5	9	4	5
Good job or income	4	4	11	4	5
Caste, religion, region etc.	2	2	0	2	1
Love and companionship	2	1	3	1	1
Consent of parents	1	2	1	0	1
Family background	1	1	0	0	1
Should know housework	1	2	1	3	1
Other qualities	2	3	4	2	3
No opinion	49	54	33	51	46

Note: The question was asked in an open-ended manner and hence the proportion of no opinion is very high as many of the youth either could not think of an answer or simply refused to answer. The figures are column percentages.

Similarly, 53 percent of married and 46 percent of unmarried youth did not provide their opinion on this question.

Advertisement in matrimonial websites and newspapers

On the question of matrimonial advertisements, the study reveals a strikingly interesting finding, indicating that only 3 percent of youth had placed a matrimonial advertisement whereas 87 percent had not. Amongst the married cohort, roughly as many youth who had a love marriage and an arranged marriage had made a matrimonial advertisement in a newspaper/website (4 percent each).

Contrary to the claims of the news media that scores of youngsters are finding potential partners on matrimonial sites, evidence from the study suggests that reliance on matrimonial websites is far less than is assumed. The fact that until now a large majority of marriages are endogamous in nature and only 3 percent of the young population in our study had relied on matrimonial advertisements suggests that there is continued reliance on traditional methods of marriage, specifically within familiar kin networks.

The relationship of child's gender to parents' commitment to gender equity

In India, social norms and practices are significantly governed by patriarchal ideologies that define the roles of men and women. These views often play out alongside increasingly reshaped roles for women in society. The presence of daughters may be instrumental in fathers being more conscious of gender-related differences amongst boys and girls and hence more gender sensitive. Studies have also shown that having daughters has the potential of sensitizing parents (fathers particularly) to issues of gender equity (Warner and Steel 1999; Washington 2008).

Therefore, it would be important to examine whether there is any link between offspring's gender and parental beliefs on gender equity issues amongst married youth. This issue holds relevance in a context laden with gender discrimination in nearly all realms of life. The study inquired about young people's views on whether it is right for women to work after marriage, whether men are better leaders than women and whether wives must always listen to their husbands etc. Contrary to intuition, young married men with daughters as well as men with children of both genders were less likely to be open to the idea of women working after marriage than young married men with sons (Table 6.10).

The protectionist attitude of married youth, males particularly, is likely to contribute to the formation of such a parochial mindset. The fact that married men with daughters were more likely to be opposed to women working after marriage shows that in the case of Indian youth, there is a reversal of the idea of gender sensitive parenting. Young fathers with sons were more resistant (48 percent) to women being involved in paid work outside the home post marriage than mothers with sons (32 percent). It is possible that having sons might be connected to men's resistance to social change with regard to gender.

Education has been argued to have a liberalizing effect on people by exposing them to divergent worldviews and lifestyles. Numerous studies have suggested

TABLE 6.10 Relation between offspring's gender and the married youth's opinion on married working women (%)

| | It is not right for women to have a job after marriage | |
	Agree	Disagree
Married men with son/s	48	45
Married men with daughter/s	53	40
Married men with children of both genders	53	36
Married women with son/s	32	59
Married women with daughter/s	33	55
Married women with children of both genders	38	48

Note: The rest of the youth gave no response.

that higher educational attainment of a society leads to increased tolerance and acceptance of gender equity issues (Warner and Steel 1999). However, this may not necessarily hold true as far as opinion on women working after marriage is concerned. Examining the views of young parents with sons and daughters by their level of educational attainment, one sees that married males who were high school pass and above were more likely to not support women working after marriage (57 percent). Also, the opinion of married men with daughters who were graduates and above was divided (49 percent agree, 50 percent disagree) on this issue.

In the case of married women who are graduates and above and have sons, education can be seen to have a liberalizing effect, since they are more likely to support women's decision to work after marriage, compared to primary pass married women who are least likely to do so.

Opinion on leadership and gender differences is closely connected to the gender of the child. Results demonstrate that the presence of a daughter in young men's lives does not necessarily make them more sensitive on matters related to gender equity. Close to half of the young men, irrespective of whether they have a son or a daughter, believed that men are better leaders (Table 6.11).

There is a visible difference in the proportion of married and unmarried youth who agree that wives should always listen to their husbands (Table 6.12) and in this case too it can be seen that parenting daughters does not have much of a positive impact on young men (Table 6.13). Nearly three out of five young married men with daughters expect that wives should listen to their husbands. What is equally alarming is that young women with daughters did not appear to be broad minded on this question with 53 percent of them endorsing that wives must obey their husbands. It is clear that in contrast to the gender sensitive parenting argument made earlier, married men with daughters are more conservative in attitudes than married women with sons, in relative terms.

The assumption that young men with daughters are more likely to be cautious towards concerns of gender equity and equality, since they have the potential to create

TABLE 6.11 Relation between offspring's gender and married youth's opinion on women in leadership positions (%)

| | Overall, men prove to be better leaders than women | |
	Agree	Disagree
Married men with son/s	49	41
Married men with daughter/s	49	40
Married men with children of both genders	51	35
Married women with sons	35	50
Married women with daughter/s	39	45
Married women with children of both genders	36	45

Note: The rest of the youth gave no response.

TABLE 6.12 Relation between marital status and opinion on wife's position vis-à-vis her husband (%)

Wives should always listen to their husband

	Agree	Disagree
Married youth	55	35
Unmarried youth	48	44

Note: The rest of the youth gave no response.

TABLE 6.13 Relation between offspring's gender and married youth's opinion on wife's position vis-à-vis her husband (%)

	Wives should always listen to their husbands	
	Agree	Disagree
Married men with son/s	61	33
Married men with daughter/s	59	35
Married men with children of both genders	62	26
Married women with son/s	47	44
Married women with daughter/s	53	36
Married women with children of both genders	51	37

Note: The rest of the youth gave no response.

gender barriers for their daughters, does not hold true for all cases. These findings also reveal that changes associated with accepted traditional norms about the role of men and women in society have not adapted to keep pace with India's rapid economic growth and rise in opportunities for women. The increased opportunities to benefit from economic liberalization and cultural globalization have not necessarily led to concomitant attitudinal and behavioral changes. Young people have not necessarily been able to embrace new ways of thinking about gender and family. This evidence corroborates the argument of social scientists who dispute the assumption that socio-structural change will necessarily accompany changes in individual attitudes and values (Gusfield 1967).

Discussion and conclusion

The marriage system in India has experienced a number of changes such as increase in women's age at marriage and the near universal adoption of dowry as a condition for marriage. Both these developments have been attributed to changes in socio-economic factors and demographic condition of marriages including the deficit of marriageable women (a phenomenon known as the 'marriage squeeze') (Banerjee 1999; Srinivasan and Lee 2004; Uberoi 2006). However, it is imperative to ascertain whether, along with the changing socio-economic and demographic conditions, political and constitutional efforts, young people's marital preferences and outcomes reflect some of these changes or whether most marriages continue to be largely determined by religious and caste affiliations of individuals.

Using nationally representative data, the chapter has demonstrated that while arranged marriages continue to be the dominant and popular form of marriage in India, the acceptance of inter-caste marriage has increased. However, the reported outcome of such marriages continues to be low. Also, while young people are now delaying their decision to get married, young men continue to have greater agency and choice to do so than young women. Similarly, religion appears to be a bigger fault line than caste in marriage markets since the acceptance for and the reported outcome of inter-religious marriage is much less than that for caste.

The findings discussed above hold immense sociological significance. First, despite popular media representations and new public imaginations of marriage, self-choice marriages have not replaced arranged marriages, and nor has divorce replaced life-long marital unions. The widespread inclination towards arranged marriages among youth (both married and unmarried) indicates that marriages arranged by parents are not likely to become obsolete any time soon. Even as new forms of marriage have emerged, they continue to hold the hallmarks of arranged marriage. Thus, it would be safe to suggest that the practice of arranged marriage is changing in form and not declining and it is not headed towards obsolescence any time soon.

Second, in globalizing India, marriage continues to be a family affair – the pre-rogative of parents and family elders and is guided by tradition and convention. This contrasts sharply with the assumption of economic and lifestyle modernity being accompanied by a subsequent attitudinal and behavioral change. Instead, these findings demonstrate that modernization, which is often viewed as a struggle to incorporate new patterns within old boundaries (Pathak 1998), need not always lead to conflict and upheaval in traditional values.

Third, the fact that a decline in the proportion of married youth is accompanied by very high support for arranged marriage provides a glimpse into how a change in people's ways of thinking and continuity of tradition coexist. Young individuals' experience of modernity has a peculiar manifestation, that is, modernity maybe practiced alongside tradition. Despite the deep effects of globalization, the case of Indian youth in the global scenario appears distinct, where support for arranged marriage can be found not just among parents, but amongst their offspring too.

Fourth, rather than simple adoption of Western practice of self-choice mar-riage, the results point to a hybridization of Western and Indian practices. In India, the colloquial opposite of an arranged marriage is 'love marriage', wherein young people choose their own spouse on the basis of love, attraction or interpersonal compatibility. While the data show that inter-caste marriage is more common among self-choice marriages, approximately only three out of ten self-choice mar-riages are inter-caste. Thus, it appears that, like their parents, young people are also following the rules of caste endogamy.

Lastly, these findings have implications for global theories of family change, which predict that arranged marriage will decline in favor of self-choice marriage (Allendorf and Pandian 2016). These findings also suggest that the prediction of family change theories was only partially accurate for India. The influence of India's caste system and the predominance of caste endogamy can possibly be seen as factors that do not sever the ubiquitous nature of arranged marriage.

The opening up of the Indian economy in 1990s fostered new economic opportunities and a decade later India saw the birth and rise of the power of new media. This facilitated some of the greatest changes in contemporary India. The onset of globalization and the simultaneous rise in consumerism have been accompanied by a desire among the youth to embrace a certain kind of modernity. In the last two decades Indians across age groups have been able to shed their inhibition and adapt themselves to new consumption patterns and experiences. Adaptability towards new leisure opportunities such as the internet, mobile phones, malls etc. has been far smoother than changes in the socio-cultural realm and ways of thinking. It is thus clear that one of the realms where Indians have chosen to negotiate economic, social and cultural modernity is in the arena of marriage.

Notes

1 For the purpose of this chapter, the terms self-choice marriage and self-arranged marriage will be used interchangeably.
2 *Gotra* is an exogamous patrilineal clan whose members are thought to share patrilineal descent from a common ancestor. It forbids marriage among people of the same *gotra* (Chowdhry 1997). Adherence to *gotra* varies from caste to caste, and from region to region.

References

Aengst, Jennifer (2014) Adolescent Movements: Dating, Elopements, and Youth Policing in Ladakh, India, *Ethnos Journal of Anthropology*, 79(5): 630–649.

Ahuja, Amit and Ostermann, Susan (2015) Crossing Caste Boundaries in the Middle-Class Indian Marriage Market, *Studies in Comparative International Development*, 3: 70–105.

Allendorf, Keera (2013) Schemas of Marital Change: From Arranged Marriages to Eloping for Love, *Journal of Marriage and Family*, 75(2): 453–469.

Allendorf, Keera and Pandian, Roshan K. (2016) The Decline of Arranged Marriage? Marital Change and Continuity in India, *Population and Development Review*, 42(3): 435–464.

Banerjee, K. (1999) Gender Stratification and the Contemporary Marriage Market in India, *Journal of Family Issues*, 20: 648.

Caldwell, J., Reddy, P.H. and Caldwell, P. (1983) The Causes of Marriage Change in South India, *Population Studies*, 37(3): 343–361.

Chowdhry, Prem (1997) Cultural Codes: Gender and Violence in Northern India, *Economic and Political Weekly*, 32(19): 1019–1028.

Chowdhry, Prem (2007) *Contentious Marriages, Eloping Couples: Gender, Caste and Patriarchy in Northern India*. Delhi: Oxford University Press.

Dube, Leela (2001) *Anthropological Debates in Gender: Intersecting Fields*. New Delhi: Sage Publications.

Dyson, Tim and Moore, Mick (1983) On Kinship Structure, Female Autonomy, and Demographic Behavior in India, *Population and Development Review*, 9(1): 35–60.

Fuller C.J. and Narasimhan, Haripriya (2008) Companionate Marriage in India: The Changing Marriage System in a Middle-Class Brahman Subcaste, *Journal of the Royal Anthropological Institute*, 14(4): 736–754.

Gore, M.S. (1965) The Traditional Indian Family, in Nimkoff, M.F. (ed.) *Comparative Family Systems*. Boston, MA: Houghton Mifflin.

Grover, Shalini (2007) *Looking Inside Marriage: Lived Experiences, Notions of Love and Kinship Support Amongst Working Women in New Delhi*, Working Paper Series No. E/285/2007, Institute of Economic Growth, Delhi.

Gusfield, Joseph R. (1967) Tradition and Modernity: Misplaced Polarities in the Study of Social Change, *American Journal of Sociology*, 72(4): 351–362.

Karve, Irawati (1965) *Kinship Organization in India*. Mumbai: Asia Publishing House.

Kaur, Ravinder and Palriwala, Rajni (eds) (2014) *Marrying in South Asia: Shifting Concepts, Changing Practices in a Globalising World*. Hyderabad: Orient Blackswan.

Kolenda, Pauline (1987) *Regional Differences in Family Structure in India*. Jaipur: Rawat Publications.

Lessinger, Johanna (2002) Asian Indian Marriages: Arranged, Semi-arranged or Based on Love?, in N.B. Benokraitis (ed.) *Contemporary Ethnic Families in the United States: Characteristics, Variation and Dynamics*. New York: Prentice Hall.

Medora, N. (2003) Mate Selection in Contemporary India: Love Marriages Versus Arranged Marriages, in R. Hamon and B. Ingoldsby (eds) *Mate Selection Across Cultures*. Washington, DC: Sage Publications.

Mody, Perveez (2008) *The Intimate State: Love-Marriage and the Law in Delhi*. Delhi: Routledge India.

Netting, Nancy S. (2010) Marital Ideoscopes in 21st Century India: Creative Combinations of Love and Responsibility, *Journal of Family Issues*, 31(6): 707–726.

Pathak, Avijit (1998) *Indian Modernity: Contradictions, Paradoxes and Possibilities*. New Delhi: Gyan Publishing.

Srinivasan, P. and Lee, G.R. (2004) The Dowry System in Northern India: Women's Attitudes and Social Change, *Journal of Marriage and Family*, 66: 1108–1117.

Still, Clarinda (2011) Spoiled Brides and the Fear of Education: Honour and Social Mobility Among Dalits in South India, *Modern Asian Studies*, 45(05): 1119–1146.

Uberoi, P. (2006) *Freedom and Destiny: Gender, Family, and Popular Culture in India*. Delhi: Oxford University Press.

Warner, Rebecca and Steel, Brent S. (1999) Child Rearing as a Mechanism for Social Change: The Relationship of Child's Gender to Parents' Commitment to Gender Equity, *Gender and Society*, 13(4): 503–517.

Washington, Ebonya L. (2008) Female Socialization: How Daughters Affect Their Legislator Father, *American Economic Review*, 98(1): 311–332.

Xaxa, Virginius (2004) Women and Gender in the Study of Tribes in India, *Journal of Gender Studies*, 11(3): 345–363.

7

LIFESTYLE AND HABITS OF INDIAN YOUTH

Vibha Attri

This chapter highlights the lifestyle and habits of the Indian youth. It explores the youth's ways of living and doing things, and how they are impacted by the interconnected processes of globalisation, liberalisation, consumerism, urbanisation and exposure to newer forms of communication technology. A KPMG survey claims that the Indian youth today are 'highly experimental', especially in terms of their lifestyle choices (Ghosh 2015). At the same time, there is a streak of conservatism entering the attitudes of this generation regarding several aspects of their daily lives and belief systems. This chapter follows the paradoxical nature of the youth's lives as it describes the nature of living arrangements of India's youth, their style preferences, their leisure lifestyles, their health-related behaviours, their engagement with various forms of media, both traditional and new, and their religious practices. Broadly speaking, it finds the youth's lifestyle preferences, practices and interests to be a mix of both the old and the new. They are a mix of global influences, with advancing technologies and rising education standards, and local customs and traditions of the past (Bobb 1999). These processes of adaptation or localising the global are recognised by Samrat Chakrabarti (2015) as the youth's attempt at constructing an identity for themselves in the face of a world larger than ever before. In a similar strain of argument, deSouza et al. posit that the Indian youth have a 'bicultural identity' which comprises 'elements of both global and local identities' (deSouza et al. 2009: xxviii) The study uses the data of the 2007 survey conducted by the Centre for the Study of Developing Societies (CSDS), and finds that the difference in attitudes among youth was a function of material and cognitive opportunities rather than individual choice. This chapter takes the analysis further and marks the changes in the lifestyle choices of the youth in India. These changes in trends reflect on the changing social world that these youths occupy, and thus provide a window into the changing social space of Indian society.

Living arrangements of youth

The study found 65 per cent or two-thirds of youth (15–34 year olds) to be living with their parents. About 31 per cent or a third were found to be living with their spouse, and the remaining 4 per cent were living with a friend, in a hostel or alone (Table 7.1). While a greater proportion of younger youth, not surprisingly, were found to be living with their parents than older youth, what is interesting is that 33 per cent of young people aged between 30 and 34 years, and a similar proportion of married youth, were also living with their parents. Youth's living arrangements also differed considerably by education, marital and employment status, and locality. It is students (92 per cent) and employment seekers (89 per cent) who live with their parents in a greater proportion compared to employed youth (62 per cent). One also sees a clear variance regarding the living arrangements of youth from different localities. In big cities, a higher proportion of youth live with their parents as compared to small cities and villages. What is interesting here is that this trend completely reverses when one looks at married youth in different localities. A higher proportion of married youth in villages lived with their parents than in big cities. The economic class one belongs to also has an impact on living arrangements. An equal proportion of youth from economically disadvantaged classes (poor and lower), i.e. 62 per cent, lived with their parents, in contrast to 71 per cent from the well-off classes. An explanation for this could be that the youth from lower class have to move out in search of employment in order to support their family. It is also a result of locality, as poor youth in villages have a higher chance of moving out in search of jobs due to fewer job opportunities in villages. There was a 10 per cent variance amongst youth from poor classes in cities and in villages who lived with their parents, with a higher proportion of youth from poor classes in big cities living with their parents.

This high incidence of youth living with their parents in India is in contrast with some Western countries such as the United States. A Pew Research Center study (Fry 2016) conducted in 2014 found only 32 per cent of American youth in the age group of 18–34 years to be living with their parents. The figure for the same age group in India is 59 per cent according to the study (Figure 7.1).

TABLE 7.1 Living arrangements of India's youth (%)

	Live with parents	Live with life partner	Live with friend/in a hostel/alone etc.
Overall	65	31	4
15–17 years	96	1	3
18–21 years	83	12	5
22–25 years	67	27	5
26–29 years	48	48	4
30–34 years	33	63	3
Big cities	71	26	3
Smaller cities	68	30	2
Villages	63	33	4

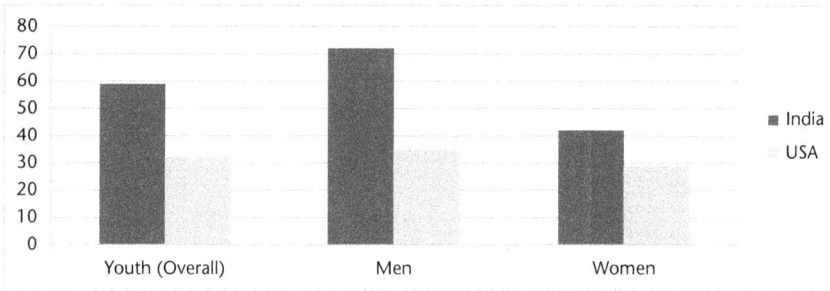

FIGURE 7.1   Living with parents: a comparison between Indian and American youth (18–34 year olds) (%)

Source: Figures for USA are from a survey conducted in 2014 by Pew Research Centre (Fry 2016).

Not just America, youth in European Union (EU) countries as a whole are also far less likely to be living with their parents than Indian youth. Eurofound's European Quality of Life Survey conducted in 28 EU countries in 2011 had found 48 per cent of 18 to 29 year olds to be living with their parents (*The Guardian* 2014). The figure for the corresponding age group in India is 68 per cent (Figure 7.2). Out of the 28 countries in which the EU survey was conducted, only in Hungary, Italy, Malta and Slovenia was there a higher proportion of youth living with their parents as compared to India.

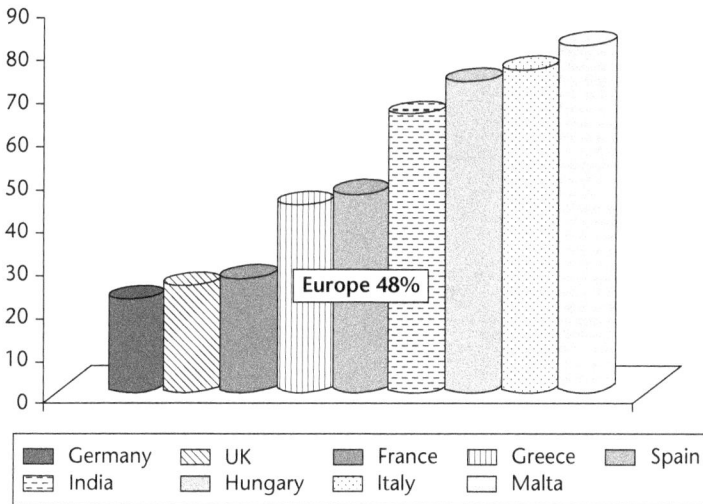

FIGURE 7.2   Living with parents: a comparison between Indian and EU youth (18–29 year olds) (%)

Source: Figures for European/EU countries are from a Eurofound's European Quality of Life Survey conducted in 2011 (published in *The Guardian* 2014).

The living arrangements of Indian youth differ significantly by gender. A greater proportion of young men (77 per cent) aged between 15 and 34 years were found to be staying with their mother and/or father than young women (49 per cent) from the same age group. This gender gap of nearly 30 percentage points is much bigger than the one seen in the USA where 18- to 34-year-old men were only 6 per cent more likely to be living with their parents than young women from the equivalent age category (Fry 2016). This wide difference in India can be attributed to marital status, since a higher proportion of young women (59 per cent) were found to be married compared to young men (39 per cent) by the study.

Educational attainment is also significantly correlated with living arrangements. A far greater proportion of highly educated youth was found to be living with their parents than youth who were less educated: 75 per cent or three-quarters of youth who had completed college education said that they were staying with their mother and/or father, as opposed to 67 per cent of high school pass youth, 41 per cent of primary pass youth and 26 per cent of non-literate youth. This pattern is unlike that in the USA, where the Pew Research Study had found a greater proportion of non-college educated youth to be living with their parents than college-educated youth (Domonosake 2016).

A little over three in every five or 62 per cent of the youth belonging to economically disadvantaged backgrounds (poor and lower class) were found to be living with their parents, compared to 68 and 71 per cent of youth from the economically well-off classes (middle class and upper class, respectively). An explanation for this could be that youth from less prosperous backgrounds may have had to move out of their homes in search of employment in order to support their families. The study, in fact, did find employment to be making a difference. Only 62 per cent of employed youth were staying with their parents, compared to 89 per cent of employment-seekers and 92 per cent of students. It also found a greater proportion of youth in big cities to be staying with their parents than their counterparts in smaller cities and villages, who are more likely to move out of their localities to bigger cities in search of employment or better education.

Style preferences and style consciousness

Contemporary social pressure on youth associated with appearance is substantial and that is why they seem to be quite conscious about how they look and carry themselves. This aspect emerges from their responses to a battery of questions on style preferences: 61 per cent said they were very or somewhat fond of wearing stylish clothes; 58 per cent said they were fond of wearing stylish footwear; 59 per cent were quite fond of keeping the latest mobile phones; 41 per cent had high to moderate fondness for buying perfumes and deodorants; 39 per cent said they liked applying fairness creams quite a lot; and 36 per cent had a high or moderate degree of fondness for visiting beauty parlours and salons (Table 7.2). A similar study done by the *Hindustan Times* amongst 5214 urban youth in the 18–25 age bracket in 15 cities[1] across India showed that India's youth spends the most on personal grooming.

TABLE 7.2 Style preference and style consciousness amongst India's youth (%)

	Quite fond	Not very fond	Not fond at all
Wearing stylish clothes	61	17	20
Keeping the latest mobile phone	59	13	27
Wearing stylish shoes/sandals	58	18	22
Buying deodorants/perfumes	41	20	37
Applying fairness creams	39	21	38
Visiting beauty parlors/salons	36	19	42

Note: The categories of 'very' and 'somewhat' fond have been merged to form 'quite fond'.

This category tops other expenses such as going to coffee shops and movies (Rs.335 or US$4.7 on an average) as well. Mobile expenses, however, remain high and seem to be rising with each passing year (Ghosh 2015).

Taking into account all the data gathered in Table 7.2, an Index of Style Consciousness was constructed (see Appendix II to find out how it was constructed) in order to measure the youth's overall style consciousness: 19 per cent of the youth were found to be very style conscious, 23 per cent to be moderately conscious, 25 per cent to be not very conscious and about 33 per cent to be not conscious about style at all.

Youth aged between 18 and 21 years (mostly college-going youth) were found to be the most style conscious (51 per cent), followed by those aged between 15 and 17 years (mostly school-going youth) at 48 per cent. A possible reason for this could be that the youth in the age bracket of 18–21 years are mostly college-going youth and the social pressure associated with physical appearance is much greater in college. Being stylish or looking good was the least important to the older age groups (Table 7.3). Contrary to popular belief, young men were found to be more style conscious than young women according to the index: 44 per cent to 39 per cent. Marriage, however, makes a difference. While married men were found to be more style conscious than their female counterparts, single or unmarried women were found to be more conscious than married men. The study found the youth living in big cities to be far more style conscious than those residing in small cities. Meanwhile, youth from small cities were found to be more style conscious than those living in villages. Not surprisingly, class matters too. A far greater style consciousness was recorded amongst economically well-off youth than those belonging to the lower economic strata, most probably because they have the economic means to buy the latest gadgets and beauty products. There also seems to be a correlation between social media usage and style consciousness. Only 23 per cent of youth with no exposure to social media said they were quite style conscious, as opposed to 73 per cent with very high exposure to social media. This was found to be more true for young women than for young men. While 54 per cent of young women with high exposure to social media were found to be quite conscious about their style and personal appearance, the corresponding figure amongst young men highly exposed to social media was just 33 per cent.

TABLE 7.3 Style consciousness amongst youth by socio-economic background (%)

	Quite style conscious	Not much style conscious	Not at all style conscious
Overall	42	25	33
15–17 years	48	28	24
18–21 years	51	28	21
22–25 years	45	23	32
26–29 years	38	25	37
30–34 years	28	23	49
Big cities	59	25	16
Smaller cities	44	28	28
Villages	36	24	40
Men	44	26	30
Women	39	24	37
Married men	30	25	45
Married women	27	23	50
Unmarried men	53	27	20
Unmarried women	57	25	18

Note: Categories of 'very style conscious' and 'somewhat style conscious' have been merged to form 'quite style conscious'.

Leisure lifestyle

The study also collected information on how frequently the youth engaged in out-door leisure activities such as watching movies in a cinema hall, eating or drinking out at a restaurant or a cafe, and going to a shopping mall: 33 per cent of the youth watched a movie in a cinema hall regularly, that is, either once a week or at least once a month. About 30 per cent regularly visited a restaurant, a hotel or a café. Meanwhile 28 per cent of the youth went to a shopping mall regularly. This indicates that, overall, movie watching was the most preferred form of outdoor leisure activity/entertainment amongst India's youth. C. Ramachandraiah, while analys-ing the mall culture prevalent amongst the youth of Hyderabad, observes that mall 'provides a space for enjoying consumption experience, both real and imaginary: a sense of feeling free, shedding inhibitions, being in a world of their own, free from the social mores and gaze of the elders' (in deSouza et al. 2009: 10).

The age of the youngsters determines how much they do these things: 18 to 21year olds were more likely than others to be going out for movies and shop-ping. Meanwhile, dining out is mostly something that 22 to 25 year olds do quite a lot. Urban youth, particularly those residing in big cities, not surprisingly, were found to be doing these activities in greater numbers (Table 7.4). The likelihood of doing these activities seems to be also dependent on a number of other socio-economic variables. Having the economic means to do these things is one such factor. Upper and middle class youth were found to be more prone to be indulg-ing in these outdoor leisure activities than lower class and poor youth. Young men were more likely to do all these things in a greater proportion than young women.

TABLE 7.4 Youth's engagement in outdoor leisure activities (%)

	Watch a movie in a cinema hall regularly	*Eat/drink in hotel/ restaurant/café/bar regularly*	*Go to shopping mall/ complex regularly*
Overall	33	30	28
Big cities	49	48	50
Smaller cities	39	31	32
Villages	25	22	17
Men	40	34	30
Women	23	24	26
Upper class	45	42	40
Middle class	39	37	35
Lower	29	25	22
Poor	22	19	18

Note: 'Regularly' means once a week or once a month.

Meanwhile, out of all these things, young women were more likely to go to a shopping mall than eat out or watch a movie.

Quite interestingly, the study found a much higher proportion of youth who had close friends from the opposite gender to be more into doing these activities than those who did not have close friends from the opposite gender (Figure 7.3). That is, young men who had close female friends were more likely to go out for a movie, eat out at a restaurant or visit a shopping mall than men who did not have close female friends. This was the case with respect to young women as well.

The study also shows that a higher proportion of youth from the southern states were fond of watching movies than the youth from other regions. In fact, youth from the southern states were found to be doing all the things in a slightly higher proportion compared to other regions. Youth from eastern regions showed the least interest in all these things.

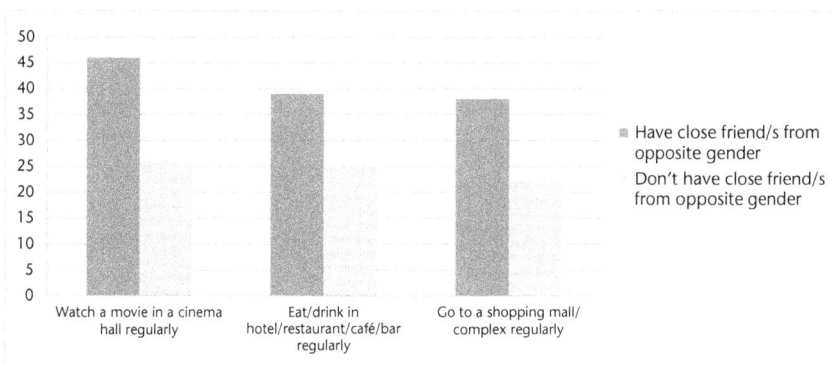

FIGURE 7.3 Engagement in outdoor leisure activities by youth with close friends from the opposite gender (%)

Note: 'Regularly' means once a week or once a month.

TABLE 7.5 Impact on youth's style by frequency of outdoor leisure activities (%)

Style consciousness	Very	Somewhat	Not much	Not at all
Regularly visit shopping mall	37	33	24	6
Rarely visit shopping mall	19	26	30	26
Never visit shopping mall	5	12	22	61
Regularly visit restaurants	34	33	23	10
Rarely visit restaurants	18	23	29	31
Never visit restaurants	7	13	23	57
Regularly visit cinema halls	30	33	26	11
Rarely visit cinema halls	17	22	27	34
Never visit cinema halls	8	12	22	58

Note: Rest of the youth gave no response. 'Regularly' means once a week or once a month; 'Rarely' means few times a year or very rarely.

There also seems to be a connection between youth's style consciousness and the frequency of their outdoor leisure activities. For instance, while only 5 per cent of those who had never gone to a shopping mall were found to be quite style conscious, the figure of high style consciousness amongst those who did so regularly was seven times more at 37 per cent (Table 7.5). Similarly, regular visitors to restaurants and cafes were five times more likely to be highly style conscious than those who never visited restaurants.

Health-related behaviour

Youth is a crucial period for establishing a positive healthy lifestyle and this chapter tries to gauge eating, drinking and smoking habits of the youth and their level of physical activity. The study found that 87 per cent of the youth ate green vegetables often, that is, either daily or a few days a week (Table 7.6); 73 per cent said they ate fruits often. About 30 per cent of the youth said they drank fizzy drinks like Coke and Pepsi often, and 24 per cent said they ate 'junk' food such as burgers and pizzas frequently.

The study also examined the participation of youth in doing physical exercise and playing sports. In terms of physical activity, 35 per cent of the youth played a sport often (in the 2007 study, the corresponding figure had been about 15 per cent only). Where in 2007, 55 per cent of the youth said that they never play a sport, the number dropped down to 34 per cent in 2016. Also, 31 per cent said that they do some physical exercise either daily or a few days a week.

A healthy lifestyle/nutritious food is not available equally to all. This difference can be attributed to varying socio-economic statuses such as age, class, educational level, occupation and gender. The youngest youth (15–17 years) and students were higher on all these parameters except smoking and drinking where the older (26–29 years) and the employed youth took over. Further, a low socio-economic status is related to unhealthy dietary habits. The less educated youth, the non-literates

TABLE 7.6 Health-related behaviour of India's youth (%)

	Regularly	Sometimes	Rarely	Never
Eating green vegetables	87	4	7	1
Eating fruits	73	9	17	1
Drinking Coke, Pepsi etc.	30	17	36	16
Eating junk food	24	16	32	26
Playing a sport	35	9	21	34
Doing physical exercise	31	8	19	41
Smoking cigarettes/*bidis*/*hukka*	9	3	9	75
Drinking alcohol	8	2	9	77

Note: The answer categories of 'daily' and 'few days a week' have been merged to form regularly. The rest of the youth gave no response.

and the youth belonging to lower and poor classes have a lower vegetable and fruit intake and a higher intake of cigarettes and alcohol.

Smoking cigarettes and consuming alcohol, meanwhile, do not seem to be very prevalent amongst Indian youth; at least they did not report doing so. Three in every four or 75 per cent of the youth said they had never smoked a cigarette and 77 per cent said that they had never had alcohol. Since questions related to smoking and drinking suffer from a social desirability bias, these figures should be read in that context. All the same, the study found smoking cigarettes and drinking alcohol to be more prevalent amongst older youth than younger ones, the youth belonging to less privileged backgrounds and those residing in rural areas.

Interestingly, the study found the prevalence of drinking and smoking amongst youth to be highly correlated to a household member also doing the same. Youth belonging to households in which a household member drinks alcohol were found to be five times more likely to drink alcohol than youth in whose house no family member drinks (46 per cent as opposed to 9 per cent). Youth in whose house someone smokes were found to be nearly four times more likely to smoke than youth in whose house nobody smokes (40 per cent as opposed to 11 per cent). Also, the youth who worried a lot turn to drinking and smoking as it may provide them temporary comfort and happiness: 12 per cent of the youth who did not worry at all were found to smoke, compared to 23 per cent of those who worried a lot. Similarly, 14 per cent of the youth with no anxieties were found to be drinking alcohol, compared to 19 per cent of the highly anxious youth.

In 2011, an American study by the National Center on Addiction and Substance Abuse on teenagers had found that those who in a typical day spend any time on social networking sites are at an increased risk of smoking, drinking and drug use (Keilman and McCoppin 2011). The study too has a similar finding for India. The prevalence of drinking amongst youth with no exposure to social media was found to be only 18 per cent, as opposed to 30 per cent amongst those very highly exposed to social media. A similar pattern was observed with respect to smoking as well. One in every five or 20 per cent of youth with no social

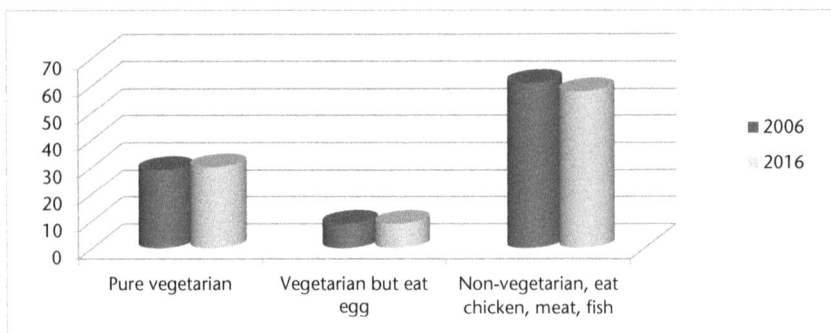

FIGURE 7.4 Dietary preferences of India's youth (18–34 year olds) (%)

Note: State of the Nation Survey conducted by CSDS in January 2006. The rest of the youth gave no response.

media exposure were found to be smokers, compared to 32 per cent of those very highly exposed to media.

Moving to dietary preferences, the study found that a majority of Indian youth (18–34 year olds) were non-vegetarians (58 per cent), 30 per cent said they were pure vegetarians and 9 per cent described themselves as eggitarians. There has been little change in this regard over the last decade. In the national CSDS study conducted in 2007, a similar proportion of youth from the same age group had described themselves as vegetarians and eggitarians (Figure 7.4). Interestingly, in the latest CSDS study, the non-vegetarians were found to be far less worried about their health and their body image than the vegetarian youth (see following chapter on youth anxieties for details).

Social media usage

Social media has undergone huge worldwide growth in popularity, resulting in it becoming a popular activity amongst the youth. It includes any medium that allows social interaction, such as Facebook, Twitter, WhatsApp and watching and sharing videos on YouTube. The study found half (50 per cent) of the youth was not exposed to social media at all. It was found that they had never used any of the popular social media platforms, be they Facebook, Twitter, WhatsApp or YouTube (see Appendix II to find out how the Index of Social Media Usage was constructed). The remaining 50 per cent were found to be exposed to social media but in varying degrees, with high usage of these platforms being at about 19 per cent, and moderate and low exposure to social media being at 13 and 18 per cent respectively.

Though the majority of the youth have an account on Facebook, followed by WhatsApp, YouTube and Twitter, when it comes to usage, a little higher proportion of youth use WhatsApp compared to Facebook on a daily basis. The study found that 75 per cent had never used Twitter, 62 per cent had never used YouTube, 54 per cent had never used WhatsApp and 51 per cent had never been on

Facebook (Table 7.7). In terms of daily usage, WhatsApp was used most (30 per cent), followed by Facebook (25 per cent), YouTube (11 per cent) and Twitter (7 per cent). Even though these figures of usage are not all that high, they have however sharply increased compared to 2014. In the 2014 study conducted by CSDS during the national elections, only 6 per cent of the 18 to 34 year olds were using Facebook on a daily basis and 82 per cent had never used it. Meanwhile, daily Twitter usage amongst the youth at that time was also extremely low at just 1 per cent and no usage of Twitter whatsoever had been very high at 96 per cent (Table 7.8).

The study found that amongst all the youth, those most exposed to social media platforms are 18 to 21 year olds, those who are students, those who are highly educated, those who live in big cities, those who belong to the upper class and those who are unmarried. This pattern remains unchanged while looking at the various platforms individually.

Interestingly, youth who said they took selfies regularly were found to be more active on social media. Amongst those who said that they took selfies regularly, 62 per cent were found to be very exposed to social media. Meanwhile, amongst those who never took selfies, only 2 per cent were found to be highly exposed to

TABLE 7.7 Social media usage amongst youth (15–34 year olds) (%)

	Use daily	Use a few days a week	Use a few days a month	Use very rarely	Never use
WhatsApp	30	5	2	7	54
Facebook	25	8	3	11	51
YouTube	11	8	3	12	62
Twitter	7	5	2	8	75

Note: The rest of the youth gave no response.

TABLE 7.8 Change in social media usage between 2014 and 2016 amongst 18–34 year olds (%)

	2014	2016
Facebook usage		
Daily	6	25
Sometimes	8	11
Rarely	3	11
Never	82	50
Twitter usage		
Daily	1	7
Sometimes	2	7
Rarely	1	8
Never	96	74

Note: Figures for 2014 are from National Election Study Pre-Poll conducted by CSDS during the Lok Sabha elections. In 2016, the categories of 'few days a week' and 'few days a month' were merged to form 'sometimes'.

social media. Youth who were conscious of their style and looks were also found to be far more exposed to social media than youth who were not. The study found a difference of 33 per cent amongst the very style conscious youth and the not at all style conscious youth in this regard.

Mobile phone and laptop penetration, and internet usage

The penetration of mobile phones amongst India's youth has increased tremendously over the last decade. Four in every five (81 per cent) youth owned a mobile phone in the study, while 43 per cent had a smartphone and 38 per cent had a basic phone. This proportion is over two times more than the figure of mobile ownership recorded in the 2007 study (34 per cent) (Figure 7.5). Personal computer and laptop ownership amongst the youth has also increased in a major way in a decade. While only 8 per cent youth households owned a computer or a laptop in 2007; the figure recorded in the 2016 study was 24 per cent, a three-fold increase.

Even as ownership of these gadgets has gone up, access to the internet on them is quite low: 30 per cent of the youth who owned a personal computer or laptop did not have access to internet on it. Meanwhile, 58 per cent of those with a mobile phone had no access to internet on it. Overall, the study found (when it was conducted in early 2016) that 64 per cent of the youth had no immediate access to the internet whatsoever. This includes those who did not have both a phone and a computer, and those who had both or either one of the two but without an internet connection. Only 36 per cent were found to have immediate access to the internet, either on one gadget or both gadgets.

Having a smartphone makes a huge difference to how much a person uses Facebook, Twitter and email, watches YouTube videos, takes selfies, plays video games and listens to the radio. Youth with smartphones were found to be more into all these activities than youth with a simple phone and those without any type of phone. Interestingly, having a smartphone instead of a simple phone had the greatest impact on Twitter usage. Smartphone users were twelve times more likely to regularly use Twitter than simple phone users. They were ten

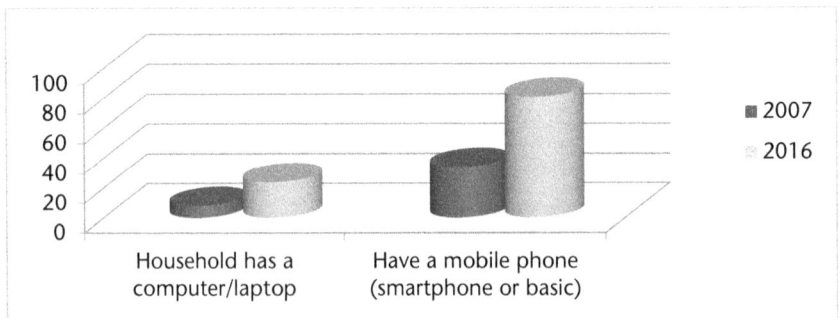

FIGURE 7.5 Mobile ownership amongst India's youth (%)

TABLE 7.9 Impact of a smartphone on a young Indian's life (%)

	Play video games regularly	Take selfies regularly	Use Facebook regularly	Use Whats App regularly	Watch videos on YouTube regularly	Use Twitter regularly	Listen to radio regularly	Check or send emails regularly
Basic phone	9	9	9	7	4	2	18	6
Smartphone	44	54	66	73	41	25	31	41

Note: Regularly here means either 'daily' or a 'few days a week'.

times more likely to regularly watch videos on YouTube and use WhatsApp, seven times more likely to regularly use Facebook and check or send emails, six times more likely to regularly take selfies and five times more likely to regularly play video games (Table 7.9).

Interestingly, the youth's increasing usage of social media via smartphones does not mean that they have cut down on their book-reading habits. The study found that 31 per cent of the youth to be very fond of reading books and 25 per cent to be somewhat fond of the activity. About 18 per cent said they were not too fond of reading books and 26 per cent were not fond of it at all. By comparing these figures with those recorded in 2007, book readership amongst youth is seen to be on the rise. In 2007, only about 22 per cent had reported reading books/magazines and periodicals a lot. Moreover, time spent on social media is not affecting the youth's regularity of reading books. In fact, the study found that the greater the exposure of youth to social media, the greater was their fondness for reading books.

News media exposure

The study also tried to measure the youth's news consumption through various news mediums – newspaper, television and the internet. The traditional mediums still dominate: 57 per cent of the youth watched news on TV regularly, that is, either daily or a few days a week. About 53 per cent read newspapers regularly and only about 18 per cent read news on the internet regularly (Table 7.10). Both TV news viewership and newspaper readership has gone up amongst youth compared to 2007. A decade ago, about 49 per cent youth were regular newspaper readers and about 48 per cent were frequent TV news viewers (Figure 7.6). However,

TABLE 7.10 Exposure of youth to news media (%)

	Regularly	Sometimes	Never
Watch news on TV	57	19	22
Read newspapers	53	20	26
Read news on the internet	18	14	63

Note: 'Regularly' means those who said 'daily' or a 'few days a week'. 'Sometimes' means those who said a 'few days a week' or 'very rarely'.

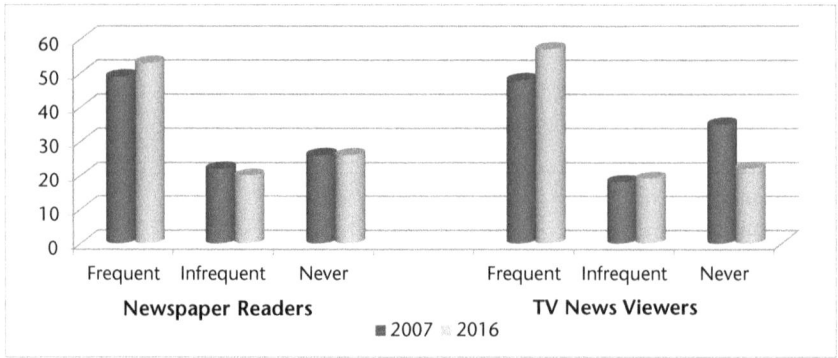

FIGURE 7.6 Newspaper readership and TV news viewership amongst India's youth 2007–2016 (%)

Note: The rest of the youth gave no response. Figures are for the 15–34-year-old age category for both years. Newspaper readership in 2007: the categories of 'daily' and 'frequently' have been merged to form 'frequent readers'; the category of 'rarely' has been put into 'infrequent readers'. Newspaper readership 2016: the category of 'regularly' has been shown as 'frequent readers'. Categories of a 'few days a month' and 'rarely' have been merged to form 'infrequent readers'. TV news viewership 2007: categories of 'daily 'and 'more than once a week' have been merged to form 'frequent viewers'. TV news viewership 2016: the category of 'regularly' has been shown as 'frequent viewers'. Categories of a 'few days a month' and 'very rarely' have been merged to form 'infrequent viewers'.

given the exponential growth of the news media sector in India in the last decade, the 4 per cent rise in the readership of newspapers and the 9 per cent increase in viewership of TV news amongst youngsters should be viewed as being modest.

Overall, it was found that 16 per cent of the youth did not seek news from any of the three mediums – newspaper, TV or the internet. In other words, they did not consume news at all: 23 per cent of the youth were highly exposed to news media (out of which 8 per cent were very highly exposed and 15 per cent highly exposed), 28 per cent were moderately exposed and 17 and 16 per cent had low and very low news media consumption, respectively (see Appendix II to find out how Index of News Media Exposure was constructed). The degree to which the youth consume news on media is linked to their socio-economic status. The higher their socio-economic status, the higher is their exposure to news media. Educated youth, youth belonging to the upper class and youth living in big cities were found to be more exposed to the news media than less educated, less privileged and less urban youth, respectively. In terms of age, 18 to 21 year olds were found to be the most exposed to news media and the oldest youth, that is, 30 to 34 year olds, were the least exposed.

Participation in religious activities

The study found India's youth to be quite religious. About 78 per cent of the youth prayed quite often (either regularly or sometimes), 68 per cent said they go to a religious place of worship frequently and 49 per cent said they watched religious shows on television. Another 46 per cent engaged in activities such as singing religious songs, *bhajans* or took part in *satsangs* and the same percentage of youth kept fasts either regularly or sometimes and finally, 39 per cent said that they read a religious book (Table 7.11).

Collating the responses to all these individual questions together, an Index of Religiosity was constructed (see Appendix II to find out how the index was constructed) in order to measure the youth's overall religiosity. It was found that only 4 per cent of youth was not religious at all. About a third (36 per cent) had low religiosity, a quarter (25 per cent) were moderately religious, another quarter (23 per cent) were highly religious and about one in every eight (12 per cent) were found to be extremely religious in terms of their practices.

Comparisons with past studies reveal that India's youth seem to be praying or visiting religious places of worship far more than they were two to three years ago (Table 7.12). According to a survey conducted by *India Today*, of the youth residing in the Silicon Valley of India, that is Bangalore, 67 per cent visit a place of worship once a week, while in Jaipur, the figure shoots up to 81 per cent. Less and less youth are in favour of banning religious procession. They seem to be, however, engaging relatively less in other religious activities such as *bhajans*, *kirtans* and keeping of fasts. Eighty-one per cent of the youth feel the need for a uniform civil code for all religions and 52 per cent agree with the demolition of illegally constructed places of worship (Prasannarajan 2005)

TABLE 7.11 Youth's participation in religious activities (15–34 year olds) (%)

	Regularly	Sometimes	Only on festivals	Never
Do *puja*/*namaz*/prayer/*paath*	38	40	14	7
Go to temple/mosque/church/*gurudwara* etc.	20	48	23	9
Watch religious shows on TV	13	36	13	36
Do *bhajan*/*kirtan*/*satsang*	11	35	22	31
Keep *vrats*/*upwaas*/*rozas*/fasts	11	35	32	22
Read a religious book	8	31	13	45

Note: The rest of the youth gave no response.

TABLE 7.12 Youth's participation in religious activities 2009–2016 (%)

	2009*	2014	2016
Do *puja*/*namaz*/prayer/*paath*	73**	73**	79
Go to temple/mosque/church/*gurudwara* etc.	52**	56**	68
Watch religious shows on TV	–	–	50
Do *bhajan*/*kirtan*/*satsang*	53*	58*	47
Keep *vrats*/*upwaas*/*rozas*/fasts	53*	55*	47

Note: Figures are for the 18–34-year-old age category for all years. Figures for 2009 and 2014 are from NES Post-Poll surveys conducted by CSDS during the Lok Sabha elections. 2009: * categories of 'daily' and 'weekly' have been merged; ** categories of 'frequently' and 'occasionally' have been merged. 2014: * categories of 'daily' and 'weekly' have been merged; ** categories of 'frequently' and 'occasionally' have been merged. 2016: categories of 'regularly' and 'sometimes' have been merged.

The study found age to make a significant difference to youth's religiosity. As they grow up, the young seem to get more religious. While 30 per cent and 34 per cent of the 15 to 17 year olds and 18 to 21 year olds were found to be highly religious, respectively, the figure of high religiosity amongst older youths (22–25 year olds, 26–29 year olds and 30–34 year olds) was in the range of 37–39 per cent. According to the study, young women in India were more likely to be highly religious than young men. The difference amongst the two genders in terms of high religiosity was recorded at seven percentage points. In fact, young women across all religious groups, except Muslims, were found to be more religious than their male counterparts. Amongst Muslims an equal proportion of young men and women were found to be highly religious. Interestingly, the study found the highly educated youth to be more religious than those less educated than them. Only 19 per cent of non-literate youths were found to be highly religious, compared to 39 per cent youths who had completed graduation. Youth in small cities and villages reported a higher level of high religiosity (38 and 37 per cent, respectively) than youth in big cities (33 per cent). Christian youth were found to be the most religious (in religious practice) followed by Muslim, Sikh and Hindu youth. A strong relationship also exists between class and religiosity. In terms of Hindu castes, upper caste youth were more highly religious (41 per cent) compared to youth from Other Backward Castes (OBCs) (35 per cent), Dalits (33 per cent) and Adivasis (29 per cent). Finally, in terms of class, youth from economically well-off backgrounds were more highly religious than those belonging to lower and poor economic status. The gap between rich and poor is of 14 percentage points.

Conclusion

Based on the chapter's findings, it can be argued that mass media and an expanding commodity culture have differentially incorporated the youth across the boundaries of gender, caste and class. Their practices of consumption reveal the meanings, salience and impact of globalisation and are closely tied with their everyday identity. While the youth appear to be caught up by the powerful market forces that fashion them as consumers (Lukose 2009), their choices, decisions and desires are reflective of the demands of the past and the expectations for the future.

The analysis suggests that the young have taken to new forms of consumerism that rests on the interplay of regional identity and transnational cosmopolitanism in ways that might be less polarising. The successful expansion of new cultural forms, styles and fashion goes hand-in-hand with the continued salience of the family, religion and region.

Furthermore, the youth are not simply imitators of the West; they easily blend a global cosmopolitanism and their local contexts. As members of societies that are rapidly transformed by the twin forces of globalisation and liberalisation, these kind of consumer practices and discourses have become an increasingly important marker of belonging and social citizenship (Lukose 2009). Navigating through status, aspiration, desire, sociality and social mobility, youth cultural practices foreground consumer citizenship as constitutive of young people's lives in liberalising India.

Note

1 The cities where the study was conducted were Delhi, Lucknow, Jaipur and Chandigarh in the north, Kolkata, Patna and Ranchi in the east, Mumbai, Ahmedabad, Pune and Indore in the west, and Chennai, Bangalore, Hyderabad and Kochi in the south.

References

Bobb, Dilip (1999) Present Generation of Indian Youth Is in Every Sense a Paradoxical One: Survey. *India Today* November 30. Available at: www.indiatoday.in/magazine/society-the-arts/story/20050131-present-generation-of-indian-youth-is-in-every-sense-a-paradoxical-one-survey-788328-1999-11-30 (accessed on 28 May 2018).

Chakrabarti, Samrat (2015) Young India, New Hunger for Identity. *The Hindu* August 29. available at: www.thehindu.com/features/magazine/young-india-new-hunger-for-identity-through-pop-culture/article7590672.ece (accessed on 28 May 2018).

DeSouza, Peter Ronald, Kumar Sanjay, and Shastri, Sandeep (2009) *Indian Youth in a Transforming World*. New Delhi: Sage Publications.

Domonosake, Camila (2016) For First Time in 130 Years, More Young Adults Live with Parents Than with Partners. NPR. Available at: www.npr.org/sections/thetwo-way/2016/05/24/479327382/for-first-time-in-130-years-more-young-adults-live-with-parents-than-partners (accessed on 8 September 2016).

Fry, Richard (2016) For First Time in Modern Era, Living with Parents Edges Out Other Living Arrangements for 18- to 34-Year-Olds. Pew Research Centre: Social and Demographic Trends. Available at: www.pewsocialtrends.org/2016/05/24/for-first-time-in-modern-era-living-with-parents-edges-out-other-living-arrangements-for-18-to-34-year-olds/ (accessed on 7 September 2016).

Ghosh, Paramita (2015) Saving and Splurging: What's on Young Consumers' Minds. *The Hindustan Times* September 3. Available at: www.hindustantimes.com/india/saving-and-splurging-what-s-on-young-consumers-minds/story-6cf3unpWaz1VHyUfOZw3IN.html (accessed on 28 May 2018).

Guardian, The (2014) Europe's Young Adults Living With Parents: A Country by Country Breakdown. *The Guardian* 24 March. Available at: www.theguardian.com/news/datablog/2014/mar/24/young-adults-still-living-with-parents-europe-country-breakdown (accessed on 7 September 2016).

Keilman, John and McCoppin, Robert (2011) Study: Teen Users of Facebook, Myspace More Likely to Drink, Use Drugs. *Chicago Tribune* August 24. Available at: http://articles.chicagotribune.com/2011-08-24/news/ct-met-social-menace-20110824_1_social-media-teen-substance-abuse-teen-users (accessed on 29 September 2016).

Lukose, R.A. (2009) *Liberalization's Children: Gender, Youth and Consumer Citizenship in Globalizing India*. Delhi: Orient Blackswan.

Prasannarajan, S. (2005) Indian Youth Not Oriental Stereotypes but Connoisseurs of Cultural Connectivity: Survey. *India Today* January 31. Available at: www.indiatoday.in/magazine/religion/story/20050131-indian-youth-not-oriental-stereotypes-but-connoisseurs-of-cultural-connectivity-survey-788338-2005-01-31 (accessed on 4 June 2018).

8

ANXIETIES AND EMOTIONAL DISTRESS

Shreyas Sardesai

Nervous about speaking in front of an audience, tense about finding or losing a job, uncomfortable about travelling by the underground train, avoiding going to the market for fear of a terrorist attack, dreading an upcoming mathematics exam, or just simply worried about attending a family gathering – anxiety can manifest itself in many different forms amongst people. It is one of the most common psychological traits. Occasional anxiety is a natural and normal part of life. We can all be anxious and indeed show some kind of anxiety or the other; and being anxious about something may not be so bad as it may help us in some cases to perform better or improve a certain aspect about ourselves. However, when anxiety is persistent, wide-ranging, touches extreme levels and starts dominating and affecting our lives, the situation changes as it can lead to physical and mental disorders and affect those around us. While anxiety is found amongst both the young and the old, the former are particularly vulnerable to it. In the United States, for instance, a recent study, published in the *Journal of Clinical Psychiatry*, in which researchers analysed data collected from a random sample of people from ages 21 to 100 years, found that people in their twenties and thirties reported having the highest levels of depression, anxiety, and stress, plus the lowest levels of happiness, satisfaction and well-being compared to older people who were found to be the happiest (Oaklander, 2016). In India too, the young generation exhibits similar tendencies.

A highly anxious young generation

The study found the Indian youth to be a highly anxious generation, with worry and stress weighing them down – be it a 15 year old about to finish school or a 34 year old who has settled down in life. Young Indians across age groups are suffering from fairly high disquietude, even though the degree of such anxiety and its causes may differ somewhat.

During the study, the youth were asked 14 questions related to anxiety. These questions probed their worry levels regarding employment, education, personal health, parents' health, personal looks, marriage, maintaining family traditions, family problems, losing a friend, English-speaking skills, sexual harassment, road accidents, mob violence and terrorist attacks. Taking the responses to all these questions into consideration, an Index of Anxiety was constructed (see Appendix II to find out how it was constructed). The results showed over half (55 per cent) of India's youth (15–34 year olds) to be highly anxious and another quarter (26 per cent) to be moderately so. Only about one in every seven (14 per cent) was found to be not too anxious, and just 5 per cent showed no anxiety at all. A small caveat is in order here. Being highly anxious does not mean that a person could be suffering from an anxiety disorder. That is certainly not for us to determine and is the job for a mental health expert. Moreover, these are self-reported levels of anxiety and there may be a difference in how the youth perceived themselves and their actual condition.

When each of the 14 items that went into constructing the index was looked at individually, parents' health emerged as the matter that the young in India worried the most about, followed by their own health. Family problems and maintaining family traditions were also matters of high anxiety for the Indian youth, followed by anxiety about jobs and one's looks. Matters that caused the least amount of worry to them were sexual harassment and quite surprisingly, marriage (Table 8.1).

TABLE 8.1 Level of worry amongst youth regarding select matters (%)

	Worry (quite a lot + somewhat)	*Worry quite a lot*	*Worry somewhat*	*Worry very little*	*Don't worry at all*
Parents' health	87	68	19	5	7
Personal health	83	54	29	8	7
Family problems	82	57	25	8	8
Maintaining family traditions	77	48	29	11	11
Job/employment	73	46	27	10	14
Body shape/weight/ looks	69	38	31	15	14
Losing a friend	60	35	25	14	22
Road accident	57	27	30	18	23
Studies/education	54	33	21	14	28
Riots or mob violence	49	23	26	21	26
Inability to speak good English	45	23	22	17	34
Terrorist attack	44	24	20	17	34
Marriage	38	18	20	17	39
Harassment/teasing	35	18	17	16	44

Note: The rest of the youth gave no response.

Anxiety amongst the youth based on age

While on the whole India's youth come across as being highly anxious, some age groups within them are more anxious than others: 18 to 21 year olds, for instance, seem to be the most anxious of all. Overall, the study found that three out of every five of them (61 per cent) had high levels of anxiety. This is higher than the extreme worry levels seen amongst other age brackets: 57 per cent amongst 15 to 17 year olds, 58 per cent amongst 22 to 25 year olds, 51 per cent amongst those aged between 26 and 29 years, and 47 per cent amongst 30 to 34 year olds. In fact, anxiety peaks at the early age of 18 to 21 years and drops thereafter as the young grow older; 18 to 21 year olds are those just out of school and making sense of the new world around them, and as they enter college, many students experience several firsts which include making new friends, encountering a new lifestyle and exposure to new cultures and different ways of thinking. Many amongst them also start worrying about their future prospects in the job market. The study found them (18–21 year olds) to be more worried than the other age groups about jobs, marriage and harassment (Table 8.2). The age groups 15 to 17 years and 22 to 25 years also showed fairly high levels of anxiety. The former age group was found to be distinct from others when it came to worrying about studies, looks and body image, losing a friend and lack of good English-speaking skills. Anxiety amongst the latter group (22–25 years) was found to be mostly on account of jobs followed by road accidents, riots, terrorist attacks and marriage. Marriage is also something that caused distinct worry amongst the 26 to 29 year olds. Meanwhile, the oldest amongst the young (30–34 year olds) were found to worry much more than others only about two things – their personal health and family problems.

TABLE 8.2 Worry regarding select matters by age group (%)

	15–17 years	18–21 years	22–25 years	26–29 years	30–34 years
Job/employment	68	78	78	72	71
Studies/education	83	74	58	47	39
Maintaining family traditions	75	77	78	74	78
Family problems	75	80	83	82	85
Riots or mob violence	48	50	52	47	48
Road accident	54	58	59	56	55
Terrorist attack	42	49	47	42	41
Personal health	82	82	84	83	85
Body shape/weight/looks	74	72	70	71	65
Inability to speak good English	61	56	48	40	36
Losing a friend	69	66	62	62	54
Parents' health	87	89	87	87	86
Marriage	31	42	41	41	36
Harassment/teasing	32	42	37	33	33

Note: Worry in this table includes the categories of 'worry quite a lot' and 'worry somewhat'.

TABLE 8.3 Ranking of anxieties of the youth by Age group

Rank	15–17 years	18–21 years	22–25 years	26–29 years	30–34 years
1.	Parents' health	Parents' health	Parents' health	Parents' health	Parents' health
2.	Studies	Own health	Own health	Own health	Family problems
3.	Own health	Family problems	Family problems	Family problems	Own health
4.	Family problems	Job	Job	Family traditions	Family traditions
5.	Family traditions	Family traditions	Family traditions	Job	Job
6.	Personal looks	Studies	Personal looks	Personal looks	Personal looks
7.	Losing a friend	Personal looks	Losing a friend	Losing a friend	Road accident
8.	Job	Losing a friend	Road accident	Road accident	Losing a friend
9.	Poor English	Road accident	Studies	Studies	Riots
10.	Road accident	Poor English	Riots	Riots	Terrorist attack
11.	Riots	Riots	Poor English	Terrorist attack	Studies
12.	Terrorist attack	Terrorist attack	Terrorist attack	Marriage	Poor English
13.	Harassment/teasing	Marriage	Marriage	Poor English	Marriage
14.	Marriage	Harassment/teasing	Harassment/teasing	Harassment/teasing	Harassment/teasing

Hierarchy of anxieties

Youth across all five age groups worry most (and almost equally so) about their parents' health, their personal health and about family matters (Table 8.3). Harassment or teasing meanwhile is the least of their worries followed by marriage. Overall, the top three anxieties of youth aged between 18 and 21 years, 22 and 25 years and 26 and 29 years are the same – parents' health, personal health and family problems, in that order. In fact, these three aspects, along with maintaining family traditions, figured in the list of top five anxieties for each and every age group. Worry about jobs is amongst the top five anxieties of every age group barring the 'still in school' age group of 15 to 17 year olds. In the hierarchy of anxieties, worries about personal looks and losing a friend are somewhere in the middle amongst all groups.

Difference in degree of anxiety between youth in urban areas and rural areas

The study found anxiety amongst youngsters to be more prevalent in urban areas than in rural areas and more particularly amongst those residing in cities, and further amongst those in big cities. As opposed to 87 per cent youth in big cities who reported high or moderate anxiety, youth in smaller cities showed slightly lesser anxiety at 85 per cent. Youth in villages were found to be the least anxious with three-quarters (76 per cent) of them feeling anxious.

In fact, youth living in big cities showed much greater anxiety than youth of small cities and villages on almost all matters. The difference in degree of anxiety between youth residing in these three locations was greatest with respect to body image. The level of worry amongst big-city youth about body image was found

TABLE 8.4 Level of anxiety regarding select matters amongst youth by locality (%)

Worried/anxious about . . .	Big cities	Smaller cities	Villages
Job/employment	77	74	72
Studies/education	66	60	58
Maintaining family traditions	78	75	76
Family problems	80	80	82
Riots or mob violence	52	54	46
Road accident	63	63	50
Terrorist attack	52	52	39
Personal health	88	82	81
Body shape/weight/looks	76	67	69
Inability to speak good English	53	49	47
Losing a friend	67	67	57
Parents' health	91	88	85
Marriage	41	41	35
Harassment/teasing	45	39	31

Note: Worry in this table includes the categories of 'worry quite a lot' and 'worry somewhat'.

to be 76 per cent, which is seven percentage points higher than the worry level amongst rural youth (69 per cent) and nine points higher than the anxiety level amongst small-city youth (67 per cent) (Table 8.4). With respect to studies too, big-city youth showed a significantly higher level of anxiety than small-city and village youth – six and eight percentage points more, respectively. Anxiety levels of big-city youth were also greater than small-city youth on matters such as harassment, work, the inability to speak good English, personal health, parents' health and maintaining family traditions. Anxiety levels amongst youth in big cities and small cities are more or less similar when it comes to matters such as marriage, terrorist attacks, road accidents, riots, family problems and losing a friend. On all these issues, they have much greater anxiety than rural youth, who show the least anxiety on all issues barring one – body image. On this issue, the youth of rural areas were found to be a bit more anxious than small-city youth.

Rise in anxiety with higher economic status and education

The study found youth from economically better-off backgrounds to be more anxious. High anxiety amongst youth belonging to the upper class was found to be 12 per cent more than high anxiety amongst youth who are poor (Table 8.5). Education too seems to significantly impact anxiety levels. Graduate youth were found to be two times more highly anxious than non-literate youth. They were also one and a half times more highly anxious than youth who had completed only primary education. Gender, meanwhile, seems to only make a marginal difference as young men were found to be only 3 per cent more anxious than young women.

Questions on anxiety

This section presents a deeper analysis of each of the 14 questions that were asked in the study in order to understand the anxieties of the Indian youth and illustrates some of the most striking findings.

TABLE 8.5 Level of anxiety amongst youth by educational qualification and economic status (%)

	Highly anxious	Somewhat anxious	Not much anxious	Not at all anxious
Upper class	59	26	11	3
Middle class	58	24	13	5
Lower class	56	27	14	4
Poor	47	25	18	11
Graduate or above	64	23	9	3
High school pass	50	28	16	6
Primary pass	42	28	21	9
Non-literate	27	26	31	16

Anxiety about parents' health

As mentioned earlier in this chapter, of all the various anxieties, it is the concern about the health and well-being of one's parents that makes young people in India most anxious. Overall, nearly seven out of ten youth were found to worry a great deal about their parents' health. This high worry for parents' health was much greater amongst unmarried/single youth compared to married youth – 74 per cent as opposed to 65 per cent. Anxiety levels amongst youth about parents' health were also found to be linked to the amount of influence that their parents have had on them. Three in every four youth who said that the biggest influence in their life had been their parents worried a lot about their parents' health, as opposed to two in every three youth who said that their spouse or sibling had been the biggest influence in their life. Interestingly, high anxiety about parents' health was found to be greatest amongst youth residing in the northern states of the country at 81 per cent.

Anxiety about personal health

Anxiety about one's own health and fitness follows the concern for parents' health as the second strongest anxiety amongst India's youth. It has also gone up significantly in the last decade. While the youth study conducted in 2007 found 74 per cent to be worrying (greatly or somewhat) about it, in 2016 a much larger proportion of youth (83 per cent) said they were anxious about it. Out of this 83 per cent, 54 per cent belonged to the greatly worried category. This figure is quite alarming, although just how many of them are hypochondriacs or suffer from abnormal chronic anxiety cannot be ascertained by us. Economic status and worry about personal health are strongly correlated. Youth belonging to better and more privileged economic backgrounds were found to be much more anxious about their health than those who were not so well off. The reason for this greater worry amongst upper class youth may well be linked to their dietary preferences and lifestyle. The analysis found worry about personal health to be particularly high amongst youth who ate junk food or drank fizzy drinks on a regular basis. Health anxiety was also found to be quite high amongst those who exercised regularly or played a sport. It could be that the former worried about health because they have poor eating and drinking habits, and the latter worried because they are health conscious. Interestingly, the study found youth who were vegetarian to be showing much higher anxiety about their health than youth who were non-vegetarian. While 68 per cent falling in the former category were found to be highly anxious about personal health, the figure was nearly 20 per cent less amongst those who ate meat.

Anxiety about maintaining family traditions

In the order of anxieties amongst India's youth, anxiety about maintaining family traditions came third. High anxiety about it was found to be the greatest amongst

Hindu and Muslim youth (about 50 per cent) and least amongst Christian youth (30 per cent). It was also found to be the greatest amongst highly religious youth (59 per cent). Married youth were found to be more greatly worried about maintaining family traditions (51 per cent) than youth who were single (47 per cent). Moreover, amongst married youth those whose marriage was an arranged one had a much higher anxiety (51 per cent) about maintaining family traditions compared to those whose marriage was a love marriage (43 per cent). Marriage, especially an arranged marriage which involves a greater family participation, raises an individual's involvement in family matters and decision-making.

Anxiety about family problems

The marital status of the youth also seems to determine their worry levels about family problems. High anxiety about family problems was found to be greater amongst married youth (60 per cent) than amongst single youth (53 per cent). Youth who lived with parents or with their spouse were also found to be more highly worried about family problems (57 per cent) than youth who lived with friends, in a hostel or all by themselves (48 per cent). On the whole, anxiety about family problems amongst the youth has gone up since the study conducted in 2007. About 88 per cent worry (highly or somewhat) about it now, as opposed to 73 per cent a decade ago.

Anxiety about jobs

Anxiety (high or somewhat) about jobs has also seen a rise in the past ten years, from 70 to 73 per cent. The study found unemployed youth and students to be worrying much more about jobs than employed/working youth. Education and locality make a difference and the worry levels about jobs across the three categories – unemployed youth, students and working youth – went up if they were graduates and were located in urban areas. Youth who said they prefer a government job were found to worry far more (55 per cent) about jobs than youth who said they prefer a private job (48 per cent) or having their own business (39 per cent). It could be seen as an indicator that youths who are worried are looking for stability, and hence going into the less risky government sector. Similarly, youth who said they would prefer a permanent job even if it meant drawing a lesser salary were found to be more worried (57 per cent) about jobs than youth who said they would either prefer a job with a good income (44 per cent), a job which has good people around (45 per cent) or a job that gives them satisfaction (51 per cent).

Anxiety about studies

With its strong emphasis on exams and academic outcomes, school emerges as a significant stressor amongst youth, with the worry regarding studies being greatest (83 per cent) amongst the school-going age group of 15 to 17 year olds.

Very interestingly, worry about studies amongst youngsters was also found to be linked to their father's education. It was found that higher the father's educational qualification, higher was the likelihood of the teenager or young adult to worry about studies. Only about a quarter of the youth whose father had completed primary education were found to be highly worried about studies. In comparison, the proportion of those highly worried about studies was a third amongst those whose fathers had studied up to middle pass, half amongst those whose fathers had studied until intermediate or completed graduation, and two-thirds amongst those whose fathers were post-graduates. Anxiety about studies was also found to be linked to the type of institution a person has studied in. Being or having studied in a private college or a private school increases the level of worry of the youth about studies. About 70 per cent of school-going youth (15–17 year olds) studying in a private school were found to be highly worried about studies as opposed to 62 per cent of school-going youth studying in a government school. Similarly, 64 per cent of college-going youth (18–23 year olds) studying in a private college were greatly worried about studies, as opposed to 59 per cent of college-going youth studying in a government college.

Anxiety about personal looks and body shape

The study found two out of five youth to be highly anxious about the way they looked and their body shape. This anxiety with respect to one's looks and physique was found to be particularly high amongst upper class youth compared to poorer youth. Meanwhile, young men were found to be more worried about their personal looks than young women, except in big cities. The youth in the youngest category (15–17 year olds) were also found to be more worried about their looks than those slightly older (18–25 year olds) than them, except in big cities. Taking selfies on the phone also seems to be connected with worrying about personal looks. Those who took selfies daily were nearly two times more likely to highly worry about personal looks than those who never took selfies – 60 to 32 per cent. Similarly, those who said they were very fond of applying fairness creams were also twice as likely to worry about their looks as compared to those who did not use fairness creams – 63 to 30 per cent. Quite interestingly, non-vegetarians were found to be the less worried about their looks and body image compared to vegetarians. Two in every three non-vegetarian youths said they were either highly or somewhat anxious about their body shape and looks as opposed to four in every five vegetarian or 'eggitarian' youth.

Anxiety about losing a friend

Youth with close friends from another religion, caste and gender were found to be more anxious about losing a friend than those who did not (Table 8.6). The pattern with respect to religion was seen amongst youth belonging to all religious groups, i.e., young Muslims, Hindus, Christians and Sikhs. Those who said they have a close friend from a religion other than theirs showed much higher anxiety about 'losing a friend' than their co-religionists who did not have a close friend

TABLE 8.6 Anxiety about losing a friend (%)

	Worry about losing a friend			
	Quite a lot	*Somewhat*	*Very little*	*Not at all*
Overall	**35**	**25**	**14**	**22**
Those with a close friend from opposite gender	43	25	15	15
Those without any close friend from opposite gender	34	26	12	24
Those with a close friend from another caste	40	26	14	17
Those without any close friend from another caste	26	23	12	35
Those with a close friend from another religion	39	27	14	16
Those without any close friend from another religion	33	21	13	29

Note: The rest of the youth gave no response.

from another religion. Even in terms of caste, young upper castes, Other Backward Castes (OBCs), Dalits and Adivasis who had a close friend from another caste turned out to be more worried about 'losing a friend' than their counterparts who had no close friends from a caste other than theirs. Similarly, men and women with friends from the opposite gender were also found to worry more about 'losing a friend' than those men and women who said they did not have a close friend from the opposite gender. This is particularly stronger in the case of women.

Anxiety about road accidents

According to government statistics, 1.46 lakh (146,000) people were killed in road accidents in India in 2015 and a majority or over half (54 per cent) of them were from the age group 15 to 34 years old (Hindu, 2016). Moreover, within this broader age group of 15 to 34 years old, it is the 18- to 24-year-old category to which 53 per cent of the victims belonged (GOI, no date). It is little surprise then that the data in the study found anxiety (quite a lot and somewhat combined) about road accidents to be the highest amongst this age group at about 59 per cent. This is also the age when many young people learn how to drive a car or ride a bike or a scooter. It is also the age when most of them move out of their secure environments and begin to travel much more.

Anxiety about riots and mob violence

With respect to anxiety about mob violence and riots, the study found Muslim youth to be the most anxious about it, followed by Christian and Sikh youth (Table 8.11). Amongst Muslim youth, those residing in small cities were found to be twice as highly anxious about riots breaking out than those living in big cities, 35 per cent as opposed to 16 per cent. The study also found that youth who had faced discrimination on account of their religion were more likely to be highly worried about riots and mob violence than youth who had not, 36 per cent compared to 23 per cent. Meanwhile, young people who have a friend from another religion seemed to worry slightly more about a riot taking place in their area than youngsters who said they did not have a friend from another religion.

Anxiety about the inability to speak good English

The worry about the inability to speak good English was found to be greater amongst the more educated youth than the less educated ones. It is also very high amongst the youngest cohort (15–17 year olds) in big cities. In fact, the 15 to 17 year olds across all three locations (big cities, smaller cities and villages) showed much higher anxiety than the oldest cohort (30–34 years) on this issue. The youth residing in the northern and southern Indian states were found to be more highly anxious about their English-speaking skills (34 and 29 per cent, respectively) than youth living in states located in the eastern and western parts (18 and 16 per cent, respectively). A high level of worry about English-speaking skills was also found to be much greater amongst youth thinking of studying abroad or finding a job abroad than those who were not planning to go abroad – 34 to 23 per cent.

Anxiety about a terrorist attack

Degree of news media exposure seems to determine anxiety levels about a terrorist attack taking place. While only one in five youth with low exposure to news media was found to be highly worried about terrorist attacks, amongst youth with high news media exposure the proportion was one in three. Terrorist attacks being a more urban phenomenon, the study found youth in big and small cities to be much more highly worried (27 per cent each) about terror attacks than rural youth (21 per cent). The study also found Muslim and Sikh youth to be the most highly anxious (33 and 31 per cent, respectively) about a terrorist attack taking place than Christian and Hindu youth (26 and 23 per cent, respectively).

Anxiety about marriage

Marriage, the study found, is not a big worry for the majority of Indian youth. Overall, only about 18 per cent of them were found to be highly worried about it and another 20 per cent were somewhat anxious about it. Within the broader category of youth, however, the level of worry differed depending on one's age. Two in every five (41 per cent) of those aged between 18 and 29 years were highly worried about marriage. This is largely the age group that consists of mostly those who are either thinking of marriage or are newly married. These worry levels dropped to 36 per cent amongst the 30–34 year olds, nine out of ten of whom were found to be married in the study. Having married outside one's religion makes a huge difference to one's anxiety about marriage. About 45 per cent of those youth who have married someone from outside their religion were found to worry a lot about their marriage as opposed to 18 per cent of those who have married co-religionists (Table 8.7). Marriage outside of caste also makes a similar difference in this respect, although to a lesser degree. The kind of a marriage one has had, love or arranged, also determines the level of anxiety about one's marriage. Youngsters who have had a love marriage were found to be slightly more greatly worried about their marriage than youth who have had an arranged marriage, 20 per cent as opposed to 17 per cent. However, within both these types of marriages, the religion or caste of the spouse makes a big difference. While 38 per cent of those whose marriage is an inter-caste or an inter-religious love marriage reported worrying a lot about their marriage, amongst those whose marriage is an intra-caste or intra-religious love marriage, the level of worry was found to be three times less at 12 per cent. Similarly, youth with an arranged marriage outside of their caste or religion were twice as likely to highly worry about marriage as youth with an arranged marriage within their community, 33 per cent as opposed to 17 per cent.

Parental influence on the decision to marry is also a factor. Single youth who said that their parents will influence their decision to marry or married youth who said that their parents had influenced their marriage decision were found to be over two times more likely to highly worry about their marriage than youth who denied parental influence on the issue of marriage – 26 per cent as opposed to 11 per cent. When analysing by locality, the study found the city youth to be more anxious about marriage than the village youth. Within cities, both big and small, the 26 to 29 year olds were found to be the most worried about it. In villages, it was the

TABLE 8.7 Anxiety about marriage (%)

	Worry about marriage			
	Quite a lot	*Somewhat*	*Very little*	*Not at all*
Overall	**18**	**20**	**17**	**39**
Those who have married outside caste	33	15	18	30
Those who have married within caste	18	17	14	45
Those who have married outside religion	45	8	5	41
Those who have married within religion	18	17	15	44
Those whose love marriage is outside caste/religion	38	15	17	26
Those whose love marriage is within caste/religion	12	18	15	29
Those whose arranged marriage is outside caste/religion	33	14	9	41
Those whose arranged marriage is within caste/religion	17	17	14	46

Note: The rest of the youth gave no response.

18 to 21 year olds who were the most worried about marriage. Finally, and rather interestingly, anxiety about one's looks and body shape amongst the youth may also be shaping their worry about marriage. Nearly a third of those highly worried about their looks and body shape were also found to worry highly about marriage. In comparison, only about 7 per cent of those not worried at all about their looks worry highly about marriage. The study also found a link between taking selfies on one's phone and applying fairness creams on one's face and worry levels regarding marriage. While 28 per cent of those who took selfies on their phone daily were found to worry highly about marriage, the figure dropped to 18 per cent amongst those who never took their own pictures on the phone. Likewise, while 26 per cent of those fond of applying fairness creams showed high anxiety about marriage, the figure of anxiety amongst those not at all fond of it was 17 per cent.

Anxiety about harassment and teasing

On the issue of harassment and teasing, young women, not surprisingly, more than young men, were found to worry 'a lot' about it: 23 per cent to 16 per cent. The gap between the genders widens further to 13 percentage points when we take into account moderate worry as well. This anxiety about harassment is particularly strong amongst young women living in the northern states followed by the southern states: 58 per cent of young women in North India and 45 per cent in South India said they worried either a lot or somewhat about teasing and harassment. Anxiety about harassment was found to be greater amongst young women living in cities as compared to women living in villages, and within the broader category of cities, it was stronger in the bigger cities than the smaller ones. Age also makes a difference to how women worry about harassment and teasing: 18- to 21-year-old women were the most worried about harassment followed by 22- to 25-year-old women. Women in the age category 30–34 years were the least worried of all about this issue. Interestingly, young women who said that they have been discriminated against on account of their gender in the recent past were also more likely to worry highly (33 per cent) about harassment than women who had not been discriminated against on grounds of gender.

Emotional distress amongst the youth

Even as the youth in India show very high levels of overall anxiety (55 per cent), the incidence of emotional distress amongst them is considerably lower. After taking into account youth responses to questions on frequency of depression, loneliness, worthlessness and suicidal thoughts (see Appendix II to find out how Index of Emotional Distress was constructed), it was found that only about 7 per cent of India's youth suffer from high emotional distress. About one in every four youth (24 per cent) fall in to the moderately distressed category, 18 per cent in the low distress category and over half of them (51 per cent) reported no emotional distress whatsoever.

Both anxiety and distress seem to have an impact on each other. About 10 per cent of the highly anxious were found to be highly emotionally distressed, as opposed to only 2 per cent of the least anxious youth. Similarly, the greater the level of emotional distress, the greater is the likelihood of the youth being anxious. Three in every four or 75 per cent of those with high emotional distress said they had very high anxiety levels, as opposed to just 44 per cent of those who showed no distress whatsoever.

Analysis of the study found high emotional distress to be particularly high (at least double the overall average) amongst youth who drink alcohol, those who smoke, those who have put out an advertisement for marriage, those who regularly use social media, those who are extremely religious, those who are fond of visiting beauty parlours or salons, those who had a love marriage and young working women, especially those who are single (Table 8.8). A note of caution is in order here. This does not mean that all youth who belong to these categories suffer from high emotional distress. This only means that going by the study, the likelihood of finding emotionally distressed people amongst these categories was significantly greater than it was amongst other groups.

Also, the direction of causality with respect to some of these behavioural aspects seems to be the other way around. That is, it is not the presence of these traits and practices that may be leading to emotional distress amongst the young generation but instead it is distress that may be leading to such behaviours. The study found many of these behavioural traits to be much greater amongst the youth with high emotional distress than those with no distress at all. For instance, 31 per cent of the

TABLE 8.8 Categories amongst which high emotional distress was found to be much higher than average along with distress levels (%)

	High emotional distress	Moderate emotional distress	Low emotional distress	No emotional distress
Overall	7	24	18	51
Those who drink alcohol	22	28	11	39
Single women who are working	22	20	20	38
Those who have put out a matrimonial ad	21	33	15	31
Those who smoke	18	30	13	39
Those who are very religious	15	25	15	45
Those who are very fond of visiting salons/parlours	14	34	14	38
Those with very high social media exposure	14	26	20	43
Working women	14	24	16	46
Those who had a love marriage	13	25	21	42

Note: These figures only point to a correlation, not causality. Causality can only be speculated and could well be in the reverse direction.

TABLE 8.9 Impact of emotional distress on lifestyle and behaviour (%)

	Drink alcohol regularly	Smoke regularly	Eat Junk food regularly	High media exposure	High social media exposure	High religiosity	High aspirational lifestyle	Given a matrimonial ad	Style conscious (high and moderate)	Take selfies (daily and weekly)
High distress	31	31	51	40	52	52	32	10	53	36
Moderate distress	11	15	42	28	47	47	31	5	52	31
Not much distress	6	9	40	27	35	34	27	3	43	31
No distress	8	9	37	17	29	29	24	2	36	24
Net of extremes	**8.9**	**8.4**	**1.4**	**2.4**	**1.8**	**1.8**	**1.3**	**5**	**1.5**	**1.5**

Note: Net figures have been calculated by dividing High distress figures by No distress figures.

highly emotionally distressed youth were found to be drinking alcohol regularly, as opposed to 8 per cent of youth who suffered from no distress at all (Table 8.9). Similarly, the higher the distress, the greater is the tendency of youth to eat junk food regularly, smoke regularly, be highly style conscious and indulge in shopping and eating out regularly.

Work or studies-related stress

Overall, 19 per cent of the youth reported feeling stress from their studies or their job 'very often'[1] (Table 8.10). This stress was greater amongst those who worried a lot about their studies and about their job than those who did not. Amongst those who were very anxious about their studies, a third (34 per cent) were found to feel stressed very often, as opposed to just 6 per cent amongst those who did not worry at all about studies. Similarly, there was a 20-point gap in terms of high stress levels amongst those who worried a lot about a job than those who did not worry at all. Worrying about education or jobs is also correlated with how much one discusses these issues with one's parents. The study found that those who discussed career or education with their parents often were over four times more likely to feel stressed often than those who never discussed these things with their parents. Parental influence on these matters shows a similar result. About 30 per cent of those who said that their parents will have or have had a high influence on their career- or education-related decisions were found to feel stressed very regularly, as opposed just 8 per cent

TABLE 8.10 Categories amongst which stress was found to be much higher than average along with stress levels (%)

| | Feel stressed from work/studies | | | |
	Very often	Sometimes	Very little	Never
Overall	**19**	**29**	**14**	**32**
Those who worry a lot about studies	34	31	12	22
Those living in small cities	32	31	11	23
Those who discuss career/education with parents often	31	33	13	22
Those who reported high parental influence on career/education	30	28	11	28
Those who worry a lot about job/s	29	31	12	24
Working women	26	24	11	33
Those in a professional job (doctors, lawyers, teachers, etc.)	25	36	12	25
15–17 year olds	25	28	15	28
Those who discuss career/education with parents sometimes	24	36	13	23
Students	24	34	14	26

Note: These figures only point to a correlation, not causality. Causality can only be speculated and could well be in the reverse direction.

amongst those who denied any parental influence on these matters. The study also found that the youngest amongst the young (15–17 year olds followed by 18–21 year olds) felt the weight of stress most, as compared to their older counterparts. The older youngsters (30–34 year olds) were least likely to feel stress. Stress levels were also found to be greater amongst youth residing in smaller cities than big ones. Feeling stressed also has a strong connection with education. The more educated youth reported feeling, the greater stress than the less educated youth. In terms of job types, youth with professional jobs (scientist, doctor, lawyer, teacher, etc.) were found to be the most stressed, followed by youth who were in a government job. Young students too showed higher stress levels than others. Young farmers, young housewives and those who were unemployed showed the least amount of stress. Interestingly, the study also found young working women to be more highly stressed than young working men, 26 per cent as opposed to 17 per cent.

Tension and depression amongst Indian youth

About one in eight (12 per cent) of 15 to 34 year olds reported feeling depressed very often in the study (Table 8.11). The study found the incidence of depression to be the greatest amongst the youth who said they often feel lonely (62 per cent), followed by those who often felt worthless (54 per cent) and those who often felt stressed due to work or studies (43 per cent). It was also found to be quite high

TABLE 8.11 Categories amongst which mental tension/depression was found to be much higher than average along with mental tension levels (%)

	Feel mental tension/depression			
	Very often	*Sometimes*	*Very little*	*Never*
Overall	12	27	20	37
Those who often feel lonely	62	26	7	5
Those who often feel worthless	54	29	9	7
Those who often feel stressed from work/studies	43	31	13	13
Those who faced a lot of discrimination in last 5 years	25	34	22	10
Those who are fully dissatisfied with life	22	26	10	39
Those who worry a lot about marriage	22	25	17	32
Those who worry a lot about their poor English	21	28	19	30
Those who worry a lot about studies	19	29	19	31
Those with high exposure to media	19	31	21	28
Those who had a love marriage	19	28	20	32
Those who are highly religious	17	32	20	30
Unmarried/single Women	17	27	22	31

Note: These figures only point to a correlation, not causality. Causality can only be speculated and could well be in the reverse direction.

amongst youngsters who said they felt fully dissatisfied with life (22 per cent). Such people were, in fact, two times more likely to be often depressed than those who were fully satisfied with life. Anxiety and depression are correlated. Depression was particularly strong amongst those with high anxiety about matters such as marriage, English-speaking skills and studies, in that order. An experience of discrimination is also connected to depression. Youngsters who reported facing discrimination on several grounds, such as gender, religion, caste, state and economic class, were two times more likely to be highly depressed than youngsters who had not faced discrimination on any of these grounds. Type of marriage also seems to make a difference. About one in every five or 19 per cent of married youth whose marriage was a love marriage reported being depressed very often, as opposed to 11 per cent with an arranged marriage. High depression was also found in a much higher proportion (19 per cent) amongst those who were also highly exposed to media. It was also much stronger amongst highly religious youth when compared with the less religious. The direction of causality, of course, could be the other way around, i.e., depression could be leading to greater media exposure and more religiosity. In terms of locality, youth in rural areas were more likely to be depressed than youth in urban areas. Amongst urban areas, it was the city youth more than the mega-city youth who had higher depression. The level of education of youngsters was found to be related to their depression levels. The more educated were more likely to be highly depressed than the less educated: 14 per cent amongst graduates and 6 per cent amongst non-literates. In terms of gender, women reported higher depression than young men, 15 per cent as compared to 10 per cent. Moreover, amongst young women it was single/unmarried women who were found to be more highly depressed at 17 per cent. Married young women also had fairly high depression levels at 13 per cent. This was even higher amongst married women who have had a love marriage (19 per cent). Type of marriage also made a difference amongst men: 17 per cent of married young men with a love marriage had high depression. The incidence of depression was also quite high (14 per cent) amongst youth with a job. Interestingly, the very stylish or style conscious youth were also found to be more depressed than those who were not: 51 per cent of them were depressed often or sometimes, as opposed to 31 per cent amongst those who were not at all style conscious.

Loneliness amongst Indian youth

The study found less than one in ten (8 per cent) young Indians to be extremely lonely (Table 8.12). These were those who said they felt lonely very often. On doing some deeper analysis, the loneliest youth were found to be located amongst those who often felt worthless: 57 per cent of these youth said they felt lonely very often. Higher than the average incidence of frequent loneliness was also found amongst those highly exposed to media (18 per cent). It could be that being lonely is turning them towards media as a means to overcome their loneliness. Similarly, those who ate junk food such as burgers, pizzas and chips daily were also more

TABLE 8.12 Categories amongst which the feeling of loneliness is higher than average along with loneliness levels (%)

	Feel lonely			
	Very often	Sometimes	Very little	Never
Overall	**8**	**24**	**21**	**43**
Those who often feel worthless	57	30	6	7
Those with very high exposure to media	18	32	22	28
Those who are fully dissatisfied with life	17	22	18	39
18–21-year-old women	16	24	24	35
Those who eat fast food daily	16	29	16	36
Those thinking of looking for a job abroad	13	24	19	41
Those who are very style conscious	13	32	24	30
Middle class in villages	13	27	19	40
Upper class in mega cities	12	25	19	40
Those who are very worried about their looks/weight	12	29	21	36

Note: These figures only point to a correlation, not causality. Causality can only be speculated and could well be in the reverse direction. Mega cities include Delhi, Mumbai, Kolkata, Chennai, Hyderabad, Bangalore, Ahmedabad, Pune, Surat and Jaipur.

likely to experience higher loneliness than those who ate junk food less frequently. Once again, the direction of causality could be reverse, that is, loneliness leading to a greater propensity to eat junk food. Dissatisfaction with one's life also correlates with loneliness. About 17 per cent of those fully dissatisfied with life were found to feel lonely very often as opposed to 8 per cent amongst those who were happy with the way their life was going. Loneliness was also found to be greater amongst 18 to 21 year olds (11 per cent), particularly amongst women belonging to this age category (16 per cent). The study found loneliness to be higher than average amongst the highly style conscious youth, those thinking of looking for a job abroad and those extremely anxious about their looks and body shape. In villages, the highly lonely youth were found to be more likely to belong to the middle class than other classes and in the mega cities the rich youth were more likely to be highly lonely.

Worthlessness amongst Indian youth

If a high degree of loneliness was found amongst only 8 per cent of the youth, the incidence of feeling worthless is even less at 5 per cent (Table 8.13). However, just as loneliness seems to be determined by worthlessness, the latter too seems to be impacted by the former. Amongst those who said they feel lonely very often, the prevalence of a feeling of high worthlessness was six times the overall average. Once again, as in the case of loneliness, exposure to news media, religiosity and dissatisfaction with life are also linked to the intensity/regularity of feeling worthless. So is the consumption of junk food. Anxiety about jobs, marriage, one's looks

TABLE 8.13 Categories amongst which the feeling of worthlessness is much higher than average along with levels of this feeling of worthlessness (%)

	Feel worthless			
	Very often	Sometimes	Very little	Never
Overall	5	15	15	61
Those who often feel lonely	32	31	13	24
Those who watch/read/listen to news a lot	13	21	18	48
Those who are very highly religious	12	19	19	47
Those who are fully dissatisfied with life	11	15	14	57
Those who eat junk/fast food daily	10	16	22	49
Those who worry a lot about marriage	9	20	17	50
Those with a desire of settling abroad	9	17	15	58
Those who are fully dissatisfied with current job	9	16	19	49

Note: These figures only point to a correlation, not causality. Causality can only be speculated and could well be in the reverse direction.

and not being able to speak good English may also be contributing to a feeling of worthlessness. High worthlessness was also found to be greater than average amongst the very style conscious youth, and 18 to 21 year olds, particularly women and those living in rural areas, were also more likely to feel highly worthless than other youth. Living in a mega city seems to reduce the likelihood of feeling worthless: 70 per cent of youth residing in mega cities said they never feel worthless, as opposed to about 60 per cent in smaller cities, towns and villages. Interestingly, the study found the feeling of being 'good for nothing' to be higher than average amongst those who regularly participated in the activities of a religious or spiritual organisation. Perhaps a feeling of worthlessness is what is making them participate in such activities.

Suicidal thoughts amongst Indian youth

There is now plenty of data from various authoritative sources to suggest that India has amongst the highest suicides rates in the world. The World Health Organization (WHO) estimates that about 170,000 deaths by suicide occur in India every year, the second highest in the world after China (Padmanabhan, 2012). According to a paper published in *The Lancet* journal in 2012, a large proportion of these deaths occur between the ages of 15 years and 29 years, especially amongst women. Suicide is in fact the second most important cause of death amongst youngsters in the 15 to 29 age group after transport accidents (Patel et al., 2012). Every year, about 30 to 40 people per 100,000 Indians aged between 15 and 29 kill themselves. This accounts for about a third of all suicides in the country (Mukunth, 2014). The National Crime Records Bureau (NCRB) data from 2015 reveal that every hour, one student commits suicide in India. As per NCRB data as many as 8,934 students across India took their lives in 2015 and in the five years leading to 2015, 39,775 students killed themselves (Saha, 2017). And this could just be the tip of the iceberg as the number of attempted suicides, many of which are unreported, could be much higher.

The study tried to measure the level of suicidal proclivities amongst young Indians. About 3 per cent of the total sample said they had suicidal thoughts very often and another 6 per cent had such thoughts sometimes (Table 8.14). The propensity to get suicidal thoughts very often was found to be ten times greater (31 per cent) than the average amongst those youngsters who felt worthless very often. It was five times greater than average amongst youth who said they often felt lonely or often felt depressed and three times higher amongst those who felt stressed from work or studies very often. The tendency to feel suicidal was also found to be more prevalent amongst those who ate junk food daily and those who regularly participated in the activities of a religious or a spiritual organisation. The latter could be causing the former, which is to say the feelings of ending one's life could be leading to these habits and practices. Higher suicidal tendencies were also found to be significantly greater than the average amongst those with a high aspiration of going abroad, amongst those who worried a lot about marriage and about their English-speaking skills, and amongst those with high exposure to news media. Dissatisfaction with one's current job or with one's life also leads to suicidal thoughts but not to the extent witnessed amongst some other categories. Only 6 per cent of those completely unhappy with their job and 5 per cent of those

TABLE 8.14 Categories amongst which suicidal tendencies are higher than average along with levels of this tendency (%)

	Feel suicidal			
	Very often	Sometimes	Very little	Never
Overall	**3**	**6**	**6**	**79**
Those who often feel worthless	31	16	14	38
Those who often feel lonely	16	13	8	62
Those who often feel depressed	14	12	9	62
Those who participate regularly in religious/ spiritual organisations' activities	11	12	5	68
Those who often feel stressed	10	7	8	72
Those who eat junk/fast food daily	9	13	6	69
Those with a high aspiration to go abroad	9	7	7	75
Those who worry a lot about marriage	7	8	7	72
18–21-year-old women	7	5	8	75
Those who are very religious (in practice)	6	10	14	65
Those who are fully dissatisfied with current job	6	8	7	72

Note: These figures only point to a correlation, not causality. Causality can only be speculated and could well be in the reverse direction.

completely dissatisfied with their life felt suicidal very often. The highly religious and the highly style conscious also seem to be more likely to feel suicidal than the less religious and the less style conscious. As in the case of worthlessness, youth in mega cities were the least likely to feel suicidal than youth living elsewhere. Rural youth were found to be the most highly suicidal (5 per cent). The study also found young women between the ages of 18 and 21 to be two times more prone to getting suicidal thoughts than all youth.

Seeking medical help for mental health issues

The study asked the youth whether they had ever consulted a doctor for therapy related to mental problems. Only 6 per cent said they did so, a figure that is alarming given that the study also found 55 per cent of the youth to be highly anxious and about 31 per cent to be having high or moderate emotional distress (Table 8.15). While it is true (and the study finds) that the more anxious and the more emotionally distressed were more likely to have consulted a psychiatrist or mental health expert, the figures even amongst them were alarmingly low. Perhaps the stigma around mental health issues is preventing treatment and in some cases even acknowledgment. Amongst youth who were very anxious, only 8 per cent had consulted a doctor; and amongst the highly distressed only 18 per cent or about one in five had gone to a therapist. More shockingly, only one in every five youth (21 per cent) who got suicidal thoughts very often had sought therapy (Table 8.16). The practice of consulting a doctor for mental therapy was also found to be significantly greater than the overall average amongst those who had faced a lot of discrimination, those who suffered from a high feeling of worthlessness, and those who were extremely lonely or very depressed. But once again, these are worryingly low figures given the level of affliction. Type of marriage also makes a difference. Youths who had a love marriage or preferred a love marriage were also more likely to have consulted

TABLE 8.15 Proportion of youth who have sought psychiatric help based on level of emotional distress and anxiety (%)

	Consulted a doctor for therapy
Overall	6
Anxiety	
Very anxious	8
Quite anxious	6
Somewhat anxious	5
Not much anxious	5
Not all anxious	2
Emotional distress	
High emotional distress	18
Moderate emotional distress	8
Low emotional distress	8
No emotional distress	2

TABLE 8.16 Categories of youth who are more likely to have consulted a therapist (%)

	Consulted a doctor for therapy
Overall	6
Those who often feel suicidal	21
Those who have faced a lot of discrimination	17
Those who often feel worthless	15
Those who often feel lonely	15
Single youth who would prefer a love marriage	13
Those who are very depressed	10
Upper class in mega cities	10
Those who had a love marriage	9
Those who often feel stressed	9
30–34-year-old graduates	9
30–34 year olds in mega cities	9

a doctor than youth with a preference for arranged marriage. Economically well-off youth and 30 to 34 year olds residing in mega cities were also found to have consulted a doctor for therapy much more than the overall average. Young women were slightly more likely to have consulted a therapist than young men, particularly women belonging to the 18–21 years and the 26–29 years age groups.

Conclusion

Overall, it appears that the young in India are a greatly anxious generation who seem to be worrying about a whole host of matters at the same time. While different age groups amongst the young have different worries, what is uniform and consistent across age groups are the anxieties related to parents' health, personal health, family problems and maintaining family traditions. These four matters seem to be causing a great deal of worry amongst the Indian youngsters, whatever their age. On the whole, anxiety amongst youth seems to be more of an urban phenomenon than rural, with the highest anxiety levels being recorded amongst youth residing in big cities. Anxiety levels also seem to be dependent on educational and economic status, with the more educated and economically better-off sections amongst the youth having much higher anxiety than the rest. Meanwhile, even as one notices high levels of anxiety amongst them, the study did not find many youths to be emotionally distressed. The two conditions are different although they were found to be inter-related – those with higher anxiety were more likely to be emotionally distressed. Emotional distress as measured by us through the incidence of loneliness, depression, worthlessness and getting suicidal thoughts, does not seem to be widespread amongst the youth, with over half of them not having any of these conditions in the study. Nonetheless, there is a fairly significant proportion of youth (about one in every three) who was found to suffer from either all these conditions or at least some of them and worryingly about four-fifths of them have not yet sought medical help.

Note

1 The question on work or education-related stress was not included in the overall Index of Emotional Distress.

References

GOI (Government of India) (no date) Total Number of Persons Killed in Road Accidents in India. Available at: https://data.gov.in/catalog/total-number-persons-killed-road-accidents-india (accessed on 15 December 2016).

Hindu, The (2016) 1.46 Lakh Lives Lost on Indian Roads Last Year, *The Hindu*, 10 June. Available at: www.thehindu.com/news/national/146-lakh-lives-lost-on-indian-roads-last-year/article8710699.ece (accessed on 15 December, 2016).

Mukunth, Vasudevan (2014) Four Charts Show Why India's Youth Suicide Rate Is Amongst the World's Highest, Scroll.in. Available at: https://scroll.in/article/694364/four-charts-show-why-indias-youth-suicide-rate-is-among-the-worlds-highest (accessed on 20 October 2017).

Oaklander, Mandy (2016) Old People Are Happier than People in Their 20s, *Time*. Available at: http://time.com/4464811/aging-happiness-stress-anxiety-depression/ (accessed on 14 December 2016).

Padmanabhan, Anil (2012) Is India a Suicide Country?, *Mint*, 1 July. Available at: www.livemint.com/Opinion/Jd5s2dNLL2lyCHBUjd9dIK/Is-India-a-suicide-country.html (accessed on 20 October 2017).

Patel, Vikram, Ramasundarahettige, Chinthanie, Vijayakumar Lakshmi, Thakur, J.S., Gajalakshmi, Vendhan, Gururaj, Gopalkrishna, Suraweera, Wilson and Jha, Prabhat (2012) Suicide Mortality in India: A Nationally Representative Survey, *The Lancet*, 23 June, 379(9834): 2343–2351.

Saha, Devika (2017) Every Hour, One Student Commits Suicide in India, *Hindustan Times*. Available at: www.hindustantimes.com/health-and-fitness/every-hour-one-student-commits-suicide-in-india/story-7UFFhSs6h1HNgrNO60FZ2O.html (accessed on 20 October 2017).

9

EXPERIENCES OF DISCRIMINATION

Shreyas Sardesai

Discrimination, a prejudicial treatment of people based on negative stereotypes about the communities to which they belong, is detrimental to the harmony and integration of any society. It is generally understood as biased behaviour that harms or disadvantages a specific member of a group or the group as a whole. It stems from deeply entrenched beliefs of superiority vis-à-vis others and can be perpetrated on the basis of a range of factors such as caste, religion, race, region, class, sex, sexual preference, age or disability. While all these types of discrimination can be experienced by a person belonging to any age group, the impact of discrimination on the young can be particularly severe. As they grow up, the young have increasingly greater interactions with others in their micro-system and are therefore at a higher risk of witnessing discrimination or being recipients of it. Such experiences at a young age can not only have terrible consequences for their health, self-esteem and inclusion in society, but can also lead to alienation or violent behavioural tendencies. It is therefore essential that stereotypes and prejudices are confronted with evidence based on the youth's actual attitudes and experiences of discrimination.

Measuring discrimination faced by India's youth

Keeping this in mind, the CSDS-KAS Youth Study 2016 asked young respondents five questions regarding their encounters with bias. The questions probed whether they had in a span of five years faced discrimination because of their region, caste, gender, religion or their economic status. Based on their answers, it was found (see Appendix II to find out how the Index of Experience of Discrimination was constructed) that about 2 per cent thought they had faced discrimination either on all five grounds or on four of the five grounds; 7 per cent had faced discrimination on two or three grounds and 8 per cent on just one

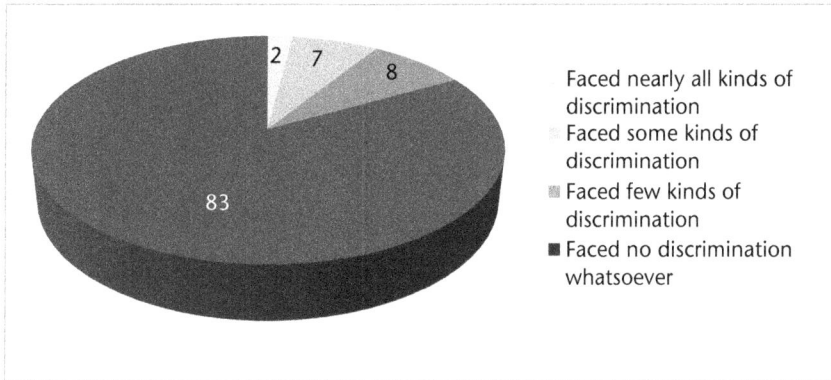

FIGURE 9.1 Measuring discrimination faced by India's youth (%)

Note: See Appendix II to find out how the Index of Experience of Discrimination was constructed.

out of the five grounds. This means that one in every six youth (17 per cent) had faced discrimination on at least one count in a span of five years (Figure 9.1). A note of caution is in order here. It must be kept in mind (throughout this chapter) that these are self-reported figures of discrimination and that there may well have been under-reporting by respondents as many may not have perceived an actual act of discrimination as being so. However, since discrimination often occurs at a personal, individual level, people's perception should be treated as a credible, though not the only, source of information regarding such practices. When analysed by different socio-demographic variables, the otherwise underwhelming figures present a telling picture.

When looked at by age, this figure of 17 per cent increased to 22 per cent among the 18–21 year olds (Table 9.1). This is precisely the period of life when most Indian youth are out of school and increasingly start interacting with the wider world, hence increasing their chances of encountering prejudice in some form or another. Meanwhile, the 15–17 year olds or those still in school reported least discrimination (11 per cent). Put differently, they were two times less likely to have experienced discrimination than the 18–21 year olds.

TABLE 9.1 18–21 year olds more likely to have experienced discrimination than others (%)

	Faced nearly all kinds of discrimination	*Faced some kinds of discrimination*	*Faced few kinds of discrimination*	*Faced no discrimination whatsoever*
15–17 years	2	3	6	89
18–21 years	3	10	9	78
22–25 years	1	7	9	83
26–29 years	2	7	9	82
30–34 years	2	6	7	85

TABLE 9.2 Are educated youth better at judging discrimination? (%)

	Faced nearly all kinds of discrimination	Faced some kinds of discrimination	Faced few kinds of discrimination	Faced no discrimination whatsoever
Graduate or above	2	8	10	80
High school pass	2	7	6	85
Primary pass	1	7	5	88
Non-literate	2	3	7	88

TABLE 9.3 Youth in small cities more likely to have faced discrimination than those in big cities (%)

	Faced nearly all kinds of discrimination	Faced some kinds of discrimination	Faced few kinds of discrimination	Faced no discrimination whatsoever
Big cities	1	5	8	86
Smaller cities	4	10	8	78
Villages	2	7	8	83

An analysis by educational qualification also shows a similar pattern. The highly educated youth reported having had faced discrimination much more than the less educated youth (Table 9.2). Whereas one in every five graduate youth reported having been discriminated against in some way or the other, among high school pass youth the figure was 15 per cent and among primary pass and non-literate youth it was even lower at 13 and 12 per cent, respectively. It could be argued that such a pattern is visible because education and the opportunities that come with it might have made these respondents more aware of the different manifestations of discriminatory attitudes and practices. This also means that many among the less-educated youth could also have been victims of prejudice in some form or the other but may not have realised it. This is of course just a supposition.

In terms of locality, the incidence of discrimination was found to be the highest in smaller cities, where 22 per cent of the young respondents reported having had experienced some discrimination or the other. Rural youth came next at 17 per cent. Youth in big cities, meanwhile, reported the least amount of discrimination, with only 14 per cent of them reporting as having been discriminated against on at least one of the five grounds (Table 9.3).

The overall study findings with respect to Indian youth's experiences of discrimination could tempt one to conclude that discrimination is not a big problem in India. However, in a country where social exclusion, particularly on the grounds of caste, has become a social norm, for anyone to come to such a conclusion would be highly naive. Moreover, the fact that the study finds every sixth youth to have experienced some form of discrimination in the recent past could be considered by some to be a fairly high occurrence. Also, to reiterate the point made earlier, what should also be kept in mind is that these are self-reported levels of discrimination and it could be the case that an individual who may well have faced discrimination had not viewed it as such, thereby not reporting it as discrimination to us in the study. The lower than expected figures could also be on account of the survey design having missed out youth living in hostels, many of whom migrate from remote parts of the country (particularly the north-eastern states and Jammu and Kashmir) to 'mainland India' for education and jobs. Their experiences of discrimination have been widely reported in the media in recent times and it is very possible that the study did not capture them well. Moreover, the study was not conducted in the north-eastern states (except Assam) and in Jammu and Kashmir, hence the experiences of youth living in these states have also not been factored into this analysis. A possible explanation for the low self-reporting can also be found in sociology. Farver et al. (2007) posits that various social groups prepare their members for the larger world through a process of socialisation. This cultural socialisation, which is prevalent in all social groups, makes the individual learn important skills for social survival. In the context of this study, a possible outcome of this process of cultural socialisation could be that ideas of discrimination, which are so prevalent in Indian society, might become so deeply entrenched in the everyday lives of individuals that they cease to seem extraordinary, which might explain why only a few people are consciously aware of them.

There is however some reason to believe that discrimination experienced by the youth has declined over the years. Nearly a decade ago, in 2007, when a similar question was asked of Indian youth in the first CSDS-KAS Youth Study, responses acknowledging discrimination had been of a higher proportion. The questions asked then had also probed the issue of discrimination on the basis of caste, economic status, gender, religion and region. However, the wording of the question in that study was slightly different from the one asked in 2016. In 2007, the question probed the frequency of discrimination experienced, with the answer categories offered being 'Often', 'Sometimes' and 'Never'. In 2016, the question simply probed the experience of discrimination with the answer categories just being 'Yes' and 'No'. Moreover, the respondents in 2007 were not given any recall period similar to the 2016 study. Nevertheless, for the purposes of a rough comparison, if we ignore the differences in the framing of the question and treat those who answered 'Often' and 'Sometimes' in 2007 as Yes/having experienced discrimination and those who said 'Never' or those who did not give an opinion as No/not having experienced discrimination, then we find that overall after taking all five questions into consideration, in 2007 about 15 per cent of the youth had reported facing a lot of discrimination, 22 per cent had faced some discrimination, 18 per cent had faced little discrimination and 44 per cent had not experienced any discrimination whatsoever. However, if we were treat only those who answered 'Often' as having experienced discrimination and the rest as not having experienced any, then the story is somewhat like what we find in 2016.

TABLE 9.4 Experience of discrimination based on economic status among youth (%)

	%
Youth (overall)	9
Upper class	7
Middle class	7
Lower class	9
Poor	11
Poor in big cities	12
Poor who are 18–25 years old	14
Poor who are Muslim	14
Poor in smaller cities	16
Poor who are graduates	18

Experience of discrimination based on economic status

The study found economic background and caste to be the strongest grounds for discrimination out of all the five questions asked. This had been the case in 2007 as well, but to a much higher degree (perhaps due to different wording of the question). Overall, 9 per cent of the young respondents in 2016 said they had been discriminated against based on their economic status (Table 9.4). Not surprisingly, the poorer the youth, the greater was their likelihood of having experienced discrimination on economic basis. Whereas 11 per cent of youth belonging to the poorer sections and 9 per cent from the lower class said they had faced discrimination on economic grounds, among youth belonging to the upper and middle classes only 7 per cent said so. On disaggregating the responses of the poor further, it was found that the feeling of economic discrimination was strongest among poor youth who were graduates (18 per cent). It was also quite strong among poor youth in small cities (16 per cent), followed by big cities (12 per cent). The experience of discrimination on economic lines was also much higher than average among young Muslims who were also poor and aged between 18 and 25 years.

Experience of discrimination based on caste

Caste too was found to be among the top grounds of discrimination, although its incidence appears to have gone down as compared to 2007. Overall, 9 per cent of Indian youth reported having had experienced caste-based discrimination in the five years preceding the study (Table 9.5). In 2007, 7 per cent had said they had experienced it frequently and 23 per cent reported experiencing it sometimes. Once again, it needs to be re-emphasised that these figures cannot be compared strictly with 2016 because of the difference in wording of the question. The sense of caste-based discrimination in 2016 was found to be greatest among young Dalits

TABLE 9.5 Experience of discrimination based on caste among youth (%)

	%
Youth (overall)	*9*
Hindu upper caste	5
Hindu upper OBC	7
Hindu lower OBC	7
Hindu Dalit	15
Hindu Adivasi	11
Muslim	10
Graduate Dalit	18
Graduate Muslim	13
Graduate upper OBC	10

at 15 per cent, followed by young Adivasis (11 per cent) and thereafter young Muslims (10 per cent). Hindu upper caste youth were least likely to say that they had been treated unfairly based on their caste, with only 5 per cent saying so. Other Backward Caste (OBC) youth, be they from the upper or the lower sections, reported similar levels of caste discrimination at 7 per cent. Being more educated made a difference in perception of caste discrimination among Dalits, Muslims and upper OBCs. Young graduates belonging to all these three communities were more likely to report unfair treatment based on caste than the less educated in these communities: 18 per cent of young Dalit graduates, 13 per cent of young Muslim graduates and 10 per cent of young upper OBC graduates reported facing discrimination based on their caste identity.

Experience of discrimination based on religion

Discrimination on the basis of religion was reported by 5 per cent of all young respondents (Table 9.6). However, this overall figure does not reveal the true picture because the religion of a person made a huge difference to their response. There are significant variations when we look at this finding by the religious community of the respondent. Muslim youth were much more likely than others to have reported religion-based discrimination. About one in every seven or 13 per cent of them said they had been discriminated against based on their Muslim identity. If we disaggregate Muslim responses to this question further, we find that Muslim youth living in smaller cities were most likely to have been victims of religious bias: 27 per cent reported having faced discriminatory treatment for being Muslims. This is twice what all Muslim youth had reported. Muslim youth who reported being highly religious were also much more likely than other Muslim youth to have reported religious discrimination. A little over one in five of them (22 per cent) said they had experienced religious discrimination. Other categories among Muslim youth who reported

TABLE 9.6 Experience of discrimination based on religion among youth (%)

	%
Youth (overall)	5
Hindu	4
Muslim	13
Christian	6
Sikh	2
Muslim men	14
High school pass/graduate Muslims	15
Lower class/poor Muslims	16
Highly religious Muslims	22
Muslims in smaller cities	27

relatively higher faith-based discrimination are those belonging to the poor and lower classes, graduate and high school pass Muslims and Muslim men. Youth from the Christian faith, also a religious minority, also reported a slightly higher than average discrimination at 6 per cent. This sentiment however is not shared by young people belonging to another minority community – the Sikhs. In fact, of all religious groupings, Sikh youths were least likely to have experienced any discrimination based on their faith. Only 2 per cent said so. Meanwhile, 4 per cent of youth belonging to the majority Hindu community reported unfair treatment based on their religion.

Experience of discrimination based on region or state

Discrimination on account of one's state or the region to which one belongs was reported by only 5 per cent of the young respondents (Table 9.7). This sentiment was particularly strong among youth from the southern and eastern states who

TABLE 9.7 Experience of discrimination based on region or state among youth (%)

	%
Youth (overall)	5
Region	
From south and has travelled to another state	6
From east and has travelled to another state	10
From west and has travelled to another state	2
From north and has travelled to another state	4
State	
From Bihar and has travelled to another state	15
From Uttar Pradesh and has travelled to another state	12
From Tamil Nadu and has travelled to another state	14

had travelled outside their states and more particularly among youth from Bihar, Tamil Nadu and Uttar Pradesh who had gone beyond their state borders: 15, 14 and 12 per cent of such youth, respectively, reported having had experienced discrimination outside their state. The study was not conducted in the north-eastern states (barring Assam) and Jammu and Kashmir; hence we are unable to say anything about the discrimination faced by youth from these regions, which is a very real problem.

Experience of discrimination based on gender

Gender discrimination was experienced by 5 per cent of the total sample, and young women, not surprisingly, were more likely to have experienced it than young men: 8 to 3 per cent (Table 9.8). Among young women, the experience of gender discrimination was greatest among those living in the southern states (12 per cent), those who were Dalit and Muslim (10 per cent each) and those in the age bracket of 18 to 21 years. Women living in small cities were also more likely to have experienced gender discrimination than other women.

TABLE 9.8 Experience of discrimination based on gender among youth (%)

	%
Youth (overall)	5
Men	3
Women	8
Women living in small cities	9
18–21 year old women	9
Muslim women	10
Dalit women	10
Women in southern states	12

TABLE 9.9 Experience of gender discrimination among young women may be leading to greater anxiety about harassment (%)

	Worry a lot about harassment	*Worry somewhat about harassment*	*Worry little about harassment*	*Never worry about harassment*
Women who have experienced gender discrimination	33	24	15	25
Women who have not experienced gender discrimination	23	20	14	38

TABLE 9.10 Young women who have experienced gender discrimination found to be less patriarchal in mindset (%)

	Very patriarchal	Somewhat patriarchal	Not much patriarchal	Not patriarchal at all
Women who have experienced gender discrimination	10	29	37	23
Women who have not experienced gender discrimination	21	26	31	23

Note: See Appendix II to find out how the Index of Patriarchal Mindset was constructed.

A young woman's experience of discrimination also seems to be correlated with anxiety about harassment. Young women who reported unfair treatment based on their gender were found to be more likely to be highly anxious about sexual harassment and teasing than women who did not report any gender discrimination (Table 9.9). The former were also found to be more likely to be less patriarchal or hold anti-women views than the latter (Table 9.10). What is striking though is that a sizeable proportion (39 per cent) of those young women who reported gender-based discrimination also hold patriarchal views.

Experience of discrimination and emotional distress

The long-term detrimental effects of discrimination on emotional health and well-being have been soundly established by various studies. In a review conducted in the US to compare 121 studies, it was found that as many as 76 per cent of all studies find a significant association between discrimination and mental health outcomes such as depression and anxiety.[1] In fact, recent studies in the US have found a significant association of discrimination with a number of psychological and physiological ailments such as increased symptoms of depression (Greene et al., 2006), increased chances of substance abuse and cardiovascular problems (Karlamangla et al., 2010; Ogden, 2012), and less healthy pregnancy in African-American women (Hilmert et al., 2014).

Similar studies for the Indian context are not yet available, but our study brings out some important implications of the psychosocial experience of discrimination. Our study shows that the experience of discrimination may be making the youth more emotionally distressed. One in every six (17 per cent) respondents who reported having faced a lot of discrimination also reported high emotional distress (Figure 9.2) and one can see a pattern here. The prevalence of high distress among those who faced no discrimination whatsoever was substantially lower at 6 per cent, which is less than one in ten.

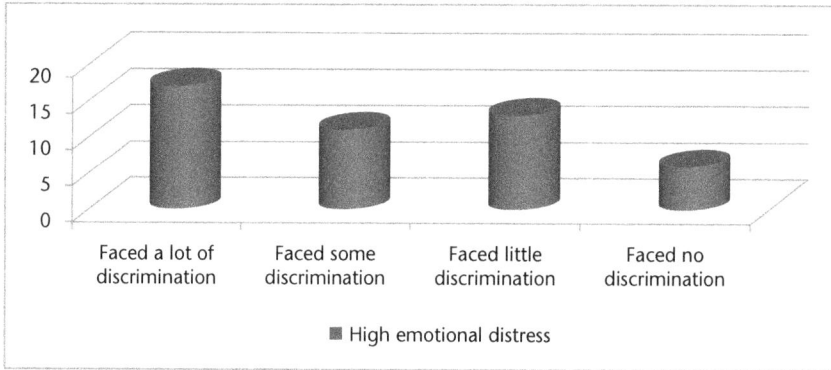

FIGURE 9.2 Experience of discrimination linked to emotional distress (%)

Note: See Appendix II to find out how the Index of Emotional Distress was constructed.

In fact, when we unpack both the Discrimination Index and Emotional Distress Index, we find that discrimination based on each of the grounds (caste, gender, religion, caste, economic status and state) was found to be linked to all questions of emotional distress (stress, depression, loneliness, worthlessness and suicidal thoughts) asked in the survey. Those youths who had experienced discrimination based on caste, gender, religion, economic status and state were more likely to feel stressed, depressed, lonely, worthless and suicidal than those who had not experienced such discriminations (Table 9.11). Moreover, barring economic status, discrimination based on all other grounds seems to have the highest impact in net terms (*experience divided by not experienced*) on getting suicidal thoughts. Gender discrimination in fact has the strongest effect on getting suicidal thoughts. Youth who had experienced gender discrimination were 2.11 times more likely to feel suicidal than youth who had not encountered such prejudicial treatment. Caste-based discrimination comes next. Youngsters who had been discriminated based on their caste identity were 1.87 times more likely to feel suicidal than those who had not. Meanwhile, out of all forms of discrimination, discrimination based on economic status has the strongest impact on feeling worthless. Those who had experienced discrimination based on their economic background were 1.77 times more likely to feel worthless than those who had not. Caste, religion and region-based discriminations were also linked quite strongly to the feeling of worthlessness among youth.

Having experienced discrimination also impacts on anxiety levels among the young. Whereas three-quarters of youth who had faced a lot of discrimination in a span of five years reported high anxiety levels, only half of those (53 per cent) who faced no discrimination at all reported similar anxiety levels (Figure 9.3).

TABLE 9.11 Youth who have been discriminated against are more likely to feel stressed, depressed, lonely, worthless and suicidal (%)

	Stressed often or sometimes	Depressed often or sometimes	Lonely often or sometimes	Worthless often or sometimes	Suicidal often or sometimes
Experienced caste discrimination	54	51	42	30	15
Not experienced caste discrimination	48	38	31	18	8
Net (experience/not experienced)	1.12	1.34	1.35	1.66	1.87
Experienced gender discrimination	59	56	49	29	19
Not experienced gender discrimination	48	38	31	19	9
Net	1.22	1.47	1.58	1.52	2.11
Experienced state-based discrimination	59	51	41	27	15
Not experienced state-based discrimination	48	38	31	19	9
Net	1.22	1.34	1.32	1.42	1.66
Experienced religious discrimination	51	50	43	29	15
Not experienced religious discrimination	49	38	31	19	9
Net	1.04	1.31	1.38	1.52	1.66
Experienced economic discrimination	57	52	45	32	13
Not experienced economic discrimination	48	38	31	18	9
Net	1.18	1.36	1.45	1.77	1.44

Note: Net figures have been calculated by dividing experienced by not experienced.

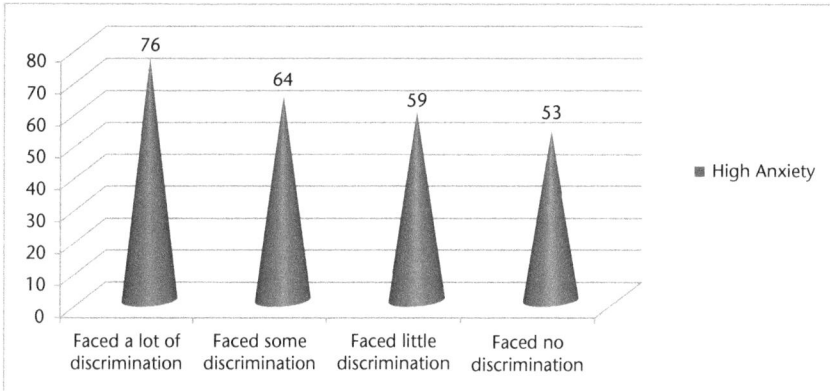

FIGURE 9.3 Degree of discrimination faced correlated to anxiety levels (%)

Note: See Appendix II to find out how the Index of Anxiety was constructed.

Discriminatory attitude greater among those who are discriminated against

The study also found that there is a strong link between being a victim of discrimination and being discriminatory in attitude. In other words, the study reveals that those who claimed to have had been discriminated against on the basis of their religious background, gender, economic class, caste or state were also more likely to discriminate or hold discriminatory views towards others than those who had not experienced any discrimination. Over one in every three youth (36 per cent) who reported facing a lot of discrimination were also discriminatory in their attitude towards others. This is two times more than the discriminatory attitude witnessed among those who said they had faced no discrimination at all (Figure 9.4).

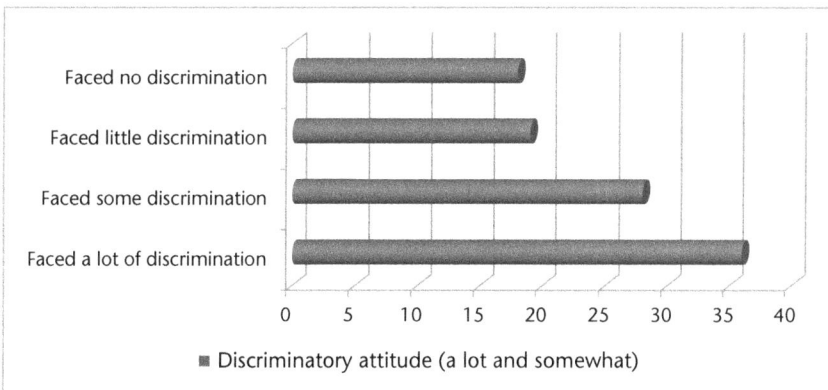

FIGURE 9.4 Discriminatory attitude greater among those who have faced discrimination (%)

Note: See Appendix II to find out how the Index of Discriminatory Attitudes was constructed.

TABLE 9.12 Link between discrimination and discriminatory attitude, disaggregated (%)

	%
Faced discrimination on grounds of religion and won't prefer a neighbour from another religion	35
Have not faced discrimination on grounds of religion and won't prefer a neighbour from another religion	21
Faced discrimination on grounds of caste and won't prefer a neighbour from another caste	25
Have not faced discrimination on grounds of caste and won't prefer a neighbour from another caste	17
Faced discrimination on grounds of region and won't prefer a neighbour from another state	31
Have not faced discrimination on grounds of region and won't prefer a neighbour from another state	22

This 'the discriminated becoming discriminatory' finding also held true for the individual questions on discrimination: 36 per cent of young people who said they faced discrimination on the grounds of their religion also said they would feel uncomfortable having someone from another religion as their neighbour. This figure of discomfort of having a neighbour from another religion was, by contrast, much less (21 per cent) among those who had not faced discrimination based on their religious identity (Table 9.12). This difference can also be seen in the caste-related question. Whereas 25 per cent of those who reported facing discrimination on the basis of caste said that they would not prefer their neighbour to be from another caste, the proportion of those holding the same view was 17 per cent among those who had not faced any discrimination on account of their caste. Finally, those who had received unfair treatment based on their region/state were also more likely to feel uncomfortable having a neighbour belonging to a different region/state than those who had not been discriminated against based on their place of residence: 31 to 22 per cent.

This finding of someone who has been discriminated against also being intolerant is not unique to India alone. A study done by the European Union Agency for Fundamental Rights (FRA) in 2008–9 among 3,000 Muslim and non-Muslim young people in France, Spain and the UK about their experiences of and attitudes towards discrimination, social marginalisation and violence has also suggested a similar correlation. The study concluded that:

> young people who felt highly alienated or excluded and those who had been a victim of either emotional or physical violence themselves because of their cultural or religious background, skin colour or language were highly likely to be involved in using emotional violence towards others.

(FRA, 2010: 71)

This section measured the discriminatory treatment experienced by India's youth. In a positive sign, the study finds that most young people have not been discriminated against at all. Nevertheless, it does find that a significant proportion (one in every six) of the youth have experienced discrimination at least once in recent times, either on the grounds of caste, religion, gender, region or economic status. Out of all these grounds, the study finds economic background and caste to have been the most prevalent basis for discrimination. About one in every ten youth reported having faced discrimination on the basis of their economic status and their caste. Caste-based discrimination was most likely to have been experienced by Dalit youth. Muslim youth were found to be more likely to have experienced discrimination because of their religion. The analysis of the discrimination data consistently finds educational attainment to be enhancing perceptions of discrimination. The more educated youth, be they Dalit, Muslim or poor, were found to be more likely to report experiences of discrimination than the less-educated youth from these categories. There also seems to be a correlation between discrimination experienced by youth and their emotional state of mind. Youth who have experienced a high amount of discrimination also reported higher emotional distress and a greater degree of anxiety. The study findings related to discrimination also seem to suggest that those youths who have been discriminated against are also more likely to discriminate against others, thus pointing to the complex power dynamics involved in the process and practice of social stratification, which belies any simplistic generalisations. Overall though, one could confidently say that youth experience discrimination acutely, which has significant social, cultural, economic and emotional impact for society at large.

Note

1 For a more detailed explanation regarding the possible physiological repercussions, and for a more in-depth view, one can visit the following link: www.ncbi.nlm.nih.gov/books/NBK284777/.

References

Farver, J.M., Xu, Y., Bhadha, B.R., Narang, S. and Lieber, E. (2007) 'Ethnic identity, acculturation, parenting beliefs, and adolescent adjustment: A comparison of Asian Indian and European American families', *Merrill-Palmer Quarterly*, 53(2): 184–215.

European Union Agency for Fundamental Rights (FRA) (2010) *Experience of Discrimination, Social Marginalisation and Violence: A Comparative Study of Muslim and non-Muslim Youth in Three EU Member States*. Available at: http://fra.europa.eu/sites/default/files/fra_uploads/1202-Pub-racism-marginalisation_en.pdf (accessed on 25 December 2016).

Greene, M.L., Way, N. and Pahl, K. (2006) 'Trajectories of perceived adult and peer discrimination among black, Latino, and Asian American adolescents: Patterns and psychological correlates', *Developmental Psychology*, 42(2): 218–236.

Hilmert, C.J., Dominguez, T.P., Schetter, C.D., Srinivas, S.K., Glynn, L.M., Hobel, C.J. and Sandman, C.A. (2014) 'Lifetime racism and blood pressure changes during pregnancy: Implications for fetal growth', *Health Psychology*, 33(1): 43–51.

Karlamangla, A.S., Merkin, S.S., Crimmins, E.M. and Seeman, T.E. (2010) 'Socioeconomic and ethnic disparities in cardiovascular risk in the United States, 2001–2006', *Annals of Epidemiology*, 20(8): 617–628.

Ogden, J. (2012) *Health Psychology: A Textbook*. New York: McGraw-Hill International.

APPENDIX I

METHODOLOGY

Study design and sample

Sampling strategies

This study is based on a sample survey of 6122 respondents aged between 15 and 34 years across 19 major states of India. The survey was conducted by Lokniti, Centre for the Study of Developing Societies (CSDS), Delhi, in the months of April and May, 2016.

The primary objective was to target a sample of 6500 respondents aged between 15 and 34 years nationally, excluding Jammu and Kashmir and many of the small states. The second objective was to give more weight to urban youth (particularly those living in the largest and large cities in terms of population) than rural youth in the overall sample.

To fulfill these twin objectives, sampling was done in the following way:

First, a list of all assembly constituencies (ACs) of the 19 states was obtained where we had decided to conduct the study, namely, Andhra Pradesh, Assam, Bihar, Chhattisgarh, Delhi, Gujarat, Haryana, Jharkhand, Karnataka, Kerala, Madhya Pradesh, Maharashtra, Odisha, Punjab, Rajasthan, Tamil Nadu, Telangana, Uttar Pradesh and West Bengal. Subsequently, all ACs were listed out, along with their level of urbanity (as per the Census of 2011) in percentage terms.

Then a target was set of about 72 interviews to be conducted in each assembly segment. As the overall target was of 6500 interviews, this meant that we had to sample 90 assembly segments across the 19 states.

Next, since one of the objectives was to ensure that a larger proportion of the sample fell in urban areas, we decided to divide the number of ACs where the study was to be conducted (90) in an urban–rural proportion of 67 per cent to 33 per cent. About 69 per cent of India's population is rural and 31 per cent is urban according to the Census of 2011. However, we decided to more or less inverse this proportion keeping in mind the objective of our study. This meant that out of the 90 ACs that had to be sampled, 60 had to be urban and 30 rural.

Once this was decided, the multi-stage stratified random sampling method was adopted:

> Stage 1 involved the selection of urban and rural ACs.
>
> Stage 2 involved the selection of polling stations (PSs) within the selected urban and rural ACs.
>
> Stage 3 involved the selection of respondents within the selected PSs.

Stage 1

Selection of urban ACs

Step 1. From the state-wise list of ACs, those ACs falling within the Lok Sabha or parliamentary constituencies (PCs) of the ten largest cities of India in terms of population (Delhi, Mumbai, Ahmedabad, Kolkata, Chennai, Bangalore, Hyderabad, Pune, Surat and Jaipur) were arranged in ten separate strata. These ten largest cities are spread across eight states. Delhi's PCs are New Delhi, South Delhi, East Delhi, West Delhi, North West Delhi, Chandni Chowk and North East Delhi. Mumbai's PCs are Mumbai South, Mumbai North, Mumbai South Central, Mumbai North Central, Mumbai North West and Mumbai North East. Kolkata's PCs are Kolkata Dakshin, Kolkata Uttar, Dum Dum, Jadavpur and Barrackpore. Chennai's PCs are Chennai North, Chennai Central and Chennai South. Bangalore's PCs are Bangalore North, Bangalore Central and Bangalore South. Hyderabad's PCs are Hyderabad, Secunderabad and Malkajgiri. Within all these PCs, only those ACs with an urban population of over 35 per cent were listed for sampling. They were all listed in ten separate strata as per their official AC number. Following this, three ACs from within each strata/city (3×10=30) were chosen randomly, using the systematic random sampling method.

Step 2. ACs of the largest city (in terms of population) of the remaining 11 states were listed as per their official AC number in 11 separate strata. Following this, one AC from each city was chosen randomly. The reason a city was chosen, even in small states like Assam, Jharkhand etc., was to ensure an adequate urban sample from them/the regions in which they fell, for the purposes of analysis.

Step 3. The remaining ACs in all states which are 30–100 per cent urban were listed in another stratum. States were ordered in terms of the share of their 15- to 34-year-old urban population in India's total 15–34-year-old urban population (from high to low) and the ACs within them were ordered in terms of their official AC number. Once this was done, 11 ACs were chosen randomly using the systematic random sampling method.

Selection of rural seats

Step 4. The remaining ACs which are under 30 per cent urban were listed in another stratum. States were ordered in terms of the share of their 15- to 34-year-old rural population in India's total 15–34-year-old-rural population (from high to low) and 30 assembly segments were chosen randomly using the systematic random sampling method. Having followed this method, the sample was as depicted in Table A1.

Stage 2

Selection of polling stations

We decided to sample four PSs from within each AC using the systematic random sampling method. In ACs sampled from within the ten largest cities, the largest cities of each state and the 30–100 per cent urban category, PSs that were urban in nature were sampled randomly. While this was a straightforward exercise for the first two categories (ACs sampled from the ten largest cities and the largest cities) since all PSs within them were urban in nature, for the third category (30–100 per cent urban) where some PSs were rural in nature we adopted a slightly different method. For this category, the random sampling of urban PSs was done only after having first identified all urban PSs (*as indicated on the electoral roll of each polling station*) within the 19 sampled ACs. Finally, in the ACs sampled from the rural category (<30 per cent urban), four PSs each were randomly sampled. These were almost all likely to be of a rural nature, but if by chance an urban PS was selected, it was replaced by a rural one situated right next to it/close to it.

Stage 3

Selection of respondents

The selection of 18- to 34-year-old respondents was done from within the latest electoral rolls of PSs that were sampled in Stage 2. The random sampling was systematic as respondents were selected at regular intervals. Since not all voters in an electoral roll (our sampling frame) fall in the 18 to 34 year age group, the fixed interval method could not be strictly implemented. Instead a suitable respondent closest to a fixed selection point was selected. Taking into consideration a lower completion rate in urban areas in our past surveys, 30 respondents were randomly selected for interviews in urban PSs and 25 in rural PSs of which investigators were expected to interview 15–16 people. This meant that on average 62 respondents aged between 18 and 34 years were to be interviewed in every AC, making the targeted sample of this age group about 5580 respondents in the total targeted sample of 6500 respondents. In percentage terms this was to be about 86 per cent of the entire targeted sample and hence quite representative of their actual proportion in the total 15–34-year-old population of India, which is 83 per cent. This

TABLE A1 Sample spread across 19 states

	Assembly seats from the 10 largest cities of India spread across 8 states	Assembly seats from the largest cities of remaining 11 states	Assembly seats that are 30–100% urban from remaining assembly seats of all 19 states	Assembly seats that are <30% urban from remaining assembly seats
South				
Andhra Pradesh	—	1 AC (Vishakhapatanam)	1 AC (Narasaraopet)	2 ACs
Telangana	3 ACs (Hyderabad)	—	1 AC (Ibrahimpatanam)	1 AC
Tamil Nadu	3 ACs (Chennai)	—	3 ACs (Krishnagiri, Udumalaipatti, Kovilpatti)	1 AC
Karnataka	3 ACs (Bangalore)	—	2 ACs (Belgaum Dakshin, Hassan)	2 ACs
Kerala	—	1 AC (Kochi)	1 AC (Ponnani)	1 AC
East				
Assam	—	1 AC (Guwahati)	—	1 AC
Bihar	—	1 AC (Patna)	—	3 ACs
Jharkhand	—	1 AC (Jamshedpur)	—	1 AC
Odisha	—	1 AC (Bhubaneshwar)	1 AC (Rourkela)	2 ACs
West Bengal	3 ACs (Kolkata)	—	1 AC (Bally)	2 ACs
West				
Chhattisgarh	—	1 AC (Raipur)	—	1 AC
Madhya Pradesh	—	1 AC (Indore)	1 AC (Amlai)	2 ACs
Maharashtra	6 ACs (Mumbai, Pune)	—	2 ACs (Amaravati, Ulhasnagar)	2 ACs
Gujarat	6 ACs	—	1 AC (Morbi)	1 AC
North				
Haryana	—	1 AC (Faridabad)	1 AC (Jagadhari)	1 AC
Delhi	3 ACs (Delhi)	—	—	NA
Punjab	—	1 AC (Ludhiana)	1 AC (Pathankot)	1 AC
Rajasthan	3 ACs (Jaipur)	—	1 AC (Dholpur)	2 ACs
Uttar Pradesh	—	1 AC (Kanpur)	2 ACs (Rampur, Etawah)	4 ACs
Total	**30 ACs**	**11 ACs**	**19 ACs**	**30 ACs**

assumption more or less worked as eventually the final achieved sample was 6122, of which 5220 were 18 to 34 year olds (85 per cent).

Since electoral rolls do not have information of citizens below 18 years of age, a different approach was adopted for sampling/interviewing 15 to 17 year olds. Apart from the randomly selected 18 to 34 year olds in every PS, as many as 20 households were randomly selected for interviews per PS. This means that in addition to their task of getting in touch with the randomly sampled 18–34-year-old respondents in a PS, field investigators were asked to knock on the doors of these 20 randomly sampled households in the same PS and check if they had a 15 to 17 year old residing there. From these 20 households, the investigators were expected to interview two to three respondents aged between 15 and 17 years, ensuring that at least one male or one female was also interviewed from among them. This meant that on average about ten respondents in the 15 to 17 year age group were interviewed in every AC, making the targeted sample of this age group around 900 respondents in the total targeted sample of 6500 respondents. In percentage terms this was about 14 per cent of the entire targeted sample and hence quite representative of their actual proportion in the total 15–34-year-old population of India, which is 17 per cent. The final achieved sample of 15 to 17 year olds was 902. This is 15 per cent of the total achieved sample of 6122.

Fieldwork

The fieldwork of the survey took place in the months of April and May 2016. Before going to the field, field investigators (FIs) were given training in the survey method and interviewing techniques at day-long training workshops conducted in each of the 19 states. The FIs conducted face-to-face interviews with the respondents at the place of residence of the respondent using a standardised questionnaire in the language spoken and understood by him/her. A total of 6122 interviews were conducted across the 19 states. Before being finalised, the entire questionnaire was piloted and tested in Delhi. Most questions in the questionnaire were structured, i.e. close-ended. However, there were some that were kept open-ended in order to find out the respondent's spontaneous feelings about an issue without giving him/her a predecided set of options. During the survey, around 35–40 minutes was requested from the respondent to administer the survey. The questionnaires that returned from the field were checked/reviewed for incompleteness and coding errors. The checking and the subsequent data entry took place at the CSDS office in Delhi. The analyses presented in this report have been done using a standard social science statistical package (SPSS).

Sample profile and data weighting

The achieved sample is quite representative of India's 15–34-year-old population. The proportion of various demographics in the sample largely matches with the actual proportion of those groups in India's 15–34-year-old population, except in

TABLE A2 Profile of the raw sample and the weighted sample

	Actual proportion in 15–34-year-old population of India according to Census 2011 (%)	Raw proportion in achieved sample (%)	Proportion after weightage by actual state population proportion and age group proportion* (%)	Proportion after weightage by actual state population proportion, age group proportion and locality proportion** (%)
15–34 years old Urban	33.3	65.2	58	32.9
15–34 years old Rural	66.7	34.8	42	67.1
15–17 years old	17.2	14.8	17.2	17.2
18–21 years old	23.1	9.6	23.1	23.1
22–25 years old	21.4	20.4	21.4	21.4
26–29 years old	17.4	18.7	17.4	17.4
30–34 years old	20.9	36.6	20.9	20.9
15-34-year-old Muslims	14.5	11.5	11.2	10.3
15-34-year-old Christians	2.2	2.5	2.7	3.0
15-34-year-old Sikhs	1.8	2.1	2.0	1.7
15-34-year-old Scheduled castes	16.8	17.7	17.3	18.5
15-34-year-old Scheduled tribes	NA	6.7	6.6	9.2
15-34-year-old Other backward castes	NA	42.3	42.4	43.7
15-34-year-old Women	48.4	41.8	40.7	40.5

Note: *This weight was applied only for analysis by locality; **This weight was applied for a generalised analysis of Indian youth.

terms of locality as we made a deliberate choice to oversample urban respondents. While making generalised claims about the Indian youth, we ensured that the achieved sample was weighted in such a manner that it mirrored (nearly) the actual profile of India's 15–34-year-old population as per Census 2011 data (Table A2, Column 4). For such generalised analysis, the sample was weighted by three weights: 1) the proportion of the 15–34-year-old population of a state in the total 15–34-year-old population of the 19 states where the survey was conducted; 2) the actual proportion of different age groups (15–17, 18–21, 22–25, 26–29 and 30–34) in the larger 15–34-year-old population of the 19 states; and 3) the actual proportion of urban and rural youths in the larger 15–34-year-old population of the 19 states. While analysing only by locality, i.e. big cities, small cities and villages or biggest cities, big cities, small cities and villages, the achieved sample was weighted only by the first and second weights mentioned above, not the third.

APPENDIX II

CONSTRUCTION OF INDICES[1]

1. Index of Anxiety

The index was constructed by taking into account 14 questions asked during the survey. They are:

Q13a: How much do you worry about job/occupation?

Q13b: How much do you worry about studies?

Q13c: How much do you worry about maintaining family traditions?

Q13d: How much do you worry about family problems?

Q13e: How much do you worry about riots or mob violence in your city/village?

Q13f: How much do you worry about a road accident?

Q13g: How much do you worry about a terrorist attack?

Q37a: How much do you worry about your health?

Q37b: How much do you worry about your body shape/weight/looks?

Q37c: How much do you worry about your inability to speak good English?

Q37d: How much do you worry about losing a friend?

Q37e: How much do you worry about your parents' health?

Q37f: How much do you worry about your marriage?

Q37g: How much do you worry about harassment/teasing?

For each question, the response options offered to the respondent were 'quite a lot', 'somewhat', 'very little' and 'not at all'.

Step 1: An answer that was either 'quite a lot' or 'somewhat' was assigned a score of 1. An answer that was either 'very little' or 'not at all' was assigned a score of 0. A no response/no opinion to the question was also assigned a score of 0.

Step 2: The scores of all 14 questions were summed up. The resulting summated scores ranged from 0 to 14.

Step 3: The summated scores were distributed across five newly created categories that indicated different degrees of anxiety. Summated scores that ranged from 12–14 were categorised as 'Very anxious'. Summated scores that ranged from 9–11 were categorised as being 'Quite anxious'. Summated scores ranging from 6–8 were categorised as 'Somewhat anxious'. Summated scores that ranged from 3–5 were categorised as 'Not much anxious' and summated scores that totalled 0–2 were categorised as 'Not anxious at all'.

	Summated score	*Weighted distribution (%)*
Very anxious	12–14	23.6
Quite anxious	9–11	31.1
Somewhat anxious	6–8	25.7
Not much anxious	3–5	14.0
Not anxious at all	0–2	5.5

2. Index of Attitude Towards Reservation

This index was constructed by taking into account seven questions asked during the survey. They are:

Q61a: Should reservation for SCs and STs in government jobs continue?

Q61b: Should reservation for SCs and STs in government colleges/universities continue?

Q61c: Should reservation for OBCs in government jobs continue?

Q61d: Should reservation for OBCs in government colleges/universities continue?

Q62a: Should reservation for SCs and STs in private jobs be implemented?

Q62b: Should reservation for OBCs in private jobs be implemented?

Q62c: Should reservation for backward Muslims in government jobs be implemented?

In Q61a and Q61b, the possible response options were 'yes', 'no', 'only for SC', 'only for ST' and 'less quota'. In Q62a, the possible responses were 'yes', 'no', 'only for SC' and 'only for ST'. In Q61c, Q61d, the possible response options were 'yes', 'no' and 'less quota'. In Q62b and Q62c, the response options were 'yes' and 'no'.

Step 1: An answer that was 'yes' or 'only for SC' or 'only for ST' or 'less quota' was assigned a score of 1. Meanwhile, a 'no' response was assigned a score of 0. A no response/no opinion to the question was also assigned a score of 0.

Step 2: The scores of all seven questions were summed up. The resulting summated scores ranged from 0 to 7.

Step 3: The summated scores were distributed across six newly created categories that indicated different degrees of support for reservation. A summated score of 7 was categorised as 'Very high support'. These are respondents who indicated complete or partial support for reservation in all seven questions related to reservations. Summated scores of 5 or 6 were categorised as 'High support'. A summated score of 4 was categorised as 'Moderate support'. Summated scores of 2 or 3 were categorised as 'Low support'. A summated score of 1 was categorised as 'Very low support'. Finally, a summated score of 0 was categorised as 'No support'.

	Summated score	*Weighted distribution (%)*
Very high support for reservation	7	23.4
High support for reservation	5–6	13.5
Moderate support for reservation	4	12.6
Low support for reservation	2–3	12.5
Very low support for reservation	1	3.1
No support for reservation	0	35.0

3. Index of Discrimination

The Index of Discrimination was constructed by taking into account five questions asked during the survey. They are:

Q25a: In the last five years have you ever faced discrimination on account of your state/region?

Q25b: In the last five years have you ever faced discrimination on account of your caste?

Q25c: In the last five years have you ever faced discrimination on account of your gender?

Q25d: In the last five years have you ever faced discrimination on account of your religion?

Q25e: In the last five years have you ever faced discrimination on account of your economic status?

The possible response options to all five questions were 'yes' and 'no'.

Step 1: A 'yes' response was assigned a score of 1. A 'no' answer was scored as 0. No response to the question was also scored as 0.

Step 2: The scores of all five questions were summed up. The summated scores of all questions ranged from 0 to 5.

Step 3: The summated scores were distributed across four new categories. Summated scores that were either 4 or 5 were categorised as 'Faced a lot of discrimination'. In other words, those falling within this category had answered either all five or four of the five questions in the affirmative. Summated scores that were either 2 or 3 were categorised as 'Faced some discrimination'. A summated score of 1 was categorised as 'Faced little discrimination'. Finally, 0 was categorised as 'Faced no discrimination at all'.

	Summated score	*Weighted distribution (%)*
Faced a lot of discrimination	4–5	1.9
Faced some discrimination	2–3	7.0
Faced little discrimination	1	8.1
Faced no discrimination at all	0	83.0

4. Index of Discriminatory Attitudes

This index was constructed by taking into account seven questions asked during the survey. They are:

Q42a: Would it create discomfort/problems for you if they were your neighbours – people who cook non-veg food?

Q42b: Would it create discomfort/problems for you if they were your neighbours – people from another caste?

Q42c: Would it create discomfort/problems for you if they were your neighbours – people who drink alcohol?

Q42d: Would it create discomfort/problems for you if they were your neighbours – people from another religion?

Q42e: Would it create discomfort/problems for you if they were your neighbours – people from Africa?

Q42f: Would it create discomfort/problems for you if they were your neighbours – people from another state?

Q42g: Would it create discomfort/problems for you if they were your neighbours – a man and woman living together outside of marriage?

In each question, the possible response options were 'yes', 'no' and 'maybe'.

Step 1: An answer that was either 'yes' or 'maybe' was scored as 1. No response to the question was also scored as 1. A 'no' answer was assigned 0 points.

Step 2: The scores of all seven questions were summed up. The resulting summated scores ranged from 0 to 7.

Step 3: The summated scores were then distributed across four newly created categories that indicated different degrees of discriminatory attitude. Summated scores ranging from 5–7 were categorised as 'Very discriminatory'. Summated scores of 3 or 4 were categorised as 'Somewhat discriminatory'. Summated scores of 1 or 2 were labelled as 'Not too discriminatory'. Finally, a summated score of 0 was categorised as 'Not at all discriminatory'.

	Summated score	*Weighted distribution (%)*
Very discriminatory	5–7	8.6
Somewhat discriminatory	3–4	10.5
Not too discriminatory	1–2	24.9
Not at all discriminatory	0	56.1

5. Index of Electoral Participation

The Index of Electoral Participation was constructed by taking into account five questions asked during the survey. They are:

Q18a: In the last ten years, have you attended an election meeting during any election?

Q18b: In the last ten years, have you taken part in a procession or a rally during any election?

Q18c: In the last ten years, have you done door to door campaigning during any election?

Q18d: In the last ten years, have you donated or collected money during any election?

Q18e: In the last ten years, have you distributed leaflets or put posters during any election?

The possible response options to all five questions were 'yes' and 'no'.

Step 1: A 'yes' response was assigned 1 point. A 'no' response was scored as 0. Those who did not answer the question were also assigned a score of 0.

Step 2: The scores of all questions were summed up. The summated scores of all questions ranged from 0 to 5.

Step 3: The summated scores were then distributed across six newly created categories that indicated different levels of electoral participation. A summated score of 5 was categorised as 'Very high electoral participation'. These are basically those respondents who said that they participated in all five election-related activities. A summated score of 4 was labelled as 'High electoral participation', 3 as 'Moderate electoral participation', 2 as 'Low electoral participation', 1 as 'Very low electoral participation' and 0 as 'No electoral participation'.

	Summated score	Weighted distribution (%)
Very high electoral participation	5	2.5
High electoral participation	4	2.1
Moderate electoral participation	3	3.6
Low electoral participation	2	7.5
Very low electoral participation	1	9.7
No electoral participation	0	74.5

6. Index of Emotional Distress

This index was constructed by taking into account four questions asked during the survey. They are:

Q39b: How often do you feel mental tension/depression?

Q39c: How often do you feel lonely?

Q39d: How often do you feel that I am not worth anything?

Q39e: How often do you get thoughts of suicide/ending your life?

In each question, the response options offered to the respondent were 'very often, 'sometimes', 'very little' and 'never'.

Step 1: The response categories of 'very often' or 'sometimes' were defined as being distressed, and the categories of 'very little' or 'never', or anyone who gave 'no response' were defined as being not distressed.

Step 2: Any response belonging to the 'not distressed' category was assigned a score of 0 across all the four questions. However, responses belonging to the 'distressed' category were not treated as being equal across all questions. They were instead assigned different scores/weights depending on the nature of the question. In the question on loneliness (Q39c), response options 'very often' or 'sometimes' were assigned a score of 1. In the questions on depression (Q39b)

and worthlessness (Q39d), they were assigned a score of 2. In the question on suicidal thoughts (Q39e) they were weighted even higher and assigned a score of 3.

Step 3: The scores of all four questions were summed up. The resulting summated scores ranged from 0 to 8.

Step 4: The summated scores were distributed across four newly created categories that indicated different levels of emotional distress. Summated scores
that ranged from 6–8 were categorised as 'High emotional distress'. Summated
scores that ranged from 3–5 were categorised as 'Moderate emotional distress'.
Summated scores that were either 1 or 2 were categorised as 'Low emotional distress'. Finally, a summated score of 0 was categorised as 'No emotional distress'.

	Summated score	*Weighted distribution (%)*
High emotional distress	6–8	7.0
Moderate emotional distress	3–5	23.8
Low emotional distress	1–2	17.6
No emotional distress	0	51.6

7. Index of News Media Exposure

This index was constructed by taking into account four questions asked during the
survey. They are:

Q67h: How often do you watch news on TV?

Q67i: How often do you read the newspaper?

Q67j: How often do you listen to the radio?

Q67k: How often do you read news on internet websites?

In each question, the response options given to the interviewee were 'daily',
'few days a week', 'few days a month' 'very rarely' and 'never'.

Step 1: The response option of 'daily' was scored as 4, 'few days a week' was
scored as 3, 'few days a month' was scored as 2, 'rarely' was scored as 1 and
'never' and those who did not give a response were scored as 0.

Step 2: The scores of all questions were summed up. The summated scores of
all questions ranged from 0 to 12.

Step 3: The summated scores were then distributed across six newly created
categories that indicated the intensity of news media exposure. A summated
score of 12 was labelled as 'Very high exposure', a score of 9 to 11 was categorised as 'High exposure', 7 or 8 as 'Moderate exposure', 4 to 6 as 'Low
exposure', 1 to 3 as 'Very low exposure' and 0 as 'No exposure'.

	Summated score	*Weighted distribution (%)*
Very high exposure	12	8.0
High exposure	9–11	16.5
Moderate exposure	7–8	16.5
Low exposure	4–6	28.0
Very low exposure	1–3	15.0
No exposure	0	8.1

8. Index of Patriarchal Mindset

This index was constructed by taking into account five questions asked during the survey. They are:

Q35a: 'It is not right for women to work/do a job after marriage'; do you agree with this statement or disagree with it?

Q35b: 'Overall, men prove to be better leaders than women'; do you agree with this statement or disagree with it?

Q35c: 'Higher education is more important for boys than girls'; do you agree with this statement or disagree with it?

Q35d: 'Wives should always listen to their husbands'; do you agree with this statement or disagree with it?

Q35e: 'Girls should not wear jeans'; do you agree with this statement or disagree with it?

In each question, the response options offered to the respondent were 'agree fully', 'agree somewhat', 'disagree somewhat' and 'disagree fully'.

Step 1: An answer that was either 'disagree fully' or 'disagree somewhat' was scored as 1. Meanwhile a response that was either 'agree fully' or 'agree somewhat' was assigned a score of 0. A no response/no opinion to the question was also assigned a score of 0.

Step 2: The scores of all five questions were summed up. The resulting summated scores ranged from 0 to 5.

Step 3: The summated scores were then distributed across four newly created categories that indicated different degrees of patriarchal mindset. A summated score of 0 was categorised as having a 'Very patriarchal in mindset'. These are respondents who either agreed with all the five statements read out to them or stayed silent on the issue preferring not to respond. Summated scores of 1 or 2 were categorised as 'Somewhat patriarchal mindset'. Summated scores of 3 or 4 were labelled as 'Not much patriarchal mindset'. Finally, a summated score of 5 was categorised as 'No patriarchal mindset at all'.

	Summated score	Weighted distribution (%)
Very patriarchal mindset	0	23.5
Somewhat patriarchal mindset	1–2	28.7
Not much patriarchal mindset	3–4	29.4
No patriarchal mindset at all	5	18.3

9. Index of Religiosity

This index was constructed by taking into account six questions asked during the survey. They are:

Q46a: How often do you do *puja/namaz/*prayer/*path*?

Q46b: How often do you do *bhajan/kirtan/satsang*?

Q46c: How often do you keep *vrats/upwaas/rozas/*fasts?

Q46d: How often do you go to temple/mosque/church/*gurudwara*?

Q46e: How often do you watch religious shows on TV?

Q46f: How often do you read a religious book?

In each question, the response options given to the interviewee were 'regularly', 'sometimes', 'only on festivals' and 'never'.

Step 1: Anyone who said 'regularly' was assigned a score of 3. Anyone who said 'sometimes' was assigned a score of 2. The response category of 'only on festivals' was assigned 1 point. Those who said 'never' or those who did not give any opinion on the question (no response) were scored as 0.

Step 2: The scores of all questions were summed up. The summated scores of all questions ranged from 0 to 18.

Step 3: These scores were then distributed across six newly created categories that indicated the intensity of religiosity. Summated scores ranging from 14 to 18 were labelled as 'Very high religiosity', 11 to 13 as 'High religiosity', 8 to 10 as 'Moderate religiosity', 5 to 7 as 'Low', 1 to 4 as 'Very low religiosity' and 0 as 'No religiosity'.

	Summated score	Weighted distribution (%)
Very high religiosity	14–18	11.9
High religiosity	11–13	23.8
Moderate religiosity	8–10	24.5
Low religiosity	5–7	22.5
Very low religiosity	1–4	13.0
No religiosity	0	4.3

10. Index of Social Liberalism/Conservatism

This index was constructed by taking into account 20 questions asked during the survey. They are:

Q35a: 'It is not right for women to work/do a job after marriage'; do you agree with this statement or disagree with it?

Q35b: 'Overall, men prove to be better leaders than women'; do you agree with this statement or disagree with it?

Q35c: 'Higher education is more important for boys than girls'; do you agree with this statement or disagree with it?

Q35d: 'Wives should always listen to their husbands'; do you agree with this statement or disagree with it?

Q35e: 'Girls should not wear jeans'; do you agree with this statement or disagree with it?

Q35f: 'In life it is not very important to get married'; do you agree with this statement or disagree with it?

Q36a: Do you consider the marriage between a man and a woman belonging to different castes right or wrong?

Q36b: Do you consider the marriage between a man and a woman belonging to different religions right or wrong?

Q36c: Do you consider a man and a woman living together without marriage right or wrong?

Q36d: Do you consider a man and a woman meeting/dating each other before getting married right or wrong?

Q36e: Do you consider celebrating Valentine's Day right or wrong?

Q36f: Do you consider love affair between two women right or wrong?

Q36g: Do you consider love affair between two men right or wrong?

Q42a: Would it create discomfort/problems for you if they were your neighbours – people who cook non-veg food?

Q42b: Would it create discomfort/problems for you if they were your neighbours – people from another caste?

Q42c: Would it create discomfort/problems for you if they were your neighbours – people who drink alcohol?

Q42d: Would it create discomfort/problems for you if they were your neighbours – people from another religion?

Q42e: Would it create discomfort/problems for you if they were your neighbours – people from Africa?

Q42f: Would it create discomfort/problems for you if they were your neighbours – people from another state?

Q42g: Would it create discomfort/problems for you if they were your neighbours – a man and woman living together outside of marriage?

In Q35a–Q35f, the response options offered to the respondent were 'agree fully', 'agree somewhat', 'disagree fully' and 'disagree somewhat'. In Q36a–Q36g, the possible response options were 'right', 'somewhat right' and 'wrong'. In Q42a–42g question, the possible response options were 'yes, 'no' and 'maybe'.

Step 1: In Q35a–Q35e, 'disagree somewhat' or 'disagree fully' was assigned 1 point. Meanwhile 'agree fully' or 'agree somewhat' or 'no response' to the question were assigned a score of 0. In Q35f, 'agree fully' or 'agree somewhat' were given 1 point and 'disagree fully' or disagree somewhat' or 'no response' were scored as 0. In Q36a–Q36g, 'right' or 'somewhat right' were scored as 1 and 'wrong' or 'no response' to the question were scored as 0. In Q42a–42g, 'yes' or 'maybe' or 'no response' to the question were scored as 0. Meanwhile 'no' was scored as 1.

Step 2: The scores of all 20 questions were totalled. The summated scores of all questions ranged from 0 to 20.

Step 3: The summated scores were distributed across four newly created categories that indicated degrees of social liberalism. Summated scores between 15 and 20 were categorised as 'Very socially liberal', 10 and 14 as 'Somewhat socially liberal', between 5 and 9 as 'Somewhat socially conservative', and between 0 and 4 as 'Very conservative'.

	Summated score	Weighted distribution (%)
Very socially liberal	15–20	14.3
Somewhat socially liberal	10–14	38.1
Somewhat socially conservative	5–9	36.3
Very socially conservative	0–4	11.3

11. Index of Social Media Usage

This index was constructed by taking into account four questions asked during the survey. They are:

Q67a: How often do you use Facebook?

Q67b: How often do you use Twitter?

Q67c: How often do you use WhatsApp?

Q67d: How often do you watch videos on YouTube?

In each question, the response options given to the interviewee were 'daily', 'few days a week', 'few days a month', 'very rarely' and 'never'.

Step 1: The response option of 'daily' was scored as 4, 'few days a week' was scored as 3, 'few days a month' was scored as 2, 'rarely' was scored as 1 and 'never' and those who did not give a response were scored as 0.

Step 2: The scores of all questions were summed up. The summated scores of all questions ranged from 0 to 16.

Step 3: These scores were then distributed across six newly created categories that indicated the intensity of social media usage. Summated scores ranging from 14 to 16 were labelled as 'Very high usage', 11 to 13 as 'High usage', 7 to 10 as 'Moderate usage', 4 to 6 as 'Low usage', 1 to 3 as 'Very low usage' and 0 as 'No usage'.

	Summated score	*Weighted distribution (%)*
Very high usage	14–16	8.2
High usage	11–13	10.8
Moderate usage	7–10	13.0
Low usage	4–6	8.7
Very low usage	1–3	9.4
No usage	0	50.0

12. Index of Style Consciousness

This index was constructed by taking into account six questions asked during the survey. They are:

Q27a: How fond are you keeping the latest mobile phone?

Q27b: How fond are you wearing stylish clothes?

Q27c: How fond are you wearing stylish shoes/sandals?

Q27e: How fond are you applying fairness cream on the face?

Q27f: How fond are you buying deodorants/perfumes?

Q27g: How fond are you going to a beauty parlour/salon?

In each question, the response options offered to the respondent were 'a lot', 'somewhat', 'very less' and 'not at all'.

Step 1: An answer that was either 'a lot' or 'somewhat' were scored as 1. The answer categories of 'very less' or 'not at all' or those who did not give any opinion on the question (no response) were scored as 0.

Step 2: The scores of all questions were summed up. The summated scores of all questions ranged from 0 to 6.

Step 3: These summated scores were then distributed across four newly created categories that indicated different degrees of style consciousness. A summated score of 6 was categorised as 'Very style conscious'. Summated scores that ranged from 4 to 5 were categorised as 'Somewhat style conscious'. A score of 2 or 3 was labelled as 'Not much style conscious' and summated scores that were either 0 or 1 were categorised as 'Not style conscious at all'.

	Summated score	Weighted distribution (%)
Very style conscious	6	19.1
Somewhat style conscious	4–5	23.1
Not much style conscious	2–3	26.1
Not style conscious at all	0–1	31.7

13. Index of Travel

The index of travel was constructed by taking into account three questions asked during the survey. They are:

Q21a: Have you ever travelled outside your district?

Q21b: Have you ever travelled outside your state to another state?

Q21c: Have you ever travelled outside India to another country?

The possible response options to all three questions were 'yes' and 'no'.

Step 1: A 'yes' response was assigned a score of 1. Meanwhile a 'no' response was assigned a score of 0. Anyone who did not answer the question was also assigned a score of 0.

Step 2: The scores of all questions were summed up. The summated scores of all three questions ranged from 0 to 3.

Step 3: The summated scores were then distributed across four newly created categories that indicated different levels of travel/mobility. A summated score of 3 was categorised as 'Travelled a lot'. These are basically those respondents who said that they had travelled outside their district, outside their state to another state and outside the country. A summated score of 2 was labelled as 'Travelled somewhat', 1 as 'Travelled very little' and 0 as 'Not travelled at all'.

	Summated score	*Weighted distribution (%)*
Travelled a lot	3	3.4
Travelled somewhat	2	51.6
Travelled very little	1	32.6
Not travelled at all	0	12.4

14. Class classification

The Economic Class Index was constructed by taking into account the type of house a respondent lives in, the occupation of the respondent, the assets owned by the respondent's household and the monthly income of the household. In the case of a respondent being a student or housewife, the occupation of the main earner of the household was taken into consideration.

The index was constructed in three steps.

> **Step 1**: The first step involved defining the typical/standard characteristics of four pre-determined classes: upper class, middle class, lower class and poor.
>
> A typical upper class respondent was defined in the following terms:
>
> Type of house: a respondent who lives in a bungalow/independent house/ flat with five rooms or more; a respondent in a village living in a *pucca* house.
>
> Occupation: a respondent who is either in a professional job or is an elected official or a Class I employee in the government or a big business person or a farmer/cultivator who owns over 10 acres of land.
>
> Asset: a respondent whose household owns a car; a rural respondent whose household owns a pumping set or a tractor.
>
> Income: a rural respondent with a household monthly income of over Rs8,000 (US$112); a town respondent with a household monthly income of over Rs13,000 ($182); a city respondent with a household monthly income of over Rs17,000 ($238).

Each of the four categories above was assigned a score of 4.

> A typical middle class respondent was defined in the following terms:
>
> Type of house: a respondent in a city/town living in a house/flat with three to four rooms; a respondent in a village living in a mixed house or a *pucca-kuchha* house.
>
> Occupation: a respondent who is either in a lower professional job or is a Class II employee in the government or a medium business person or a farmer/ cultivator who owns over 5–10 acres of land.

Asset: a respondent whose household owns at least two of the following four items: a microwave, washing machine, refrigerator and power backup/ inverter.

Income: a rural respondent with a household monthly income of Rs4,000– 8,000 ($56–112); a town respondent with a household monthly income of Rs7,000–13,000 ($98–182); a city respondent with a household monthly income of Rs9,000–17,000 ($126–238).

Each of the four categories above was assigned a score of 3.

A typical lower class respondent was defined in the following terms:

Type of house: a respondent in a town/ city living in house with one to two rooms or in a mainly *kutcha* house; a respondent in a village living in a *kuchha/* mud house.

Occupation: a respondent who is either a medical technician or a Class III/IV employee in the government or a small business person/petty shopkeeper or a farmer/cultivator who owns 1–4 acres of land or a skilled worker.

Asset: an urban respondent whose household owns only LPG gas; a rural respondent whose household owns LPG gas and a fan/cooler but nothing else.

Income: a rural respondent with a household monthly income of Rs1,000– 4,000 ($14–56); a town respondent with a household monthly income of Rs2,500–7,000 ($35–98); a city respondent with a household monthly income of Rs4,000–9,000 ($56–126).

Each of the four categories above was assigned a score of 2.

A typical poor class respondent was defined in the following terms:

Type of house: a respondent in a town/city living in a *jhuggi jhopri*; a respond- ent in a village living in a hut.

Occupation: a respondent who is either an *ayah* or a maid or an unskilled worker or agricultural labourer or is unemployed.

Asset: an urban respondent whose household has none of the assets asked about in the questionnaire; a rural respondent whose household only has LPG gas.

Income: a rural respondent with a household monthly income of upto Rs1,000 ($14) only; a town respondent with a household monthly income of upto Rs2,500 only ($35); a city respondent with a household monthly income of upto Rs4,000 ($56) only.

Each of the four categories above was assigned a score of 1.

Step 2: All the scores were added up. The summated scores ranged from 4 to 16.

Step 3: The summated scores were distributed across four class categories. A respondent with a summated score of 13–16 was categorised as being 'Upper class/rich'. A respondent with summated scores of 11 or 12 was categorised as being 'Middle class'. A respondent with a summated score of either 8 or 9 or 10 was categorised as being 'Lower class'. Finally, a respondent with a summated score of 4 or 5 or 6 or 7 was categorised as being 'Poor'.

	Summated score	*Weighted distribution (%)*
Upper class/rich	13–16	18.5
Middle class	11–12	28.9
Lower class	8–10	28.9
Poor	4–7	23.6

15. Caste and community classification

Hindu upper caste: Brahmin, Bhumihar, Rajput, Kayastha, Vaish, Jain, Punjabi Khatri and other upper castes.

Hindu peasant proprietor/dominant farming castes: Jat, Reddy, Kamma, Nair, Maratha, Patel, Patidar, Velama, Kapu, Telaga, Balija, Naidu and other peasant proprietors. In some tables the peasant proprietors or the dominant farming castes have been merged with Hindu upper caste.

Hindu peasant Other Backward Caste: Gujjar, Thevar, Yadav, Kurmi, Mudaliar, Gowda, Lodh, Vanniyar, Munnuru Kapu, Koeri, Kushwaha, Mutharayars, Mudiraj, Vokkaliga, Kalinga, Lingayat, Thurpu Kapu, Gaderia, Koppulu Velama, Kunbi, Maratha Kunbi, Koli, Charan, Rabari, Bharwad, Kshatriya-Thakore (Gujarat), Chaudhary (Gujarat), Nadar, Koch, Dhangar, Vanjari, Leva Patil, Gowari, Agri, Powar, Mali/Saini, Kashyap and other peasant OBCs.

Hindu artisanal and service Other Backward Caste: Darzee, Thatihar, Lakhera, Badhai, Kumhar, Lohar, Sunar, Kewat, Dhobi, Nai, Teli (oil pressers), Jogi, Newar, Dhimar, Bhat, landless labourers, toddy tappers and other service OBCs.

Hindu Scheduled Caste: Jatav, Satnami, Balmiki, Pasi, Pano, Devendrakula Vellar, Dhobi/Kori, Khatiks, Rajbhanshis, Mala, Namasudras, Mahar, Boyar, Dom, Dhobi (non-OBC), Kewat (non-OBC), Dhanuk,, Kori, Adi Karnataka, Adi Dravida, Thiruvalluvar, Banjara, Bhovi, Holaya, Pulaya, Kuruva and other SCs.

Hindu Scheduled Tribe: Mina, Bhil, Gond, Oraon, Santhal, Munda, Kondh, Baiga, Kharia, Bhumij and other STs.

Muslim upper: Ashraf (Sayyad, Sheikh), Mughal (Khan), Muslim Rajput and other Muslim upper castes.

Muslim Other Backward Caste: Muslim peasants, traders, craftsmen, weavers and other Muslim OBCs.

Muslim other: Muslim unclassifiable

Other: Sikhs, Christians and Hindu no caste.

	Weighted distribution (%)
Hindu upper caste	13.3
Hindu peasant proprietor/dominant farming caste	7.8
Hindu peasant OBC	25.6
Hindu artisanal and service OBC	9.7
Hindu SC/Dalit	16.5
Hindu ST/Adivasi	7.6
Muslim upper	5.2
Muslim OBC	4.3
Muslim other	0.8
Other	9.1

Note

1 The questionnaire used for this study can be accessed from at: https://bit.ly/2UVLJ9p

INDEX

Page numbers for figures are given in *italics*, and for tables they are given in **bold**. Notes are given as: [page number] n [note number].

For Product Safety Concerns and Information please contact our EU
representative GPSR@taylorandfrancis.com
Taylor & Francis Verlag GmbH, Kaufingerstraße 24, 80331 München, Germany

* 9 7 8 0 3 6 7 1 4 2 0 0 1 *